AAL - 4506

25.95
70C

Effective
Social Action
by
Community Groups

Alvin Zander

Effective
Social Action
by
Community Groups

 Jossey-Bass Publishers
San Francisco • Oxford • 1990

EFFECTIVE SOCIAL ACTION BY COMMUNITY GROUPS
by Alvin Zander

Copyright © 1990 by: Jossey-Bass Inc., Publishers
350 Sansome Street
San Francisco, California 94104
&
Jossey-Bass Limited
Headington Hill Hall
Oxford OX3 0BW

Library of Congress Cataloging-in-Publication Data

Zander, Alvin, date.
    Effective social action by community groups / Alvin Zander.
  — 1st ed.
        p.   cm.—(The Jossey-Bass management series)
(The Jossey-Bass social and behavioral science series)
The Jossey-Bass public administration series)
    Includes bibliographical references.
    ISBN 1-55542-223-3 (alk. paper)
    1. Community organization—United States.   2. Social action-
-United States.   I. Title.   II. Series.   III. Series: The Jossey
-Bass social and behavioral science series.   IV. Series: The Jossey
-Bass public administration series.
    HN65.Z36   1990
    361.8′0983—dc20   89-78373
                                                       CIP

Manufactured in the United States of America

The paper in this book meets the guidelines for
permanence and durability of the Committee on
Production Guidelines for Book Longevity of the
Council on Library Resources.

JACKET DESIGN BY WILLI BAUM

FIRST EDITION

Code 9038

A joint publication in

The Jossey-Bass Management Series

*The Jossey-Bass
Social and Behavioral Science Series*

and

*The Jossey-Bass
Public Administration Series*

Contents

Preface

In almost every town in this country, citizens create groups to work for changes they believe will improve things. The members recognize that they cannot make this transformation on their own because they are not equipped to do so, a set of decision makers is in charge of the situation to be modified, or the activists need the support of neighbors. Thus, the agents of change try to persuade everyone who will listen that the proposed reform is wise. Usually, they do not have enough power to convince either neighbors or officials, and thus they need to figure out how they can become influential. In this book, I consider the origin and nature of such simple groups, their goals, the methods they use in trying to get their way, and the members' motivation to engage in what is for many of them a stressful and uncertain mission. I observe how people with little power try to develop a voice that cannot be denied.

The keen enthusiasm of activists in groups like these is well known. They believe that their purpose is just, they say so with utter conviction, and they are entirely willing to do whatever needs to be done, even if these are activities they would never attempt on their own. One wonders why they are so eager, so convinced that their cause is correct. We know a bit about how persons become loyal members of other kinds of units, such as those created to produce commercial products, solve problems, fight wars, worship a deity, or learn a lesson. We know little about why and how ordinary citizens set out to improve things on their own, however, because such groups have seldom been studied. I am not sure why. They are worthy of investigation because their goals, the beneficiaries of their actions, the methods they use to gain local influence, and the individuals toward whom they aim their efforts are not like those in other settings. Perhaps we can develop new insights into group behavior by examining these self-starting units as they work to bring about change.

There is a reasonable body of scholarly work describing some kinds of organizations created to do good for society. These include large social movements, improvement associations, pressure groups, advisory committees for counseling community staffs of administrative agencies, and unions of poor people. The kinds of entities that interest me most are different from any of these, however, because citizens create community groups for themselves, to solve problems they identify by themselves, through methods of social action they devise among themselves. Such small independent units are beholden to no other organization, and their members try to bring about change because they feel they must. Examples are block organizations, action groups in neighborhoods, and militant bodies seeking reform at city hall.

Scholarly writing about the ways social activists try to achieve their goals often emphasizes how impatient and aggressive the activists are. This fascination with hostile behavior is so dominant among social scientists that they usually call any action body a protest group. Perhaps their scholarly interest in coercive intervention exists because vigorous social action threatens the social order: stability is good and is to be protected; disorderly change is bad and is to be opposed. Threats are also more exciting to study than are sober appeals for reform, yet every follower of the news knows that means other than confrontation are used to influence those who would help introduce change. Many of these methods are gentler and more sophisticated than the pressuring and hostile acts that get much attention from the news media and from scholars. Furthermore, many change agents try to help others as well as themselves, to benefit persons outside their organizations, or to assist the community as a whole, without expecting any gain for themselves. Of course, it is useful to know when and how groups employ aggressive acts or threats. It is equally useful to learn why and how they select other methods from the wide array available to them and to compare how and when they use different procedures.

Purpose of This Volume

The purpose of *Effective Social Action by Community Groups* is to describe how community groups for social change get started, choose their objectives, and select the methods they use to convince persons whose help they need. I consider why they select one form of social action rather than another and how they use it most effectively. I also examine how they face up to any opposition or resistance offered by persons they wish to influence. I hope that such basic information will help leaders of change groups plan how their units can proceed. I also wish to help students of group behavior or social action develop a better understanding of activities within these bodies so that researchers can develop studies that will reveal what leads to what in these entities. Often, I believe, the student of group behavior begins work on a topic with a too-narrow view of the phenomenon to be examined. This volume may help scholars broaden their approach to research on small-scale social action. I present no theory, not even an elementary one, about activism by group members; I offer instead an organized set of ideas on these matters.

Intended Audience

I had two audiences in mind while writing *Effective Social Action by Community Groups*. One is composed of agents of change in communities who may want to understand how they can create and manage effective groups for social action. These people include organizers of groups, consultants to organizations, members of such bodies, and leaders of them. The other audience is made up of researchers interested in how small groups form to take action and how they succeed in these efforts. The groups under observation here have properties and purposes that make them unlike many others. They are a special breed, and they warrant special attention from students of group behavior because they are modern versions of the action groups seen throughout the history of democracy. They want their desires to be heard. They depend on their own ideas, not on those of a larger social movement. They deeply desire to attain the goals of their groups. There are thousands of such bodies in America, with thousands of members. Such groups should be given more attention by social psychologists.

I drew the ideas in this book from many sources: studies of social movements, improvement associations, pressure groups, citizen advisory groups, and unions of people receiving social welfare benefits; programs of research on the motives and goals of group members; investigations of social power; work on social conflict and intergroup relations; essays on social reform; descriptions in newspapers and magazines about groups currently devoted to social change; and my own experiences in and observations of such bodies. Given the variety of sources tapped for *Effective Social Action by Community Groups,* it goes without saying that many statements in the following pages are open to question. They are intended to be. They are opinions, mildly informed ones, about why groups of ordinary people are created and why they operate as they do. None of the statements represents a fully tested and reliable conclusion.

Overview of the Contents

Chapter One provides a summary of the main ideas in this volume, drawn together under a series of generalizations—an overview of the book. Chapter Two illustrates the varied kinds of groups that community members create to better their lives. In Chapter Three, I look at the conditions that encourage organizers to form units that are useful to themselves or to others, and I consider how such bodies are developed. The characteristics of these groups are discussed in Chapter Four to demonstrate that units with different styles of operation tend to have unlike properties. The next chapter takes up the motives of group members and how these are aroused by organizers and leaders so that participants will place a high value on their groups' objectives.

In Chapters Six and Seven, I examine eleven kinds of methods that members use to influence target persons. The first half of this discussion takes up procedures employed by those who want a situation improved in whatever way makes most sense to those whom they hope will provide such help. The reformers act as models, given the target persons information, provide them with advice, or negotiate with them. When using procedures like these, the agents of change place no restraint on the plans, decisions, or acts of the decision makers. Instead, they encourage the latter to make the most sensible moves. The second half of this discussion considers groups that constrain target persons to do exactly what activists want. The reformers try to persuade, spread propaganda, offer rewards, interfere with the work of those they hope to change, threaten them with harm, or impose penalties on them. Under each of eleven classes of social action, I consider four topics: typical examples of such action in use, why the method is chosen, its effects on those who use it or become targets of it, and how it can be employed well.

In Chapter Eight, I observe why a given group may prefer to use one method rather than another. Chapter Nine discusses the origins of social power. It examines the conditions that make influence attempts most compelling and looks at ways in which members try to prevent target persons from opposing or resisting ideas offered to them. In Chapter Ten, I turn to social change as seen through the eyes of those being asked to introduce a modification—the target persons. I observe what conditions lead them to listen to and accept the comments of the reformers. I note why the listeners oppose the ideas offered to them and how they do this. Then I consider the resistance that target persons develop because of activists' behavior and manner of presentation. Finally, I examine how target persons may deliberately try to reduce the influence of reformers or even to abolish their units.

The final chapter recalls the central ideas discussed in the previous pages and considers how these ideas can help managers and students of action groups. First, I assemble practical suggestions for organizers of groups, leading members, and consultants in community social change. Next, I consider suggestions for developing, nurturing, and directing such entities. Finally, I list a number of research questions for students of social action or group dynamics. These are researchable issues in need of study, and many of them have been noted in earlier chapters.

Walnut Creek, California   Alvin Zander
February 1990

The Author

Alvin Zander has been a student of group behavior for many years. From 1948 to 1980 he was program director in the Research Center for Group Dynamics at the University of Michigan. For twenty of those years he served as director of that center. As professor of psychology and of educational psychology, he taught courses in the social psychology of groups. During his last seven years at the University of Michigan, he served as associate vice-president for research. Zander is now retired from academic duties.

Zander earned his bachelor's degree (1936) in general science, his master's degree (1937) in public health, and his doctoral degree (1942) in psychology—all at the University of Michigan. He developed an interest in group behavior while employed as a graduate student during the Great Depression, helping small towns develop social services for which they could not afford professional fees. After a postdoctoral year (1942) with Kurt Lewin at the University of Iowa and nearly three years as a clinical psychologist and a commissioned officer in the U.S. Public Health Service during World War II, Zander returned to the University of Michigan.

Zander has conducted research on the relations among persons who differ in their ability to influence others, the impact of group membership on a person's self-regard, the nature of identification between persons, the sources of members' motivation to help their group succeed, and the origins of a group's goals. He is coeditor of *Group Dynamics: Research and Theory* (1968, with D. Cartwright) and has published the results of a program of investigations in *Motives and Goals in Groups* (1971). Zander also has written *Groups at Work* (1977), a discussion of needed research in group dynamics; *Making Groups Effective* (1982), a guide to fostering the development of well-functioning groups; and *The Purposes of Groups and Organizations* (1985), an essay on the origins and objectives of social entities.

Effective
Social Action
by
Community Groups

1

~·~·~·~·~·~·~·~·~·~·~·~·~·~·~·~·~·~·

Community Groups
as Agents
of Social Action

The problem is this: How can a group of ordinary citizens, with little experience in social action, develop enough influence in town to get things changed? The efforts of such action bodies have been a major source of vitality in democratic societies since ancient Athens. Even so, they can generate uneasiness among those who have to deal with the persons who seek a change. A wise group of would-be reformers therefore recognizes that the group must conduct its campaign for change in a way that does not arouse too much resistance among the persons approached. How do reformers do this?

We are interested here in a voluntary body composed of activists who want to change things locally but who recognize that they need the help of sympathetic neighbors and officials to achieve their objectives. They aspire, for example, to get traffic flowing more smoothly, have more flowers planted in the city park, find homes for the homeless, improve the taste of drinking water, reduce noise from the freeway, or recall a member of the board of education.

Participants in these small movements may intend to benefit themselves alone, a number of citizens whom they represent, their group as an entity (by, for example, increasing its power), or products of Mother Nature. They may use varied methods to make their influence felt, from teaching or advising, on the one hand, to bargaining, persuading, or coercing, on the other. The members of these bodies are called *agents of change* (or, alternatively, *activists, reformers, innovators,* and *initiators*). The individuals they try to reach, whether these are supervisors in administrative agencies or citizens who can influence such officers, are called *target persons* (or *decision makers* and *receivers*). How do change agents develop the enthusiasm they need to become amateur rebels?

At the outset, with the help of group members, the organizers answer a number of questions more or less firmly.

> What is wrong?
>
> Who is affected by this condition?
>
> Whom should we try to help—ourselves, others, or ourselves as well as others?
>
> What do we think should be changed? How?
>
> Who should we approach for help in creating this change? Who are our target persons?
>
> How shall we try to convince these target persons and their supporters to develop this innovation?
>
> What method shall we use in our social action? Why this one?
>
> How can we make our attempts at influence most successful?
>
> How shall we organize ourselves to act, and who will do what?
>
> How can we prepare ourselves to take action and keep up our morale?

Other decisions also have to be reached, usually after the members have made a preliminary attempt to interest the target persons. For example,

> How precisely shall we define what we wish the target persons to do?

Should we become permissive and open-minded in dealing
with target persons, or pressuring and insistent that our
views are right?
Are our objectives appropriate? Too hard? Too vague?
How can we counter the opposition that target persons offer?
How can we calm unfavorable emotional reactions to our
style, or should we?

Answers to questions like these have an impact on subsequent decisions. Suppose, for instance, that the change agents know
exactly what improvement they want the target persons to accept,
and that this change is intended to benefit only themselves. In such
a case, I suspect, they are more likely to choose a pressuring method
of action when they try to convince the target persons. This kind of
method, in turn, will require that the change agents create a formal
and more disciplined structure within their organization. Such a
pressuring method will generate a tendency among the target persons to develop negative emotions (resistance) toward the actions of
the change agents. This resistance ordinarily will cause the same
kind of reaction among the change agents. A two-way resistance
thus arises and escalates. It must be calmed by the efforts of persons
in both parties, or the change effort will fail.

Consider a contrasting example. The change agents recognize the need for a change but are not sure what ought to be done.
Furthermore, they believe that any change should benefit others,
and not themselves at all. Such views lead them to prefer a permissive method of approaching the target persons. This kind of method
causes the agents of change to want the kind of flexibility that an
informal group structure allows. When they use the gentleness inherent in one of the nonconstraining methods, they may meet either
quiet acceptance or opposition, but little resistance. In this book, we
will note other scenarios concerning what is wrong, who is to be the
beneficiary, the choice of action, and reactions from target persons.
All in all, the definition of the problem and the nature of the beneficiary affect the methods chosen by the activists. These methods, in
turn, affect the reactions of target persons, which lead the agents of
change to make further strategic moves, and so on.

In this dance of influence and counterinfluence, the main

ideas, as I see them, can be summarized in several generalizations. We shall take up each of these brief statements in turn and thereby provide ourselves with a preview of this volume's contents, its basic concepts, and the relationships among these notions.

To put the matter simply, a group for social action is organized because it is useful for the organizer, members, or others. Individuals join like-minded citizens to form a group that will work toward improving things. This brings us to our first concept about groups for influential action: *Individuals form an activist group if they believe that a specific situation should be changed and that persons acting alone cannot achieve that end.* The condition they wish to modify may be an unpleasantness that they cannot tolerate any longer or a state of affairs that could or ought to be improved— a response to a repulsive circumstance, or the recognition of an opportunity to accomplish a valued goal.

A citizen who has become aware of a need for change is more likely to organize a group if four facilitating circumstances are present (Zander, 1985). First, conditions in the community or in the behavior of influential persons are unsatisfactory or suggest an opportunity for favorable change. Second, a more satisfactory state of affairs is conceived by group developers. Third, organizers and members believe that their joint actions will succeed if they initiate an effort to make a change. Fourth, conditions in the community do not prevent the activists from taking part in its activities. By contrast, persons who believe that the current state of affairs ought to be bettered will not create a group if they cannot conceive of a way to improve things, do not think a group can create reforms, are not willing to join a group for this purpose, have no skills in being members of such a body, hold values opposed to those of most other community members, or have no faith in group work. Once a group is organized, it develops its own special characteristics. The qualities peculiar to a group are called its *properties*.

The method that members plan to use in social action determines the formality of the properties they create for their group. This second generalization is based on three central ideas. First, leaders try to create the properties that their group must have when it attempts to influence target persons in chosen ways. They thus create roles for members, relationships among members' jobs, and the tools, procedures, and plans they will need to make their efforts productive. Second, the group may be formal, informal, or in between. Formal groups are small bureaucracies that function in fixed and specified ways under close control. Informal groups have loosely delineated and flexible characteristics. In-between groups are formal in some respects and informal in others. Third, agents of change create a formal organization if they plan to employ constraining (pressuring) methods, and they create an informal organization if they intend to use nonconstraining (encouraging) methods. The logic here is that innovators who intend to press their case strongly toward a specific objective will need to have careful plans and controlled procedures in their unit. By contrast, if the initiators need a change but leave it up to the target persons to decide what is to be done and how to do it, the reformers want flexible guidelines and operations for their organization.

Members of a community group working for local change may be driven by any of four kinds of motivation. A *motive* is an individual's disposition to strive for a certain kind of satisfaction. It is an enduring disposition that a person carries with him or her from setting to setting. A different kind of motivation, which an individual develops because of qualities in a particular situation, is called a *desire.* We are interested here in the effects of four types of motivation: a *self-oriented motive,* or the capacity to be satisfied by the achievement of a personal incentive; the *desire for group success,* or the capacity to take pride in the group's achievement of its goal; the *desire to benefit others,* or the capacity to be satisfied when specific persons outside the group of activists are benefited; and the *desire to benefit the community,* or the capacity to be satisfied when improvements are made in the environs of the group.

The willingness of members to participate in the group's activities is determined by the strength of their motivation. The weight of motivation is the multiplicative resultant of three factors. The first factor is the strength of the relevant motive or desire. This is the capacity of members to achieve satisfaction from the attainment of a valued incentive, an attribute identical in each of the four kinds of motivation just described. The incentive may be a strictly personal goal or one for the group as a whole. The second factor is the value of the incentive. This is the perceived likelihood that attainment of a given incentive will provide the satisfaction that a member seeks. Members put greater value on incentives that promise more satisfaction. When a person commits himself or herself to a given objective, he or she pledges to value that incentive and to give first priority to the goal. One who makes a commitment vows to behave in a particular way when he or she takes action. Members commit themselves to their group's goal regardless of their motivation or their confidence that the group will succeed. The third factor in motivational weight is the perceived probability of success. This is the degree of confidence among members that they can reach their objective.

Leaders in a group arouse members' readiness to take action by strengthening one or all of these three aspects of motivation: members' motive (or desire), the value of the incentive, and their perception of the probability that the incentive can be accomplished. Organizers or officers of a group strengthen the motive (or desire) of colleagues in either of two ways. On the one hand, they find out what typically satisfies the members and then make that form of satisfaction more valuable. On the other, they teach them to value wishes that the participants may not already possess but should possess. Organizers heighten the importance of an incentive by demonstrating that its attainment will gratify participants. They press group members to commit themselves to behaving as the goal requires them to do, even if the participants must drop their obligations to other persons or groups. Organizers inspire confidence in success by making group members believe that they can accomplish their group's goal. The organizers declare that the group is becoming more effective and will continue to do so, that the objective is a challenge neither too hard nor too easy, that the goal is clear, that the path to the goal is known, that the necessary resources are at hand, and that groups like their own do well.

The effectiveness of activists' attempts to influence target persons is weakened if the effort arouses opposition or resistance among the receivers. Opposition is the refusal among target persons to accept the substantive content of a proposal on the grounds that it is wrong, does not make sense, is too costly, or does not seem necessary. Target persons will oppose a suggestion for change when they are sure of their own opinions, have faith in their own positions, and are committed to them. *Resistance* is an emotional response of receivers to the style that initiators use in making a proposal; reformers present their case in a way that arouses anger, fear, or defensiveness among the listeners. Activists usually try to avoid creating useless opposition or resistance among those they want to influence. Sometimes, however, they deliberately arouse these reactions in order to create disorder that may help their cause.

Activists select a method according to three considerations: how well it will work in attempts to influence listeners, how well it conforms to their own values, and what kind of satisfaction its use will provide. Judgment about what method will work best is tempered by hunches about how target persons will respond to an issue put before them and by activists' own beliefs about how to influence the listeners without arousing unnecessary opposition or resistance among them.

Agents of change avoid methods that violate their own beliefs about right or wrong public behavior. They may feel, for instance, that they must not seek power for its own sake, attack target persons, throw rocks at bank windows, or parade in a picket line. By contrast, they may believe that they should take part in a parade, write a letter to an editor, or make catcalls at a meeting of the school board. They often prefer methods that are satisfying in themselves to use, methods that release tension, provide revenge, or frighten high-status persons.

The choice of method is also affected by activists' views about who should benefit from the change they seek. If, for example, they wish to gain an objective that will benefit only themselves, they will assign more weight to their own desires than to those of the target persons and will put pressure on the latter to do what the activists desire. If, by contrast, they wish to help the target persons (but not themselves), they will give higher priority to the receivers' needs and will facilitate freedom of choice among the target persons by using permissive methods in meetings with them. If innovators simultaneously seek to benefit both themselves and others, they will prefer a course of action somewhere in between, closer to problem solving.

Agents of change use nonconstraining (permissive) methods when they want target persons to have pride in the change they develop. In such a case, the reformers act as models, information givers, advisers, negotiators, or problem solvers because they want an improvement to be made in whatever way makes most sense to the listeners, and because the change agents believe that the targeted persons will work more effectively toward the proposed end if they are not put under direct pressure or if they clearly know best about what changes ought to be made. Moreover, the actors assume that the target persons will be more motivated if they work for pride in their own achievement, rather than for some other incentive. Encouraging methods work equally well in changing overt behaviors and covert beliefs among target persons, and such procedures are less likely to arouse resistance among the individuals toward whom they are directed.

If reformers decide exactly what change must be made in a given situation and will accept no other, they use constraining (pressuring) methods. Activists attempt to persuade the listeners, bargain with them, offer them a reward, or threaten them with harm in order to give them an incentive to do as they are asked. The activists tend to use such methods when they believe that target persons prefer the current situation and will refuse to change it unless they can benefit from the change or minimize the costs of adopting a new idea. Agents of change monitor the behavior of any target persons who do agree to a change, to see if the target persons are doing what is demanded of them and to apply stronger constraints if necessary. The activists continue their close surveillance if they suspect that the target persons may only pretend to do as they were urged, in order to evade the penalties or win the rewards that agents of change can provide. Reformers can monitor overt behavior more reliably than covert beliefs, and so constraining methods are more effective in changing the overt behavior of target persons than in changing their private opinions, attitudes, or values.

Activists recognize that decision makers want to know what is in it for them if they make the transformation being proposed. Thus, reformers exert their attempts at influence in a way that can help the listeners in this respect. They employ encouraging procedures. They also arouse appropriate motives in the target persons and try to convince them that the suggested change will satisfy these motives. The reaction of a target person to an influence attempt depends on his or her view of the consequences of giving in. Target persons will be more likely to adopt the change proposed by initiators if it plainly is in their best interest to do so, and they will not adopt the new idea if it will do them more harm than good.

The general rule for influencing, then, is this: *The stronger the motive (or desire) that change agents arouse among target persons, and the stronger the probability that this motive or desire will be satisfied if target persons do what the innovators propose, the more likely agents of change are to influence target persons.* In accord with this rule, activists strengthen a relevant motive or desire in target persons by making it important to them, or by helping them recall the value they have placed on satisfying the motive or desire in the past.

If they are to be successful, agents of change need to counteract the prior reasons that target persons have had for other beliefs or behaviors, and they must get them to abandon those reasons. Otherwise, targeted people will be inclined to oppose the proposed change. The strength of the opposition among those being pressed to change depends on three factors: the amount of difference there appears to be between the proposal and the procedures or states currently supported by target persons, the degree of satisfaction that target persons derive from their current situation, and the number of features in the change agents' proposal that are not attractive to the individuals being induced to change. The innovators plan how to present their case in ways that reduce the impact of these three features.

When target persons are pressed to support a change, they are less likely to develop opposition or resistance to the proposal if they convince the change agents to engage in constructive problem solving. Target persons who are asked to introduce a change often have more legitimate and established social power than do the persons who make the request. When this is the case, target persons usually believe that their duty is to set the tone for a meeting in which initiators present a proposal. First, they assume that the innovators have a right to bring up an issue for discussion or evaluation and that they, the listeners, should understand this to be so. Second, the issue under question is taken by the pressured persons to be a dilemma (for those on both sides), and thus it is understood to deserve consideration through a problem-solving process. Third, target persons try not to become defenders of their own prerogatives or practices but attempt to listen and respond rationally to ideas offered by the initiators. Clearly, problem solving is facilitated if target persons are interested in the proposal brought before them and become convinced that the issue deserves further consideration.

Activists arouse resistance among target persons if they try to restrict the freedom of decision makers or use duplicity in attempting to win their way. Target persons are engaged in the act of resisting, as we noted earlier, when they display negative emotions, such as anger and fear, or defensive behavior in their responses to reformers. When agents of change offer a plan, their style, rather than the substantive content of their proposal, is the source of resistance. There are many examples of behavior that provokes resistance. Activists try to limit listeners' freedom by making arbitrary or obscure demands of them, threatening to harm them if they do not comply, or intimating that the activists have the support of a powerful person who can force the issue. Reformers use duplicity by reporting incorrect information, distorting arguments made against their point of view, making illogical derivations, or making promises they clearly cannot keep. They display hostility by ridiculing receivers, stating that they are angry, and demonstrating this in their tone of voice and body language. Agents of change prevent resistance among target persons by avoiding behaviors that stimulate it, getting decision makers to engage in problem solving, posing an issue (rather than pressing a favorite solution), dealing with the dominant individuals among target persons (who tend to be self-confident and not easily drawn into resisting), and proposing that the change be given a tentative trial or that part of it be put in place to see whether it works.

When target persons resist, their actions arouse similar resistance among the change agents. Members of each faction then react unfavorably toward the other, and two-way resistance develops. When target persons resist, their rejecting behaviors, directed toward the instigators of change, generate comparable responses among the instigators. These reactions, in turn, cause an increase in the resistance of the target persons. A circular causal system escalates, and a lust to outdo the other side develops among participants.

An escalation of two-sided resistance can be dampened if participants on both sides try to calm things down. For example, they may pledge to behave in a courteous and rational manner, repress their own tendencies to be fearful or hostile, come to meetings prepared to present their views clearly and thereby prevent confusion, establish ground rules for ways of working, agree on guidelines for making decisions, and point out any similarity in background and goals among the participants. The irrational tone inherent in resistance counteracts the rational aspects of any existing opposition. Thus, resistance tends to be a more powerful determinant of target persons' behavior than opposition.

Agents of change work for the pride they will feel when an innovation they developed is in place, but target persons try to avoid the embarrassment that could follow an unwise change. Innovators want to reach a stated objective because doing so will give them pride in their group's accomplishment and relieve the dissatisfaction that inspired their group's efforts. Failure is a disappointment for them, but it is not an embarrassment because the goals they set are usually difficult. Targeted persons, in contrast, derive little sense of success if they introduce the changes, for the ideas are not their own. They also fear the shame that will follow if they make blunders. They benefit little if they reject the proposal offered by the activists unless everyone agrees that the plan will not work. Thus, change agents have much to gain and little to lose by making a proposal; target persons have much to lose and little to gain by accepting the activists' plan.

When agents of change will not take no for an answer, target persons try to diminish the effectiveness of the activists' organization. They do so in several ways. They ignore the initiators and their proposals. They restrict the freedom of the change agents' actions by creating curfews, antisubversion laws, rules against demonstrating, taxes on public rallies, barriers to the use of open spaces, regulations against disturbing the peace, or laws forbidding large gatherings. They set up rival organizations and lure members of the protesting group to join those, or they back the competing units. They try to lower the morale of activists by telling them that they are not accepted or wanted in the community, and that their campaign is failing. They weaken, remove, or arrest the group's leaders.

They damage the group's reputation by sponsoring unfavorable rumors and labels. They deprive the group of space, money, personnel, and other resources. They wait for the new plan to fail, or even to create the opposite of what was intended, after it is put in place.

The central ideas of this book are contained in sixteen generalizations. A straightforward listing of these ideas helps to reveal the relationships among them and among the concepts contained in the following chapters. Thus, the sixteen ideas are repeated here:

1. Individuals form an activist group if they believe that a specific situation should be changed and that persons acting alone cannot achieve that end.
2. The method that members plan to use in social action determines the formality of the properties they create for their group.
3. Members of a community group working for local change may be driven by any of four kinds of motivation.
4. The willingness of members to participate in the group's activities is determined by the strength of their motivation.
5. Leaders in a group arouse members' readiness to take action by strengthening one or all of these three aspects of motivation: members' motive (or desire), the value of the incentive, and their perception of the probability that the incentive can be accomplished.
6. The effectiveness of activists' attempts to influence target persons is weakened if the effort arouses opposition or resistance among the receivers.
7. Activists select a method according to three considerations: how well it will work in attempts to influence listeners, how well it conforms to their own values, and what kind of satisfaction its use will provide.
8. Agents of change use nonconstraining (permissive) methods when they want target persons to have pride in the change they develop.
9. If reformers decide exactly what change must be made in a given situation and will accept no other, they use constraining (pressuring) methods.

10. The stronger the motive (or desire) that change agents arouse among target persons, and the stronger the probability that this motive or desire will be satisfied if target persons do what the innovators propose, the more likely agents of change are to influence target persons.

11. If they are to be successful, agents of change need to counteract the prior reasons that target persons have had for other beliefs or behaviors, and they must get them to abandon those reasons. Otherwise, targeted people will be inclined to oppose the proposed change.

12. When target persons are pressed to support a change, they are less likely to experience opposition or resistance to the proposal if they convince the change agents to engage in constructive problem solving.

13. Activists arouse resistance among target persons if they try to restrict the freedom of decision makers or use duplicity in attempting to win their way.

14. When target persons resist, their actions arouse similar resistance among the change agents. Members of each faction then react unfavorably toward the other, and two-way resistance develops.

15. Agents of change work for the pride they will feel when an innovation they developed is in place, but target persons try to avoid the embarrassment that could follow an unwise change.

16. When agents of change will not take no for an answer, target persons try to diminish the effectiveness of the activists' organization.

2

~~~~~~~~~~~~~~~~~~~~~~~~~~~~~~~~~~~~

Types of Groups
That Engage
in Social Action

Organizations to improve our society come in different sizes. Some are large movements; others are small groups of neighbors; still others are of proportions in between. As already noted, we are most interested here in small, voluntary community groups whose members receive no remuneration for their efforts, believe their groups' objectives must be achieved without fail, and are confident that accomplishing their goals will improve the conditions that inspired them to join. They seek the help of nonmembers, officials, or constituents of these decision makers toward implementing the changes they have in mind.

It is useful to compare six kinds of organizations that a citizen can join to foster change, regardless of such organizations' size or location. These are social movements (large or small), improvement associations, pressure groups, citizen participation groups, citizen action groups, and community groups for social action. The distinctions among these types are not sharp, as we will see, since a given kind of entity may fall under more than one of the major headings. We shall review the salient features of each type of organization.

Social Movements

A social movement is composed of persons who advocate a change in the beliefs or practices of members and nonmembers within a relatively large geographical area. Most movements perpetually try to increase the size of their membership. Some contain smaller associations or local chapters within them. Examples are Mothers Against Drunk Drivers (MADD), the National Rifle Association, the Association to Help Oliver North, the Coalition to Stop the War in Nicaragua, and the National Organization for Women (NOW). Other movements (or ways of describing movements) rely on no structures that hold believers together and are little more than particular points of view spreading among people. Eventually, if an opinion is accepted by many, a set of individuals may found a formal entity to diffuse its notions more widely. Popular views of our time that had already spread among many persons before organizations were formed to promote certain causes involve the legality of abortions, controls on research into DNA, the provision of sanctuary for illegal immigrants, private funding for rebels in Nicaragua, rules for operating nuclear power plants, restrictions on smoking in public places, and testing of citizens for exposure to the HIV virus. Whatever the main concerns are, changes advocated by members of a movement tend to be vague, difficult to achieve, and multiple, rather than clear, attainable, and singular.

The issues at the heart of a movement are usually value-laden and tend to deal with ideas more than with actions. The advocated changes are strongly in accord with what the participants think is right and against what they believe is wrong. Many movements result from actions initiated by a lone demagogue who claims there is a simple, sovereign solution to a complex set of problems (Father Coughlin, James Watt, George Wallace, Oral Roberts, Malcom X). When the demands of a movement are taken up by a formal organization, that body ordinarily is managed by members of a paid professional staff, who work out of a headquarters office to increase the influence of the organization. Movements use many methods to make their ideas acceptable. They depend most often on lobbying legislators, placing favorite issues on local election ballots, holding rallies, creating demonstrations, and inventing ways of gaining wide attention for their views. Useful writings about social movements include Gerlach and Hine (1970), Lipset and Raab (1970), Toch (1965), Wilson (1973), and Wood and Jackson (1982).

Improvement Associations

Most associations look inward and foster the beliefs or practices of their members, so that those persons can perform better in their professions, hobbies, religions, fraternal activities, patriotic societies, or businesses (Zander, 1985). Among the fifteen thousand associations in the United States (Ruffner, 1968), however, about one in four is devoted to advocating a better state of affairs in some activity outside that body. Examples of associations to improve society are the League of Women Voters, the Ku Klux Klan, the Sierra Club, Common Cause, the Independent America Party, and the John Birch Society. The larger organizations among these have paid staffs, central offices, and branches in various parts of the country. They educate their members through newsletters, conferences, journals, books, and other communications media. They seldom engage in lobbying, lawsuits, threats, or coercion. The central concerns of such bodies vary from time to time as conditions change. They tend to have a number of objectives. Readings on bodies like these are included in Hyams (1975), Lipset and Raab (1970), and Zander (1985).

Pressure Groups

These are organizations whose dominant feature is their advocacy of specific one-issue legislative actions. They are smaller than other kinds of groups for social change, some having only a few members plus a staff of careerist cause-pushers. They may be supported by wealthy sponsors, such as companies whose products or political preferences are under attack. Typical topics for pressure groups are reduction of disliked taxes, advocacy of tariffs to protect local companies from foreign competition, care for the elderly, increased funding for scientific research, subsidy of farm products, and advocacy of time for prayers in public schools. These groups depend on such methods as lobbying, getting preferred candidates on the ballot, urging that particular bills be put into the legislative hopper, collecting funds to ensure the election of politicians who agree with their views, and working in the election campaigns of favored legislators. Writings on groups like these include Barbrook and Bolt (1980), Douglas and Wildavsky (1982), and Olsen (1982).

Citizen Participation Groups

The term *citizen participation groups* designates committees that provide participants a means, mandated by law, to influence the policies and actions of administrative units in government. The invited members of these bodies serve for no compensation and usually are not professionals or even specialists in the matters on which they are asked to give advice. The term *citizen participation* is also used by sociologists and social psychologists who study why citizens participate in groups for social good, such as block or neighborhood organizations (Wandersman and others, 1987). For the present purposes, I use the term to describe a specific field of interest among political scientists.

Although government agencies have always had advisory committees, the main feature of citizen participation bodies is that their membership is drawn from the ranks of persons who are served by the entities they advise. President Lyndon Johnson fostered the use of such advisory bodies in 1964, when he declared a war on poverty. The Office of Economic Opportunity, which he created to fight this war, required that poor people be given the opportunity for maximum feasible participation in planning and monitoring the services in their communities. The war on poverty was conducted by branches of the Community Action Program (CAP) in each of nearly a thousand towns. It was locally sponsored, according to law, by either public or private agencies. Federal funds were granted to each town so that participants could do what they thought was best in their "theaters" of the war. The idea of encouraging citizen participation soon spread to other governmental agencies working in welfare, housing, reduction of poverty, health care, and urban planning. By 1978, a total of 155 federal agencies required local or regional advisory bodies. Federal guidelines were published, describing how such units should be run. The councils were regularly mandated in such legislation as the Model Cities Act, the Airport and Airways Development Act, the Federal Water Pollution and Controls Act, and the Energy Reorganization Act. The idea was also taken up by the governments of states, counties, cities, and towns. Today, as an illustration of the idea's diffusion throughout the land, Pennsylvania has 165 laws that require local advisory committees for governmental programs.

Students of politics soon became interested in this new layer of government. They believed that the creation of these bodies was stimulated by increased interest (during the 1960s) in civil rights and (during the 1970s) by the desire to hold officials more responsible for their acts (a desire that arose after the Watergate scandals), as well as by the wish among administrative officials to inform citizens and taxpayers more fully about the programs they were sponsoring, with an eye toward strengthening the support of advisers.

Daniel Moynihan, who had an active part in these developments, offers other, more abstract reasons for the creation of these advisory units (Moynihan, 1970). He believes that the planners wanted to develop a sense of power among persons in poor neighborhoods because such people too often feel that they have no control over their destinies. This opportunity for a role in policymaking was supposed to help them see that they and their neighbors amounted to something. Participation in decisions about matters that affected them would also increase the participants' sense of identification with one another, as well as their acceptance of the ideas at hand. Group decisions were expected to be more valuable to the members than private decisions and therefore more closely followed by the persons who made them.

The designers had three goals in mind for these bodies. The first was to give the users of an agency's services a say in the offerings of that organization. This implies that there was to be a redistribution of power, whereby the established holders of influence would give up some of their influence and grant it to the advisers. The second goal was to increase citizens' support for the work of the agencies. The third was to improve the services offered by these governmental units.

Unlike other kinds of bodies discussed in this chapter, units devoted to citizen participation have been studied a good deal, to see whether they accomplish what they are supposed to. Generally speaking, the answer is no. Ideas offered by citizen advisers have had little impact on the practices of the organizations they serve, according to Berry (1981), Brill (1971), Kweit and Kweit (1971), Langton (1978), Moynihan (1970), and Olsen (1982). These writers give several reasons for this failure. Members of such units were often coopted by the agencies that they were to have enlightened, so that participants did not come up with notions that differed much from those already in place. Their suggestions were neither noticed nor given weight by professionals in the organizations because the officials believed (rightly or wrongly) that the suggestions of the advisers were unworkable, naïve, or based on misinformation. The goals of the agencies were often so vague that the advisers had no clear criteria to use in selecting among alternative plans of actions. According to Brill (1971) and Moynihan (1970), members of the counseling groups often lacked the necessary knowledge to develop sound advice. They preferred confronting to conferring in dealing with officials, and they quarreled among themselves while trying to decide what counsel they should offer. Problems within units of the war on poverty were that poor people moved a lot, community activities were typically staffed by middle-class persons whose views did not match those of the counselors, lower-class people were skeptical from the outset that they could accomplish anything and were easily discouraged, and advisers representing separate groups in the communities could not agree when they joined in common conferences.

The approach also labored under several other disadvantages. Moynihan (1970) says that President Johnson regretted having urged maximum feasible participation and gave the program little support once it was under way because he was concerned about the war in Vietnam and about criticisms of the war on poverty. The government was never quite sure what it was trying to accomplish; it had a theory about the value of participation and about urging it on poor people, but it had little else. There was no remedy, Moynihan says, only an untested basis for an untried procedure. The advisory committees were supposed to use a democratic method, but this did not suit the procedures followed in most agencies of government. Furthermore, expectations of results among members of these councils (persons who were not well versed in the professional nuances of the agencies they were to advise) were in fact often unrealistic. Moynihan (1970) states that some leaders of these groups decided to overcome apathy among local citizens by rubbing their sores or discontent raw, or by arousing hatred toward certain programs or persons, so that the listeners would overcome their lethargy in fits of anger. People in the agencies and the advisory units alike were disappointed in the notion of maximum feasible participation. Moynihan (1970) believes, however, that this program for poor people gave local black leaders first-rate training and experience in influential roles just at the time when these people were becoming increasingly interested in urban politics.

Citizen Action Groups

This term is used by those who organize groups composed of persons receiving welfare funds. The aim is to ensure that these people receive everything coming to them. The welfare-rights unions were created outside the sponsorship of the Office of Economic Opportunity. Eventually, they were joined into the Association of Community Organizations for Reform Now (ACORN) (Delgado, 1986). Community neighborhood councils in large cities were similar to the welfare-rights unions, but their membership was not limited to persons on welfare. These councils are discussed by Alinsky (1971) and Lancourt (1979) as parts of the so-called back-of-the-yards movement, which arose near the stockyards in Chicago and spread to other large cities.

ACORN units were created by organizers who came to town, often uninvited, and worked to develop entities that would protect the rights of people on welfare. In contrast, organizers on Alinsky's counseling staff (devoted to advising city dwellers) ordinarily were paid to assist those who wanted to create an urban neighborhood council but did not know how to do so. Along with ensuring welfare rights, members of these bodies sought improvements in such matters as housing (cost, conditions, availability, restricted mortgages), services provided for the poor, environmental conditions, and behavior of the police. Delgado (1986) describes forty different kinds of issues taken up by ACORN bodies at one time or another.

Units engaged in citizen action preferred to confront the people they wished to influence (that is, they attended meetings of official bodies in the city and demanded, loudly, that their grievances be heard and assuaged). Delgado (1986) thinks members preferred direct action, as he called it, because they were skeptical of the results they could obtain by petitioning, lobbying, or negotiating. Alinsky, according to Lancourt (1979), preferred abrasive shouting matches in these situations because such behavior called attention to the problem brought forward by the aggrieved persons and eventually forced the listeners to sit down with the confronters and engage in good-faith bargaining. We will learn more about Alinsky's rules for behavior in such bodies later on.

According to Delgado (1986), there were ten local ACORN organizations in 1975. By 1984, there were eight thousand, in all fifty states. Delgado (1986) and Moynihan (1970) believe that these units spread because organized actions to broaden civil rights and to protest against the war in Vietnam had demonstrated that dissatisfied persons could obtain results that would be impossible without such bodies. Persons who had worked for civil rights or against the war in Vietnam were willing to serve, often to "advance revolutionary consciousness." They were trained as organizers, and many of them (usually recent college graduates) remained on the road for months, working for ACORN to create new chapters wherever feasible. Eventually, Delgado suggests, these separate entities may work together on national causes that interest them, thereby becoming a new political party. Writings about such groups are found in Alinsky (1971), Brill (1971), Delgado (1986), Lancourt (1979), Moynihan (1970), and Piven and Cloward (1977).

Community Groups for Social Action

A sixth type of group seeks to improve local or personal situations. It has appeared throughout history in all kinds of governments. Its prime characteristic, in contrast to the groups discussed so far, is that a few citizens develop a desire for a specific change in their town and attract others to join in a small social movement toward that end. These people are not appointed, elected, or recruited except by themselves, and they work for free, without financial support, advice, or assistance (save when they hire such counsel). They are not parts of a larger social movement or government plan and are seldom allied with other bodies. Some of these entities have a brief life and are concerned with only one topic; others last many years and take up numerous issues. They cannot, of course, get the relief they seek through their endeavors alone, and so they try to get help from administrative officials or from the constituents of these leaders—their target persons. The individuals they hope to help vary from group to group. They may intend to benefit their own members and no one else; particular persons outside the groups who need special assistance; individuals whom they represent; city blocks, ethnic groups, neighborhoods, or whole communities, perhaps including flora, fauna, or esthetically pleasing objects that have a right to protection. They are unique in that they use any of a wide variety of methods in working toward change, from permitting to pressuring, from helping to harming. Because bodies like these are seldom examined (except by the media, when their actions make news), let us recall a few instances of them. I sort these bodies into separate kinds of units according to who their beneficiaries are supposed to be.

Members Only. A simple example of a self-serving group is one that arose in Boston during the American Revolution. At the time, the British occupied the city and had an encampment around the area that is known today as the Commons. Soldiers' tents were placed on the side of a hill, which in the winter months was the favorite place for sledding among boys in the neighborhood. The young people were unhappy about losing their coasting place and requested a meeting with General Gage, the officer in charge of the troops, to state their grievance. He received them graciously, and after hearing their request and teasing them about their readiness to rebel as their fathers were doing, he agreed to move some tents to make room for the coasters. The neophyte protesters won their way, even though they had no right to make such an appeal.

Although these boys used a gentle approach in seeking change, one can find organized moves that are even milder. In California, for example, in the century following 1850, seventeen utopias came and went (Hine, 1953). Each of these was an isolated community of several dozen persons, who set out to devise an ideal kind of society on either religious or socialistic grounds. They qualify as would-be agents of social change because each group intended to have its community serve as a model society for the rest of the world. The members seldom attempted, however, to bring their newly perfected way of life to the attention of outsiders. They were passive idealists waiting for the rest of the population to discover and copy them; they were mostly ignored. None of them lasted longer than twenty years. They either went broke or quarreled and split up over the best course to follow. Communes in recent years, as described by Kanter (1972), are not always so passive. Some of them send speakers into surrounding areas to spread the ideas they favor.

An excellent study of a community group engaged in influential action is provided by Lindgren (1987). She describes a body that was organized twenty-five years ago to work on a single issue— namely, to oppose the construction of a bridge over a river in the center of a small city. The proposed span was to carry traffic from a busy part of town and empty it into a quiet residential neighborhood. For a quarter of a century, the group of neighbors lobbied members of the city council and officials of the state highway department, offered alternative proposals based on expert advice, held hearings, and informed townsfolk about what was happening. The body was dormant from time to time, coming back to life whenever the bridge question was again up for consideration. Their views did not always prevail, but no bridge has yet been built.

Sometimes a problem arises for a group of neighbors because another group is given something it has requested. For example, the recreation commission of a middle-sized city permitted the erection of lights on poles at a playground, so that baseball games could be played in the evenings. Over several years, the officers of the softball league had collected most of the necessary money and asked the city to put up lights. Because the poles holding the bulbs were unusually high, the resulting brightness caused an unwelcome glare around houses bordering the ballfield. The noise of the games at night was also a nuisance. As a result, an organization called Neighbors Under the Lights was formed to seek relief from these conditions. The protesters decided to bypass the city's recreation commission and put their complaint before the city council. The council heard them and proposed that leaders among the players meet with residents of the affected houses to find a solution that would please both sides. This procedure was followed, and the joint body developed a plan that called for baffles on the lights, a solid fence near the houses (to reduce noise), limited hours of play, and rules for courteous behavior when foul balls landed in neighboring yards. The city council, acting as a mediating body, approved these ideas and voted to provide funds for the changes plus a dirt berm next to the new wall, to muffle the noise still more. Clearly, neighbors and players alike were understanding of and sympathetic to the desires of the other group. The grievance was easily resolved, but it could have led to a long-term disagreement between players and residents.

Groups of activists sometimes arise because they wish to protect themselves from real or imagined threats to their values. For instance, parents in a small midwestern town believed that teachers were leaving their children's school too early, thereby curtailing the education of the children and providing inadequate services to taxpayers. The offended parents asked the school board for tighter supervision of the teaching staff. This request was denied, on the grounds that the principal of the school should be allowed to supervise his staff without outside interference by board members. Feeling that they had a case to prove, the mothers and fathers set up a watch squad. Members of this body sat in automobiles each day on the street outside the school and recorded which teachers left the building at what hours. Children were also asked to spy on their teachers and to report any wasteful practices. After several weeks, the watchers gave their findings to the principal, with a demand that these data be placed in the personnel files of the teachers and reported to the board of education. The principal refused this request because the group had previously stated its case to the board without making a favorable impression, and the teachers who left the building early had his permission to do so. They were being allowed to complete official business, perform voluntary services in town, or attend professional-improvement classes at the local university. The principal also knew that the organizing of these watchers had been primarily the work of a woman who made a career of worrying about whether she was receiving fair treatment in the community. Therefore, he did not believe that many townsfolk would side with the complaining parents. The group's style of operation and reporting generated resentment among the educators who were accused of wrongdoing. These teachers therefore agreed among themselves to provide no further voluntary services outside of school hours. Underground discussion of the issue raised so much distrust that the next school levy was voted down, and educational services had to be decreased. Here, a small-scale action aroused a large-scale reaction (Madison, 1973).

A final example of an organization for self-centered help is one that was formed in England in 1811. The participants were weavers and knitters, who worked in their homes on looms that they rented from the persons who purchased their woven and knitted products (Liversidge, 1972). Since most of the residents of several villages took part in this business, work and life in the town overlapped. The owners charged high rent for the machines and paid low prices for the finished goods. They urged the weavers to work quickly, and so the weavers made mistakes and were then ashamed of their shoddy work. The owners also preferred to hire children because children could be paid less than adults. A few community leaders complained to the bosses about these conditions, but their grievances were ignored. Some instigators declared a work stoppage, but this call was ineffective, since most of the community members were afraid to join the strike. The initiators of the protest then demanded that all weavers and knitters take part in a strike or have their looms destroyed. Soon thereafter a militant band entered the homes of a few holdouts and smashed their knitting frames. This raid, as well as a number of others, was planned and led by a former soldier, who assumed the name Ned Ludd; his followers were known as Luddites. They eventually wrecked more than a thousand machines, yet the owners refused to make the changes requested by the strikers. The bosses pushed instead for national laws against destroying industrial machinery. These laws were passed and the strike was broken.

People Outside the Group. In contrast to groups created for personal ends, some units are developed to benefit people who are not group members. Participants in such entities may gain from their own efforts, but such rewards are side effects, and acquiring them is not the prime goal. Indeed, members of bodies like these often lose money because they help finance their groups' good works and receive no compensation for the time, energy, and strain they put into a cause, although they do obtain satisfaction from helping others, even at some cost to themselves. They are altruists (Bar-Tal, 1976; Macaulay and Berkowitz, 1970).

Members of units created to help disadvantaged persons may provide direct help to the deprived. These services are expensive, and so the altruists ask townsfolk to help cover the costs. A unit may begin a program (say, to furnish food for homeless persons or to help new immigrants find homes) on the assumption that financial assistance can be obtained from kindhearted neighbors, churches, and welfare funding agencies, or a unit may start a project simply to demonstrate what can be done. Once such a program is under way, the group asks governmental agencies for continuing sponsorship, hoping that thereafter it will be supported by the government. Whether initiators of such activities look to ordinary citizens or to city officials for financial support, they must attract wide interest in their goals and must influence persons who will help carry on their activities. Often the best way to gain the help they need is to appeal to the general public, asking the public to convince local agencies that they ought to take the new program under their wing.

Capraro (1979) describes a community-development corporation created in southwest Chicago to form a coalition among neighborhood residents, local banks, and businesses. The aim of this body was to change the growing perception that the community was gradually becoming a slum. A large building in the area's business district had been vacated, and the coalition worked to make sure that the new tenants would be good neighbors, rather than proprietors of adult bookstores, bookie joints, or bars. They helped get the building refurbished and recruited reputable businesses, including a jewelry store and a delicatessen. The building's value immediately increased. This same body also renovated a large apartment house

that had previously been a haven for drug dealers and was supposed to have been torn down (Wandersman, 1984).

As another example, in a rapidly growing city there is only one road to carry traffic between the northern and southern parts of town. Everyone complains of the crowded conditions on this thoroughfare, but local officials do not wish to discuss a solution because the only place available for a parallel way is through land on the town's eastern edge, which has been set aside as an open space and is not to be used by anyone but pedestrians. Citizens who defend the open space are vociferous in their arguments against putting a road through that territory, and they readily recruit rabid supporters when that is necessary. Thus, the issue is quietly ignored by the city council, the planning commission, and the traffic commission, even though something will have to be done sooner or later. A retired civil engineer and several friends have designated themselves as a task force. Their goal is to find a route for an avenue through the open area that will be minimally offensive to all concerned. They have gathered the necessary engineering data and made detailed drawings at their own expense. The course they favor requires the widening and extending of streets close to the open space. It also calls for a limited-access road, which means that no driver will be able to leave the highway where it passes through the untouched area. They have a plan that they think will work and have presented it to various groups, asking the listeners for criticisms and suggestions. They hope to generate a favorable public response and an invitation to present their drawings before one of the braver official bodies. No member of the initiating group will benefit directly if this new road is built.

As still another example, a different kind of unit, in this city and in others nearby, was recently created to take action for the good of all. (Once again, the officials who should have sponsored helpful changes were not willing or able to do so.) The members of the helping units recognized that their communities were growing, and that it would not be long before all land suitable for parks, schools, or other public buildings was covered with houses, shops, and large buildings and that the plots would become so expensive that the cities would be unable to afford them. The helpers in each community therefore created trust funds, composed of contributions

from local citizens and firms, to buy land suitable for public use and to hold this real estate until their city governments might wish to obtain it and would be able to pay for it. The land would be sold at the price paid years before, rather than at a later, inflated price. If a community's government were to express no interest in such land, then the helping units, after a reasonable period of time, would sell it to help cover their own expenses. No one would benefit unduly from this arrangement.

Some years ago, planning groups were developed in a number of cities to examine and evaluate local social programs. These groups were created under the joint financial sponsorship of the Ford Foundation and an agency of the federal government (Marris and Rein, 1967). Staff members in both the foundation and the federal agency believed they could help improve communities' social services by asking that any studies of these programs, as well as any changes proceeding from such investigations, meet criteria created by the sponsors. They also offered funds to help establish new activities. The members of these planning groups were community leaders. Few were professionally engaged (or experienced) in alleviating local social problems. They assumed, however, that such issues demanded disinterested and objective study, along with wise social engineering. They also believed that their lack of past involvement in such programs made it possible for them to deal objectively with the facts, rather than base their decisions on compassion, as had been done too often in the past. Marris and Rein (1967), who studied these planning groups, state that most of them were not successful (that is, few of the plans created by these groups were adopted by local people). A major reason was that the group members had developed their ideas without giving sufficient consideration to conflicting interests among residents of the town, nor were their ideas generally accepted by local social workers.

Here is a final example of an altruistic group. In 1942, before laws supporting the civil rights of black Americans were common, some white college students in Iowa City met to plan how they could persuade the owners of local restaurants to serve black students. All eating places in that town were lily-white; any "colored" student who entered a restaurant was told to leave. When asked about this policy, the owners explained that white customers would

protest if a Negro were served. The activists decided to focus on this rationalization because they believed that few students would even notice, let alone object, if a black student were served. Accordingly, they interviewed owners of the student eateries. As they had expected, all the owners said privately that they were willing to serve black students but were afraid to do so. Next, the students circulated a petition on campus, in which they asked signers to say that they would not object if black students were served at a nearby table. Armed with many signatures, members of the change group again talked to the owners and displayed their petitions, showing that there was little danger of an unfavorable reaction from white customers. The owners were again asked whether they would serve black students who came into their restaurants. Most said that they would. This agreement was tested when a few black students were asked to enter each restaurant. Activists would be present to observe how they were treated. None of the black customers had any difficulty. Although the plan was simple, it took a remarkable amount of work to bring it off.

Members and Others. The most common type of group for social action benefits the participants themselves, as well as a specific set of persons they represent (or claim to). Here are some examples.

Residents on the west side of a small city in Oklahoma learned that a manufacturing firm was planning to develop a dump nearby, where toxic wastes would be buried. The townsfolk feared that these poisons might seep into the drinking water or be carried in the winds. A concerned couple brought their neighbors together to discuss this threat. They decided to hire a lawyer and to sue the firm for endangering the public's health. A committee of the members also asked state legislators to pass a law that would forbid construction of a dump near a residential part of the city. They emphasized to the lawmakers that their cause was sponsored by hundreds of persons. Most of their efforts went into recruiting new members and into earning the money needed for the lawyer's fees. They conducted bake sales, held rallies, spoke to clubs, and passed out pamphlets at local shopping malls, asking in each case for financial help. Their actions were low-key and dignified, yet many members received anonymous telephone calls and letters accusing them of being radicals and troublemakers. Their efforts failed.

A comparable group developed in New Jersey when a state-appointed environmental commission decided to get rid of radioactive waste by blending it with uncontaminated dirt and burying the mixture in an abandoned gravel quarry and in the hayfields of adjacent land (Hanley, 1986). Neighbors in the selected area heard rumors of this plan and set up a meeting with state officials to learn more about it. At this session, the farmer whose land had been chosen to be the disposal site heard for the first time that he was the designated host. Representatives of the environmental agency said that there was no danger from the material to be buried. The residents did not believe these assurances. They developed an organization to prevent creation of the dump. They blockaded the only access road, so that trucks could not reach the site, and they built a fortress of railroad ties to protect themselves from attack. They hired a lawyer to appeal for an appropriate injunction. They set up a telephone network and a warning system, so that two hundred sympathetic citizens could be gathered at the battleground on short notice. They earned funds to support their activities by holding rock concerts and walkathons. They also sold baseball caps in local stores with the slogan "Hell No, We Won't Glow!" The dump site was moved to a different location.

When an area experiences a rapid growth in population, some residents may wish to slow these changes. For example, one body was committed to the prevention of growth in a suburban town. This group was composed initially of persons who were angry over heavy traffic during rush hours, and who assembled in response to an announced forum on problems of transportation. Those who attended decided that the reason for the traffic problem was that the population of the city had grown too large for the size and layout of its streets. Many new residents had been drawn to the town because a few years earlier it had encouraged the construction of half a dozen large office buildings. Now the structures and their occupants were on hand, and the result was much heavier traffic. The assembled citizens agreed to form an organization that would prevent further growth. They soon had a chance to further their cause, when developers proposed to close a few streets and build a new shopping mall downtown. The no-growth body worked to prevent this development, got the issue placed on a citywide ballot, and stopped the mall. As a result of this election, a new law was also put on the town's books. It requires that no new structure taller than six stories and larger than ten thousand square feet be built in the city without the approval of a majority of voters in a citywide ballot. The cost of such an election is to be paid by the builder. This regulation will stay in effect until the streets are improved enough to handle automobile traffic better than they now do. The goal that the no-growth advocates seek is precise—a traffic light must not hold up a motorist for more than a stated number of seconds. (This improvement in the flow of traffic, as it turns out, has been impossible to achieve.) New building is effectively stalled for the time being because no developer wants to pay for a citywide election. Meanwhile, the group against growth has become a political pressure body and has managed to get members elected to the city council, so that the majority of council members now support the no-growth stand.

The movement for black power among young people in the southern states was a form of activism in which members of small cells worked to benefit both themselves and others in their communities. These units developed spontaneously, each on its own. There was no regional movement, nor was there any joint conspiracy among the teams in separate towns to disobey the laws that infringed civil rights. National black leaders had made the times ripe for some kind of effort to get such laws changed. Nevertheless, the leaders were surprised when youths took action without letting the veterans in on their plans (Gerlach and Hine, 1970). Their typical moves are familiar. A squad of well-dressed and courteous black youths entered an eating place and waited for service. They refused to leave when asked to do so and continued to sit quietly, sometimes for hours. Sooner or later, the manager would ask police to remove the unwanted guests, an action that won the manager publicity that was not always favorable. The same procedure was used in many other public places that barred black people, such as libraries, swimming pools, railroad waiting rooms, and even schools. Eventually, groups of white students from northern colleges journeyed south to help the black-power units conduct their campaigns. These new-age carpetbaggers were not given a friendly welcome by white residents or officials. Nevertheless, the laws restricting the access of black people to public places eventually were removed, partly as a result of the actions by these young people.

Citizens are sometimes moved to take action when they dislike a step proposed by officials. For example, a group was formed to prevent the return of an unwanted prisoner to his hometown in California. Years earlier, he had been convicted of raping and maiming a young girl in that city. His forthcoming parole from prison was publicly announced by correction officials, in accordance with the law. When the intention to parole this man became known, a number of mothers met and prepared a complaint, which they delivered to the warden of the prison. This grievance received no response. After his release, the parolee rented an apartment in his old neighborhood. The mothers began a vigil outside his building, objecting to his presence. These actions earned attention from the news media. He left two days later, under police escort. Persons who had formed the protesting group admitted to reporters that they were without pity, but they were sure no one in the town would object to their approach. No one did (Chamberlain, 1987).

As another example of a group created to benefit both itself and others, consider the vigilantes in San Francisco during the days of the Gold Rush. In 1851, the city was in a third year of rapid growth, and much easy-come-easy-go wealth was held by its young, mostly male population. Many disreputable new arrivals came to acquire some of this money, without enduring the rigors that the original finders had experienced. The methods that the newcomers employed did not win the admiration of those who reluctantly provided these funds. At the time, San Francisco had no full-fledged government or officers of the law, and so the vigilantes—mostly businessmen in town—appointed themselves the operators of a judicial system for punishing those who deserved punishment. They hoped, too, that their amateur efforts would hasten the establishment of legitimate ordinances, courts of law, and a police force. They set about punishing thieves and other wrongdoers, without using due process or asking for public approval of their moves. Hangings were conducted in the streets, in full view of the residents.

During their period of "service," the vigilantes arrested ninety-one men, hanged four of them, banished twenty-eight from the city, punished sixteen in other ways, and set sixteen free. They believed that their actions caused a drop in the rate of crime and that the goodness of these results justified their methods. They described the persons they arrested as too evil to deserve civil rights. As soon as the city created agencies and officials who could defend law and order, the vigilantes ceased their operations.

Sometimes beneficiaries are objects, or states of affairs. Some groups are developed to improve attractive objects or the products of nature. Members believe that a valuable thing or place should be protected, regardless of its value for humans. A founder of a group that works to conserve open land put it this way: "We wanted to argue for the wilderness for its own sake, instead of having to come up with a bunch of human-centered reasons about why wilderness is good. It just is. That's all there is to it" (Diringer, 1987). Arguments in favor of such a view have been offered by Christopher Stone in his 1974 book *Should Trees Have Standing? Toward Legal Rights for Natural Objects.* Stone holds that legal rights have been extended in the past to people who previously had none; likewise, it is reasonable that endangered objects can also be deserving of protection. He proposes that legal rights be granted to objects in the environment such as trees, mountains, rivers, and lakes, just as corporations have been given rights and protected by law (regardless of actions by their individual members). The beneficiary is the object itself, not the human users of it. Examples of this kind of activity are efforts to refurbish a statue; to prohibit roads in the wilderness; to prevent species of plants, animals, and birds from extinction; to name a mountain; and to preserve a historical site.

National movements to prevent cruelty to animals have been around for a long time. Their work has led to the development of federal guidelines that researchers must obey if they wish to use animals in their laboratories. Most researchers believe they have a legal and ethical responsibility to follow these regulations in caring for their animals, and they do so. The rules have provided a rationale, however, for groups on college campuses and elsewhere who protest the use of animals in medical and other research. Because laboratory animals cannot defend themselves, the protesters suspect that the researchers carelessly cause pain to the imprisoned beasts. As a result, the activists try to rescue the animals by breaking into the buildings where they are kept, destroying equipment in the laboratories, and even burning down the research structures. Defense of the defenseless can arouse extraordinary hostility.

A group in a western city conducts a watch over research that is trying to reduce the vulnerability of strawberry plants to frost. In this work, approved by the National Institutes of Health, the plants are sprayed with a solution containing bacteria that (it is hoped) will prevent the formation of ice on their leaves when the temperature falls below freezing. These bacteria have been created through genetic engineering. The members of the group objecting to these experimental activities fear that the manufactured bacteria may spread to other plants and cause unfavorable effects. To prevent such an occurrence, the watchers have destroyed the experimental strawberry plot several times, evading guards who were posted to protect the berries day and night. The members of this aggressive body call themselves the Environmental Guerrillas. One member commented on the group's behavior in this way: "I am not at all happy that it's come to this, but I don't feel I have any choice. To me, the stakes are so high, I'm willing to do that. I'm willing to make sure that none of the tests succeed. . . . What's exciting is that for once you feel empowered in a world that tries to take your power away. You're demanding that your voice be heard" (Diringer, 1987, p. A-8). For such believers (as is so often the case), might is right.

Summary

Community groups seek to acquire a say for citizens in solving local social problems, improving unpleasant situations, and creating other changes. Six separate kinds of bodies interested in social change are social movements, improvement associations, pressure groups, citizen participation groups, citizen action groups, and community groups for social action. Our major attention will be devoted to the latter two kinds of bodies because these have seldom been studied, and they are small entities created by amateurs to accomplish tasks important to them. How and why do these units develop? How do they keep up their courage? What methods do they use in their actions, and why? How do the persons they try to influence react to these bodies? These questions are considered in the following pages.

3

Conditions Favoring
the Formation of Groups

Any group is organized, putting it simply, because it will be useful for its organizers, for those who become members, or for others. A unit for social action is formed because its developers wish to remedy an unsatisfactory state of affairs or to take advantage of an opportunity to accomplish a valued end. They assume that a supportive group will work with them to do these things well. Individuals who are aware of a need for change are more likely to create an action group if they perceive that four facilitating circumstances exist. These four circumstances, as I see them, are as follows (Zander, 1985):

1. Conditions in the community or in the behavior of influential persons are unsatisfactory or suggest an opportunity for favorable change. We have seen examples of such unwanted situations in the two previous chapters.
2. A more satisfactory state of affairs is conceived by organizers.

Those who develop an organization need an idea about what a group can accomplish before they will try to establish one.

3. Organizers and members believe that they will succeed if they attempt to achieve the proposed change. They judge that their group will be able to accomplish its objectives.

4. Conditions in the community do not prevent people from establishing a unit for social action or from taking part in its activities. Potential members or observers are willing to join groups, to tolerate ambiguity during the early days of the group's life, to favor values that support an action group in the community, to forgo interest in keeping things just as they are, and to develop the knowledge and skills needed of members.

We shall consider each of these four conditions in turn.

Condition 1

An unfavorable situation, or an opportunity for improving things, is a necessary (but not sufficient) condition for organizers to begin assembling a group for action. Recall some of the circumstances that inspire the formation of such groups. Citizens dislike pollution of the air, fallout of nuclear waste, drunken drivers, dealers in drugs, inadequate care for poor people, weeds in the city park, noisy parties, or traffic-jammed streets. Opportunities for a useful change include a championship won by a local team (which calls for a celebration), a good harvest, a band to play in the park, the deeds of a local hero, the possibility of attracting a new college campus to town, or a chance to get a company to move into the area.

Situations triggering groups that will benefit their own members are usually different from those that cause groups to help nonmembers. Self-centered units are more often stimulated by displeasing conditions. For example, individuals become fearful because people of other races, ethnic origins, or socioeconomic levels are moving into local jobs. Neighbors discover that books offensive to them are on the shelves of the local library. Citizens feel that the beliefs and standards of their religion are ignored in the public schools. Protesters complain that their streets are not yet paved.

Residents unhappy about the slow progress in redeveloping the center of their city form a group called UPROAR (United Property Residents Organized Against Redevelopment). Self-centered bodies are also organized by persons who see an opportunity to help themselves. Amateur artists plan a street fair, where their works can be displayed and sold. Tennis players create a club to arrange for tournaments and lessons among members. Followers of a local baseball team form a society that meets for boosters' luncheons. Engineering professors sponsor a research park, where firms working with new technologies can be induced to settle and thereby keep the professors up to date on recent developments and provide jobs for graduate students.

Groups formed to benefit persons other than members are triggered by matters different from those just noted. In such helping bodies, organizers perceive that specific persons are in need and cannot take care of themselves because they are homeless, hungry, powerless, poor, or victims of a flood, fire, storm, or accident. The helpless ones may also be victims of drugs, alcohol, malnutrition, or inadequate health care. They are not registered to vote, do not understand the electoral process, or do not know how to make their voices heard in the community. They do not know or use the words and behavior that will make them eligible for the rewards that a city can provide.

Groups that intend to benefit both members and nonmembers are inspired by similar issues, such as pollution of local air, excessive traffic on too-narrow streets, a bad taste in drinking water, or corruption in city hall. Crimes in the neighborhood, such as breaking and entering, car theft, rape, drug dealing, and vandalism, may inspire the formation of citizen squads, whose members patrol the neighborhood to watch for suspicious persons. Likewise, everyone in a town may feel that something must be done because a local mine has been shut down, a large business has reduced the number of people it hires, a drought is affecting farmers' crops, or a forest fire has made neighbors destitute. Misfortune on a scale too large for local government to handle often requires joint action by those who need relief.

Opportunities to improve current situations for members and others include a law that bars local use of nuclear energy, a goal-setting committee for the city, or a community council composed of representatives of local clubs. Groups may honor the pioneers who first settled in the area and may create conferences on that subject. Often, as we have seen, the triggering event for organized social action is what appears to be a true grievance. Forty homes are to be destroyed to create a new entry and exit for a freeway, the only bus line in town is abolished, the odor created by a paper mill is sickening, or a whole town must be moved away from lowlands that flood annually. Yet, in some cases, such severe situations are tolerated without more than mild complaint. If asked about the unpleasant conditions, residents say that they are to be expected, are not too bad, or are a part of local life. What causes people to decide that they must act and that a group for action should be developed?

Beyond merely being aware of a deprivation, those who organize to create change must also believe that they are enduring more than they should or are receiving fewer benefits than they deserve. They decide that they are disadvantaged, in terms of what they ought to have or what others like themselves usually obtain. They are in a state of *relative deprivation* (Gusfield, 1968; Wilson, 1973; Wood and Jackson, 1982). The point is that there is no simple relationship between the quality of a given hardship (which is not always easy to measure) and the feeling of being deprived. Therefore, before organizers will try to create a group to deal with a grievance, the organizers must be convinced that the current situation is unfair and that potential members agree with that view. Accordingly, the developers point out to recruits that persons in other towns are doing better on the issue under question; for example, the others have superior housing, cleaner water, higher wages, and more bus transportation, or they collect more money in their annual campaigns to support social services. Potential members are led to see that others have a better deal and are not more deserving. It is notable, in passing, that the tendency of citizens to compare their experiences with events in other cities is used by officials in the national headquarters of the United Fund to press local units toward setting realistic goals. The central office tells fund leaders in each community how well they did in collecting money for local welfare agencies by comparison with half a dozen other cities of similar economic status. These data are used by the board of each local drive to set future objectives for the communities. A town's new goals are set higher than those of the previous year if rival towns have performed better. The success of the rival communities also affects a town's future goals more than its own scores do. Poor performances in other places, however, do not lead a town to lower its goals for local campaigns. Managers of financial drives want to do at least as well as other places but not as poorly as other places do (Zander and Newcomb, 1967; Zander, Forward, and Albert, 1969; Zander, 1971).

Organizers may also get a group under way by demonstrating to interested persons that current situations are unjust because they do not conform to accepted standards. The initiators show recruits that regulations are being bypassed with respect to such matters as disposal of toxic waste, ways of collecting funds for election campaigns, hiring minority members, following zoning regulations, or controlling fast drivers. Similarly, group developers may point to a need for change by demonstrating that a better state of affairs is possible—citizens can reasonably expect traffic to move more smoothly, ambulance service to be cheaper, air to be cleaner, or sewage treatment to be more effective. By comparison to what could be, current conditions are a form of relative deprivation.

A rapid improvement in a given situation can also make people believe that they are being deprived, despite this betterment in their condition, because a swiftly improved circumstance causes observers to expect such progress to continue. They anticipate ever better benefits, and their expectations rise, sometimes to an unrealistic level (Zander, 1971). Success breeds a desire for more success. As a consequence, people want more than they have attained so far. Any decrease in their gains, or in the rate at which these arrive, is taken to be a deprivation. Thus, recent occupants of new houses, more expensive than any in town, are against paying for paving their sidewalks. Newly promoted supervisors form a labor union to protect their status. Members of the starting team resent being replaced by those on the reserve squad. Members of a posh Italian-American club refuse to accept recent immigrants from Italy as members.

Quick changes in an unfavorable direction stimulate feelings of being disadvantaged. A factory suddenly closes, college youths are told they will be drafted for military service in an unpopular war, a bank folds, or the local team loses a championship it should have won. When a deprivation is sufficiently sudden or severe, it may cause anger among those who have to endure its consequences. They may relieve their frustration by looting, wrecking, shooting, lynching, arson, and the like (Rude, 1964). If such hostile reactions are too strong, organizers may find it difficult to form an organization—people want action, not rational planning.

When people realize that they are disadvantaged, what do they do? Often, they do nothing. Neighbors or colleagues may talk about an unfavorable situation, complain about it, and agree that something should be done, but they may not take any steps at all. They may start to form an organization but then give up the idea. Why? There are several reasons. They may not be able to invent a way to improve the current state of affairs. They decide that the problem is insoluble. They can find no leader, are embarrassed to do what needs to be done, or fear reprisal if they complain aloud. They see no chance of influencing appropriate target persons, find that mere talk about the situation is so satisfying that they do not need to take any action, or do not know what to do or how to do it. (We consider such passive behavior in Chapter Five.)

Condition 2

Recognition that something needs fixing is not enough to inspire persons toward organizing a unit for social action. Group developers must also have ideas about what can be done and about how things could be different and better. In short, they need an objective—a sound one— for the group. The goal they choose must have several qualities if they are to convince others that it is worth working for.

First, the objective must serve as an incentive to members of the body. An incentive is a state or object that, once achieved, will provide satisfaction to those who value it. The aim must be one that group members want to reach. Groups for social action, by comparison with bodies created in commerce, law, the military, religion, or education, usually have little trouble developing attractive objectives because they are created to deal with issues that matter very much to their members. The interest of college students in their groups' tasks is usually greater, for example, when they are picketing an administration building in support of a cause than when they are working in groups on assigned projects in the classroom.

Second, the objective of the group, once achieved, must provide a way to resolve the issue that originally inspired formation of the body—that is, accomplishment of the group's goal must provide a true change and a better state of affairs. Organizers will find it hard to get people to join a unit unless potential recruits think that achievement of the group's goal will improve the current state of affairs.

Third, the chosen end seems attainable because members have enough resources, ability, and experience for the task at hand. The participants have a sound procedure to follow, and the target persons are not liable to develop immovable opposition or resistance.

Fourth, developers must decide who should benefit from the activities of the group: members alone, nonmembers exclusively, members and nonmembers alike, or the environment? The focus of group effort must be defined, so that an appropriate objective, method, and structure can be selected. For example, if the body is created largely to eliminate a grievance held by members, then its objective is a self-centered one. The method will serve member-oriented desires (persuasion, propaganda, confrontation, or threats will do this), and the structure of the group must ensure that members abide by these methods. Moreover, there is no value for the organizers of a self-centered group in recruiting altruists or in asking members to serve the wants of nonmembers. If, in contrast, the unit is to help outsiders, the members and methods need to be suitable for helping these beneficiaries, and there is no use in recruiting members who have personal gripes to settle or who have militant causes in mind.

When agents of change initially form a group, it is not uncommon for members to prefer action instead of working to define an objective for their efforts. They want to do something, anything, rather than sit and talk about where their actions should lead them. This eagerness develops most often when participants are impatient. It is also likely to arise when the problem is ill defined and when a clear goal for group action is difficult to identify (Zander, 1985).

Weick (1979) believes that persons who are planning to create a group (any group) tend at first to place more emphasis on the activities that members are to undertake than on the goals they are to pursue. They pass out flyers, call for a rally, or march on city hall, without being sure what they hope to gain by these impulsive moves. They do these things regardless of the issues that have led the organizers to develop the new entity. Weick holds that a group's purposes are defined only after members have been acting together as a unit and need a reason to account for what they have done. After these initial acts, which are based on the interest that first brought them together, they may try to delineate specific aims. The group's purpose is retrospective, then, rather than prospective. Weick also says that members' personal aims are best served in a group by their employment of joint methods at the start, rather than by their effort to reach a group goal. According to Weick, members follow a simple cycle of events. They begin their interpersonal interaction in the belief that any of many diverse goals may be appropriate for the group. Next, they collaborate—by creating common means, at the outset, because common means are easier to agree on. They therefore work in coordination (but often toward separate personal goals). This close collaboration ultimately helps them to agree on what a groupwide goal could be. They return once more to collaborating and work again toward developing a common goal. This cycle is repeated as many times as necessary to develop an objective for the unit. A group's goal need not be created at the outset, Weick contends, but members initially do need to use common methods, so that the actors will not interfere with one another's moves. Members gradually shift from using goalless but common means to common and shared aims. Their search for a rationale in support of group action helps members identify useful plans and intentions for the future. They create rules and policies, so that their procedures will fulfill joint objectives. All in all, as Weick sees it, participants act first and find a purpose for their actions later. For Weick (1979, p. 195), behavior is not "goal directed" but is "goal interpreted." He means that a group project is more sensible to members once they have imported a history of group activities into it.

Although we do not know how often members act first and select a purpose later, this sequence certainly does occur, yet I suspect that it is not characteristic of effective organizations. Some groups are created simply to carry out a given step, without members' having any clear vision of what they will accomplish by doing so. Typically, those in such groups think of solutions before they define the difficulty they intend to resolve. Citizens push for a new city charter, without specifying what is wrong with the current one. Churches urge that supermarkets be closed on Sundays, without considering the inconvenience this would create for persons who work nights. In a group created for social action, it is probably less likely that the members will act without any idea about what they want to achieve, since the unit originally was formed to improve a clearly identified state of affairs. Thus, participants tend to have a fairly clear objective at the time the group is assembled. They do not need to act first and find an objective later. Weick's (1979) ideas warrant further study.

Condition 3

In order to form a group, developers not only must see that a given situation needs improvement and define how it can be changed for the better but also must believe that the work of the group can be useful. Moreover, they must know what needs to be done and see how to do it.

The first moves are to assemble potential members. The initiating step may occur in any of several ways. A problem may bring individuals together because misery loves company (Schachter, 1959). These persons discuss ways to help one another, improve their actions, or protect what is theirs. In another instance, a person with an idea for innovations recruits colleagues to meet and evaluate these notions. He posts a call for a general meeting or invites participants to join him in informing a group he wishes to get under way. Lindgren (1987) reports that the Delta Avenue Citizens' Organization began in this way twenty-five years ago. The issue that prompted organization of the unit was a plan for a new bridge, which was seen as a threat to the neighborhood. One person began questioning the need for the project and found that the neighbors he contacted in a door-to-door canvass agreed with him. The group that was formed has stayed with the same issue over the years and is still effective. Wandersman and others (1987) state that 62 percent of those recruited face to face joined a neighborhood organization, but only 10 percent of those who were not personally contacted joined this body.

Like-minded persons may assemble because the promised activity is attractive or the leadership of the group appears to be capable, and they arrange things so that they can continue to meet; or an individual with the power to make this assignment requires a number of persons to become members of a committee or task force; or several persons arouse wide attention for an issue by disseminating information, holding demonstrations, and circulating petitions, and interested persons are invited to create a unit so as to keep this interest alive.

Delgado (1986) says that organizers of unions formed to defend the rights of poor people move through seven stages, over several months, in creating such bodies: (1) learning where potential members live and what issues are most lively in the town, (2) talking to potential members, (3) creating an organizing committee of local leaders, (4) announcing a neighborhood meeting and preparing for it, (5) holding the meeting and creating an organization, (6) descending on a local target group to engage in a "baptism by fire," and (7) evaluating how well the group performed its first action.

Abraham Wandersman and his colleagues have observed who takes an active part in neighborhood organizations and why. The authors have written about these matters in an excellent series of reports (Wandersman, 1981, 1984; Wandersman and others, 1985, 1987; Prestby and Wandersman, 1985; Unger and Wandersman, 1985). These scholars write that a person's sense of community is a precursor for his or her involvement in efforts to improve his or her town. A sense of community has four elements: a feeling of belonging, called *membership*, which grows out of one's awareness of boundaries that define who can belong, one's identification with the neighborhood, and one's feelings of similarity among members; a resident's feeling that he or she will have a say in the activities of an action group and that the group can influence nonmembers;

having neighbors with values similar to one's own; and having neighbors with similar emotional ties to the history of the community. This sense of community among neighbors has been reliably measured by these researchers.

They also write that residents who interact socially with persons living near them are more likely to know about a neighborhood organization and to join it, unless their ties to friendship cliques are so strong that they ignore other matters in the community. Middle-class people are more likely to participate in an action group than lower-class people are. Among those low in socioeconomic status, however, blacks are more active than whites. Nevertheless, social background is much less important than personal characteristics in determining whether people will become agents of change. People who become involved in a group, compared to those who do not, are likely to have more skill with words and to be better able to solve problems. They have a more favorable attitude toward the neighborhood, think more highly of their own skills, believe that their participation can change things, and have a stronger sense of civic duty. They think that the changes they wish to have made are attainable and that they can bring these modifications about. Persons who do not join say that they do not have time to devote to such activities, that their schedules are too crowded, that they are not well enough to take part, or that they trust others to do the job without their contributions.

As we would expect, those who join a new group eventually must help that body deal with several questions. What kind of purpose does each member have? Why is he or she there? How can we assist one another and help the community? What jobs need to be done? Who will do what? Whom shall we try to influence? How can we get influential persons to listen to us? Who will assemble the background information we need? What can we realistically hope to accomplish? Such questions need to be answered wisely if members are to believe that the group will do well.

The members' confidence that their unit will attain its objective probably becomes greater under several conditions. First, colleagues are eager to work toward their joint objective and believe it is important to do so. Second, they are sure they can do the individual tasks they have been asked to perform. Third, participants feel that the group has adequate resources, such as money, space, tools, personnel, ability, experience, and energy. Fourth, the members have no reason to believe they will not be able to reach their group's goal (no news is good news). In fact, it is easy for members to develop confidence in their group in its early days just because their keen concern about the issue that brought them together and their vigorous creativity in planning what to do are encouraging substitutes for hard data about the unit's actual output. Ordinarily, confidence in a group's performance is high in the absence of reliable feedback about how well it really is doing (Zander, 1971, 1985). (More will be said on these matters in Chapter Five.)

Organizers of a new group try to help participants develop faith in themselves. When recruiting members, they emphasize the group's objectives and the strong likelihood that the entity will attain these goals. In contrast to the recruiting of new workers for a business firm, probably little harm is done if a new member is oversold on the idea that he or she will attain personal satisfaction within the group. Should a neophyte not be satisfied after being in the organization for a while, he or she can drop out (a step that is harder to take when one has a new position in a company). Developers make sure that the purpose of the unit is accepted by its members. They show individuals how their activities will help in attaining the unit's objective. They advocate overarching goals that encompass separate and different objectives within parts of the larger unit. They elaborate on the importance of the group's purpose through speeches, mottoes, slogans, memoranda, conferences, discussion groups, demonstrations, and displays. Above all, they make sure that the progress of the group is visible to everyone, and they publicly praise persons who take steps toward attainment of the group's objectives.

Wicker (1987) says that organizers of a group make sure that certain resources are available for a new body, so that it can become a viable entity. By *resource* he means a state, person, or object that can contribute to a planned situation and is appreciated by those in that setting. The first resource is people, especially people who know what is expected of them in that circumstance. Next are necessary tools, supplies, and equipment. The third resource is space appropriate to accommodate the activities carried out there. The fourth is specific or general knowledge that bears on the group's operation. Finally, reserves of money, supplies, plans, and persons must be ready for use, as needed. For a group to be properly developed, Wicker believes the required resources must be located, assembled at one site and one time, and given a place in the program of the unit. The finding, organizing, and gathering of resources demand that organizers of a group devote time, energy, and money toward fulfilling the plan they have in mind for the group they intend to create.

Surprisingly often, the creation of a group for social action is inspired by just one individual, who develops key ideas, assembles sympathetic associates, garners necessary resources, and gives the group faith in itself. Prophets assemble members of a new cult. A citizen starts a community council, an association for civil rights, or a cell to protect the local environment. Some persons make a hobby of developing groups for social action. One resident of San Francisco is well known for his success in having initiated various kinds of action groups in his neighborhood over many years. A man in Phoenix, Arizona, has picketed city hall for eighteen years, rain or shine, with a variety of signs attached to a pole that he holds aloft. He chooses his own issues (usually current problems in city government) and prepares his own messages—some a bit tart. He works solo except when he believes that a problem needs a stronger push. In such a case, he gets friends to join him (Vander Werf, 1987).

An organizer who seeks disciples looks for persons who have an appropriate grievance (or can be taught to feel aggrieved) and who can be shown the value of joining a body for social action. Indeed, many organizations, even when their activities are well under way, put much of their energy into passing out handbills, petitioning, parading, and persuading, simply in order to recruit more and more members to share the load and spread the word. Fuchs (1967) believes that innovators who want to get an organization going must modify their own views to some degree, so that these are not too different from those held by the persons with whom they hope to work. Fuchs illustrates this point by describing the phases that a member of the Peace Corps goes through in trying to get local people to form an organization. At first, the volunteer expects residents to say what needs to be done in the neighborhood. This almost never works; the idea of collaborating with a foreigner is uncomfortable to the natives. The newcomer becomes impatient and decides to start a project independently. It begins but soon stalls because the neighbors provide help only to placate the outsider, not to relieve any grievance they may hold. The volunteer tries to push these persons to work harder. This does not succeed. The volunteer becomes discouraged and eventually realizes that it is necessary to get to know the attitudes and worries of these potential colleagues and learn to accept those feelings as facts before the locals can be expected to recognize that things could be different. One can change others only if one changes oneself. People who write about how a counselor can help neighbors introduce an innovation make the same point. Initiators must be careful not to advance their own beliefs and preferences so strongly that members merely do as they are told, rather than working toward an end that they value (Goodenough, 1963; Lippitt, Watson, and Westley, 1958; Rogers, 1983).

Condition 4

A group for social action is more likely to be formed if developers and members live in a part of town whose residents are broadminded and tolerant of innovations. At the outset, organizers try to make citizens in the community willing to accept the work of such a body; their opposition could slow or stop the group's progress. Developers of a group also welcome other facilitating conditions in the community. Some of those are embodied in the general statements that follow.

1. Persons who have frequent and easy contact with one another are more likely to join hands in a common cause. Those who live in the same neighborhood or who share the same sidewalk, entrance, or mailbox area more often create or join an entity. Individuals from a given office, courtyard, church, pub, or club are also likely to join an organization together. A wise organizer, accordingly, recruits people from the same network—people who already know one another.

2. Studies by social psychologists support the adage that birds of a feather flock together (Berscheid and Walster, 1978; Schachter, 1959). Potential participants are more likely to join a

body if they are similar to other members in such matters as age, grievances, aspirations, attitudes, hopes, socioeconomic status, education, or interests. Above all, participants need to be alike in the values they support—that is, in their beliefs about what is right and wrong (Newcomb, 1961).

3. Recruits are best sought among people who like to work in a group or who can be induced to do so. Not everyone enjoys belonging to an organization; many people, perhaps the majority, do not (Zander, 1971). In most towns, only one-third of the residents ever join entities other than churches. In big cities, people at lower socioeconomic levels are less likely to belong than those at the middle or upper levels. Counselors on community organization for inner-city areas therefore try to give members the skills and confidence they need to take social action on joint problems. For example, according to Lancourt (1979), Alinsky and his colleagues trained urban activists to create accepting conditions that make upward mobility possible for all citizens. The activists help local residents participate in decisions that affect their lives, and they work to ensure that all persons have equal justice and civil rights. They develop neighborhood organizations that have the power to influence officials. They also provide residents with the information that members of a newly formed group need in order to feel confident that they can do what their group is supposed to do.

4. When people in an area where a group for social action is formed do not fear that local changes will cause undue stress and strain, or that creation of a body dedicated to introducing an innovation is a threat to the stability of the social order, the group's work is facilitated. In such a case, the citizens do not see the way of life in town as permanently stable; if it is modified under pressure from an action group, there is no fear that chaos will develop. Nor do the citizens view proposals by dissidents as bad simply because the changes are different from the way things have always been done.

There are times when change is in the air and people are ready for new ways. Such modification of views occurs among citizens when a new mayor comes into office, when a solution is found for a long-endured community problem, when the town is given a foundation grant to be used for its betterment, when a historical anniversary leads locals to think about the future, or when a severe crisis demands that a new procedure be put into action. Commager (1960) describes an era of reform in New England towns, from 1830 to 1860. It led to changes in such social practices as slavery, business relations, education, superstition, and sinning. These new views were based on a popular philosophy about the relations among mankind, nature, and God. The philosophy, called *transcendentalism*, held that some moral truths transcend mere proof. The most important among these is that God is benevolent, nature beneficial, and man divine. These ideas were taken to be facts, and departure from them was understood as contrary to God's purpose.

On the basis of such assumptions, all men were to be harmonized with the moral order through a crusade for reform, under religious officials who were the leaders. The campaign was comprehensive. Every institution in the community was pressed to take part and to form an interlocking directorate of reformers. The changes were sought within individuals, not within organizations, on the basis of free will, not because of obedience to dictates from others. The actions of the change agents were nonpolitical; in fact, the leaders suspected that government was the cause of many needed reforms. This movement, Commager says, was fanatical without being violent, radical without being revolutionary. There was no toppling of governments. There were no riots, no mobs, no soldiers. It was a dignified activity led by clerics, writers, and scholars who hoped to change men and women in their own hearts and minds. It was an aspect of Romanticism, prevalent in those days, which fostered a sentimental attitude toward nature, women, children, and primitive peoples. From time to time since then, we have seen comparable reforms based on similar beliefs, or we have seen bodies wanting changes based on strongly held secular views about black power, the environment, the motives of business leaders, or animal rights. These views are as firmly adhered to as the religious dogmas described by Commager (Douglas and Wildavsky, 1982; Gerlach and Hine, 1970).

5. The organizers of a group for social action are more likely to get a unit under way if they get advice from persons experienced in such matters. Some kinds of community problems are so widespread that national organizations exist to provide counselors for those who wish to form a local group. Such organizations are found

in control of pollution (Douglas and Wildavsky, 1982), promotion of peace (Woito, 1982), urban community councils (Lancourt, 1979; Delgado, 1986), improvement of agricultural affairs (Rogers, 1983), and black power (Gerlach and Hine, 1970). Where help is not available locally, it can be found in the offices of national associations set up to cope with the kinds of problems bothering citizens in the local area.

Goodenough (1963) spent many years advising citizens on how to form activist groups in communities of underdeveloped countries. He offers a list of principles for such activists. These maxims are not inappropriate for community changers in America. They resemble the kinds of procedures that developers of any organization for influential action might follow in winning the support of persons not in the group:

1. Development proposals and procedures should be mutually consistent.
2. Development agents must have a thorough knowledge of the main values and principal features of the client community's culture.
3. Development must take the whole community into account.
4. The goals of development must be stated in terms that have positive value to the community's members. They must be something that the members, as well as the agent, want.
5. The community must be an active partner in the development process.
6. Agents should start with what the community has in the way of material, organizational, and leadership resources.
7. Development procedures must make sense to the community members at each step.
8. The agent must earn the respect of the community's members for himself as a person.
9. The agent should try to avoid making himself the indispensable man in the development situations.
10. Where there are several agents at work, good communication and coordination are essential [Goodenough, 1963, pp. 22–23].

6. In most jurisdictions, laws explicate what legally based bodies (schools, unions, churches, hospitals, city councils) can and cannot do in their progams, procedures, and financial affairs. Clearly, such rules affect the functioning of the units that must operate within them. Members of groups for social change need to realize that these regulations may limit or enhance the freedom of a target group to modify its practices when pressed to do so (Funk, 1982; Warren, 1971). There is not much use in urging a board to change its way of working if this is not legally permitted. Change agents may be able to facilitate their work by getting the sponsorship of a legal body, when this move is sensible. Activists can ask to be appointed by the city council, the planning commission, the local welfare board, or another administrative body whose backing will help them win acceptance in the community.

7. Persons who are ready to create or join a group for change commonly see themselves as organizing to enhance social justice. Crowfoot, Chesler, and Boulet (1983, p. 239) believe that the major focus of such efforts is "intentional action for changes in the distribution of [social] power and related changes in values, beliefs and resources." These authors describe what they call a "new wave" in organizing for social action. The "new wave" organizers recognize that gaining local influence is not just a matter of winning local acceptance; it also requires attention to forces outside the community that make it difficult to solve problems like pollution, unemployment, excessive traffic, unclean drinking water, and illegal drugs. The moral for an organizer of an action group is that efforts for reform may need the help of agencies or persons who have the power to confront distant sources of local problems.

8. The methods that organizers plan to use once a group is under way may either win followers or repel them. Those who plan a body for change must know what methods of action will be approved and disapproved by participants and observers. (These matters are taken up in Chapters Eight and Nine.)

Summary

A group of change agents is more likely to be organized in a community when several triggering conditions exist. First, organizers perceive that a current state of affairs is unsatisfactory or presents an opportunity for improving things. Before group developers are moved to form a new unit, they must feel that the situation is unfair because it does not fulfill their expectations—it puts them at a disadvantage with respect to others like themselves, or it offers fewer benefits than they are used to receiving. In short, the deprivation must be perceived in relation to a standard they value. Otherwise, they will tolerate the unpleasant state of affairs, remain passive, and live with it.

Second, organizers must have useful ideas about what a better condition would be and how that improved condition could be reached. These ideas should appeal to potential recruits for the group. They should offer satisfying solutions, reflect members' motives, and suggest attainable objectives for group action.

Third, persons preparing to participate in a new organization need to be confident that their group's actions can succeed and provide a more satisfactory state of affairs. They develop faith in the group if most members are enthusiastic about its work, if the unit has the resources it needs, and if its leaders build confidence that the members will succeed in their joint effort.

Fourth, the beliefs and behavior of local citizens should encourage persons to establish a unit for social change, rather than making it difficult for the new body to be organized or to operate. Sometimes developers can foster facilitating conditions in a community. They may try to recruit members who already have contacts with one another, are similar in relevant ways, prefer to participate in groups, know how members should behave, and like the methods that the group's members will employ in their efforts for social action. It also helps if bystanders and target persons see the group's activities as a means to evaluate the quality of local affairs and to consider proposals for reform, rather than viewing the group's efforts as a threat to the social order. Additional facilitators are consultants on organizational development, sponsorship by a legitimate institution in the community, and citizens who recognize that the time is ripe for innovations.

4

▙▞▚▞▚▞▚▞▟▞▚▞▚▞▚▞▚▞▚▞▚▞▚▞▟

Properties and Styles
of Community Groups

The qualities peculiar to a given group are called that group's *properties*. These include such characteristics as its purposes, established procedures, style of leadership, methods for reaching decisions, quality of performance, the beneficiaries of its efforts, the motives of its members, intergroup alliances, kinds of connections among participants, and its products. We will review some of these properties of groups for social action because recalling these prepares us to understand the nature of and methods employed by such bodies. Three central ideas, I believe, describe why many of a group's properties are chosen for the group by its leaders and members.

   1. *The properties of a social action group are those that the leaders and members think the entity needs in order to effectively use its chosen method of influencing target persons.*

   Many of a group's properties (other than the usual bylaws and the style of its officers) are determined by participants after they have decided what method to use in making their case. If, for example, they want to change the opinions of elected officials on a given issue, they make their group as large as possible, so that they can claim that many people in town will vote only for officials who meet the group's demands. If a group wants to present its ideas to the traffic commission, the managers of the unit will choose a spokesperson, writers, researchers, and graphic artists to plan this presentation. The work is divided among several members. We can assume that the properties of a group will vary according to members' use of different methods (parades, rallies, teaching, counseling, persuasion, bargaining, bribes, or threats). Choice of method, in short, usually precedes much of a group's organizing.

In more general terms, a group's properties are the products of a sequence of events. A grievance or an opportunity arouses persons to organize a group for action. They define the change that they will seek (their objective), select the method they will use in attempting to influence target persons toward that objective, and develop appropriate properties for their group. This last choice is influenced by additional matters, such as the preferences of the group's leaders, the values held by persons in the surrounding community, how well the group performs, members' feelings toward the target persons, and their estimates about how those receivers will respond to the influence attempts made by change agents.

2. *The properties of a group for influential action may be formal, informal, or in between.* Formal bodies are characterized by precisely defined procedures, which members are expected to follow. They are small bureaucracies and function in specified ways. Informal groups, at the other extreme, have loosely delineated characteristics, which serve only as rough guidelines (rather than as strict standards) and are readily modified when that seems wise. Groups falling between the extremes of formality and informality are characterized by a mixture of qualities, formal in some respects and informal in others.

It seems likely that the differences between formal and informal groups develop because of the methods that members select and the kinds of demands that these methods place on persons who intend to implement them. Procedures that leave only limited freedom of choice to target persons are called *constraining* or *pressing* methods. Those that provide considerable freedom of choice are called *nonconstraining* or *permissive* methods.

3. *The more that agents of change plan to use constraining (pressing) methods in attempting to influence target persons, the more they build the properties of a formal group into their organization. The more that the agents plan to use nonconstraining (permissive) methods, the more they build the properties of an informal group into their organization.*

Suppose that change agents plan to argue their case by using heavy propaganda, bargaining closely, issuing threats of bodily harm, wrecking a meeting, or capturing hostages. Carrying out procedures like these, it seems reasonable, requires a tight organization, centralized supervision, and aggressive leaders. Members of the change groups are given strict assignments and are expected to fulfill these well. Thus, pressing and coercive methods require formal organization.

In contrast, when change agents do not intend to restrict freedom of choice among target persons, they do not need internal controls of the kind just described. If they encourage their listeners to think or plan (for example, by teaching, informing, counseling, parading, negotiating, or problem solving), they set up a general approach for these moves but keep the group's own qualities flexible. Its properties, as a result, are less formal, its purposes are less clear-cut, and its methods are more permissive. It is easily changed, both in its operation and in its structure.

In summary, members of an action group choose properties for their unit that will help them use their preferred methods well. They create either a formal body or a more informal one. The unit is more formal if members plan to use pressing methods, and it is more informal if they intend to use permissive methods.

In light of these notions, let us consider the kinds of properties that members of social action groups tend to generate. My conjectures about these group qualities are based on a mixture of personal observation, guesses, logical hypotheses, and derivations from research. None is based on objective studies of action groups. It would be good to learn someday how reliable these conjectures are.

Properties That Typify Both Formal and Informal Groups

Regardless of whether members of action groups choose to use pressing methods, permissive ones, or others, and regardless of whether the organizations are formal or informal, they usually are similar in certain respects. In my experience, the following qualities are typically found in a community group for social action.

1. Members have a singleness of purpose. They wish to change only one or a few conditions, not many.

2. Members know the purpose of their group and feel strongly that it is right and just and must be achieved. Because of their faith in the group's cause, each member expects others to work toward that end and to be zealots. (History repeatedly shows that those who "know best" tend to foster the worst. I wonder how often groups of citizens, deeply dedicated to causes, create negative consequences in their home towns.)

3. The task that members wish to accomplish requires a sequence of moves. There is a goal to achieve, and members try to attain it along a more or less clear path. When this objective is reached, their task is completed.

4. Members usually do not attempt more than a few trials toward the same objective. Thus, they are not able to evaluate reliably how well the group is doing or could do by comparing its performance on earlier attempts with its performance on later ones. Members tend to think that their group is doing well because they have no convincing evidence to the contrary. A strong desire for success leads members to view "no news" as "good news" (Zander, 1971, 1977, 1985).

5. The objective that members set is difficult for them to achieve. Often the goal is hard because leaders among the change agents are inexperienced or unskilled in proposing or producing community change, and so they feel that they can do better than is realistically possible. Moreover, they do not have reliable means of measuring how much effort is required for successful performance of one task versus another. Even if they sense that their goal is difficult, this formidability itself makes the objective attractive, for several reasons. In the first place, members recognize that they will be more satisfied if their group accomplishes a difficult task than if

it completes an easy one, and they will be more embarrassed if they fail to achieve an easy objective than if they fail to reach a hard one. Therefore, they prefer to work toward an end that is tougher for them to achieve than toward one that is simpler. Fund-raising campaigns, as an illustration, often set goals that are much too hard to achieve (Zander and Newcomb, 1967). Given the types of task that groups undertake, as well as the likelihood that they will receive little good evidence of success or failure, groups will not be inclined to lower their goals to levels that would be easier to attain. Indeed, their desire for success will so dominate their evaluation of their own work that they are more likely to raise their goals than lower them. The result is that groups tend to set and hold on to hard goals because such goals seem more worthwhile. This phenomenon has been observed in groups of many kinds (Zander, 1971, 1977).

6. As a result of groups' tendency to set unreasonably difficult goals, groups fail more often than they succeed. When a group does poorly, its members develop low morale. Their group may dissolve unless they do better with a different approach reasonably soon.

7. To increase the chances of attaining their objective, members aim their efforts toward target persons whom they think can help them in their cause. They work through such people because they recognize that they themselves do not have the right or power to change things on their own or the resources and ability to do so. They try to get assistance from persons they think will facilitate a change.

8. Much of members' planning is concerned with finding ways to influence chosen target persons. Planning may be unwise if the reformers incorrectly perceive what the target individuals are like and what will appeal to them. For example, it is not uncommon for innovators to fear decision makers, dislike them, or expect them to be negative. As a consequence, the actors choose methods that are too militant and thereby make resisters out of potential allies. In contrast, they may assume that target persons will be interested in the proposed plan when in fact they are not; thus, the activists present their case in a way that leaves the listeners cold.

9. Members may realize that their participation in a change enterprise requires them to take stands and do things of which their

neighbors disapprove. They may have to parade, picket, petition, pass the hat, pen letters to the editor, give speeches, or go to court in ways that are not typical of themselves. They behave, in short, as though they will do anything, even risk ridicule, in their efforts to bring about a change.

10. Members come from a limited geographical area. Many know one another before joining or forming the group; they are friends of friends in a network. They usually join the group because of their interest in the group's purpose, however, not because they see it as a friendship society.

11. A social action group tends to be small, with no more than twenty or thirty members and often fewer. Members keep the group's size limited because in a small unit it is easier to keep secrets from leaking and simpler to detect interlopers. Members are more likely to become deeply involved, since the work must be performed by very few persons, and each therefore gets more responsibility than would be possible in a bigger entity. Communication is easier and freer, members understand one another better, divisive subsets are less likely to form among members, and pressures toward uniformity of belief and action within the group are likely to be more compelling. All in all, small units serve better to keep up members' enthusiasm (Cartwright and Zander, 1968).

12. Ordinarily, a community group is an independent entity, with no obligation to a larger body that has appointed it as an adviser or subgroup.

13. The success and maintenance of such a small organization depend greatly on the strength and personal qualities of the group's leaders (Prestby and Wandersman, 1985). Thus, the leaders of effective community groups are vigorous and conscientious.

Comparing the Properties of Formal and Informal Groups

I suspect that formal and informal groups most often differ with respect to nine general properties (among others, perhaps):

1. The *objective* of a group is a desirable state of affairs that members intend to bring about through their joint efforts. The objective is desirable because members clearly foresee the satisfaction they will derive from achieving it. Members of formal action

groups tend to be precisely aware of what they expect to accomplish. They use direct methods to attain their ends. Members of informal groups define both their goals and their methods less well.

Leaders of formal groups prefer goals that are measurable; members can determine reliably whether the group has actually attained its objective. Leaders of formal groups also favor objectives that are accessible; members know what they must do to attain their ends (Zander, 1985). I would guess that the purposes of a formal group more often grow out of grievances held by individual members than out of opportunities for improving a state of affairs in the group or the community.

Members of informal groups tend to favor unclear objectives, which are not precisely measurable or accessible. As a result of their vague aims, however, they get less satisfaction because they cannot tell whether they have achieved them. Therefore, they often work on small and neatly stated tasks, which are more measurable and accessible than the broad objectives of their groups (Zander, 1985). For instance, they collect names on petitions, recruit more members, or hang up posters.

2. *Beneficiaries* are the persons who will be helped by achievement of the change that activists propose. Persons in formal units may try to benefit themselves or a larger group of aggrieved citizens whom they represent. Members of informal bodies may work to benefit needy and helpless persons who are not group members, the community as a whole, or themselves alone. They do not directly represent larger bodies; instead, they often speak for unspecified individuals who are unable to speak for themselves or cannot ask for help.

3. A *motive* is both the capacity to find satisfaction in the attainment of a specific incentive and a disposition to seek such satisfaction. A member's motive (as we shall see in Chapter Five) may be oriented toward the personal satisfaction of individual gains, toward the attainments of others, toward the accomplishments of his or her own group, or toward desirable outcomes for objects or natural settings. Motives are learned; they develop as experience teaches a person to value certain incentives. An *incentive* is a desired state, the objective (change) that members wish to accomplish.

Activists in a formal group are more often motivated to achieve individual gains or relieve personal fears. They see their group associates either as rivals for a share of the gains or as sources of opposition in decisions about what the group shall do. Persons in an informal group are more often motivated by a desire to win gains for others, as well as for themselves.

Participants in a formal group are more committed to working for the satisfaction of their own group or of their constituency. The members would rather apply pressure to target persons than work with them on a solution that would satisfy initiators and target persons alike. They know precisely what the correct answer is, and they see no need to bargain over it. Their sense of competition with target persons make them distrustful of their relationship with the latter.

In an informal group, the motives of members are different. Participants work toward personal gratification or toward goals that will bring satisfaction both to others and to themselves. They often look forward to satisfaction for others while expecting few personal rewards. In such cases, their fulfillment derives from others' pleasure. Their approach to target persons is ordinarily fair-minded. They are interested in what target persons think, are willing to change their own views if convinced to do so, and are ready to seek the best answer, not necessarily the one they initially develop. The members of an informal group may also be concerned with social issues of national or international import. They base their beliefs about such matters on sectarian values, rather than on religious ones (Douglas and Wildavsky, 1982), which leads them to insist that target persons also become committed to such precious beliefs as human goodness, equality, and purity of heart and mind.

4. Members of a formal group prefer activities that are under close control, are thoroughly planned, and have precise duties to be carried out under well-defined leadership. Accordingly, group officers set up strict procedures, which they require members to follow closely and are not prepared to change. Members of an informal group prefer methods that are flexible and tailored for the purpose at hand and that allow ready give-and-take between change agents and target persons. For this kind of group to function well, the members probably need to have similar values and standards of

belief and behavior. Formal groups tend to survive longer than informal ones, according to Prestby and Wandersman (1985).

5. A group's *structure* is the arrangement and connections among an organization's parts. The parts may be people, jobs, or subgroups. The connections may exist with respect to power (who has the ability to influence whom), authority (who has the right to make demands of others), attraction (who likes whom), communication (who should talk with whom on matters related to the group's work), or flow of work (who receives products from whom) (Cartwright and Zander, 1968). A formal group will probably develop exactly defined links among its parts, along with spelled-out rights and duties for members, while an informal group will have loosely defined bonds among its parts, and these will be few and uncomplicated.

To illustrate, a formal entity ordinarily has a clear hierarchy, indicating who has authority over whom among persons on several levels. It has a definition of each job to be done, and jobs are assigned to specific persons. Other relationships, such as those that concern who can and should talk to whom or the flow of work, are also delineated. An informal body, in contrast, is not likely to have a hierarchy at all. If it has one, the levels are few. Labor is divided into a limited number of jobs, and people are expected to help out wherever they are needed. Few links are specified; the rest occur as the objective, method, or situation demands.

6. In a formal body, decisions are made by a single leader or a small executive corps. These decisions are usually firm and clear. Members may provide suggestions, but they seldom participate in the final choice. Individuals who rise to positions of management tend to want satisfaction of their personal desires, and they work toward such outcomes. Leaders easily agree about what the group ought to do—its goal is clear, its way of operating is well defined, and arguments over differences in values or beliefs are rare in such a neat system.

In an informal group, matters are less shipshape. Whenever feasible, decisions are made through discussion among members. Because of this wide give-and-take and the desire of members to please all other participants, decisions are often multifaceted compromises (Warren, 1971; Warren, Rose, and Bergunder, 1974). Nevertheless, these are not weak decisions. If anything, the members of an informal group work more zealously toward their group's objectives than the participants in formal bodies do, because they have had a say in setting these objectives. Several other matters also increase members' enthusiasm. Their ideas are grounded in strongly held values and emotionally tinged attitudes. The informal bodies are small enough to allow strong social pressure among participants toward keeping joint agreements. An informal unit develops high cohesiveness among its members, which enhances their willingness to work for the cause (Cartwright and Zander, 1968). Such a body frequently has no designated leader, beyond a sort of secretary who calls meetings. The leader for any given action may be chosen from among all the members and is the one who is most suitable for that special activity or who is next in line for a turn at being the group's manager (Douglas and Wildavsky, 1982; Gerlach and Hine, 1970).

Some informal groups are created so that their members can follow a central person, one who has a special gift (charisma) for arousing loyalty and enthusiasm and who can convince disciples that he or she will relieve their difficulties. Sometimes such bodies are quasi-groups in that members talk exclusively with the central figure but not with one another (Mayer, 1966). They may be products of religious prophets (Lanternari, 1963), gurus, political extremists, or convinced dissidents. (I knew a university faculty member who believed that research in genetic engineering should not be allowed on her campus. She gathered a set of persons around her, so that her objection would appear to have the support of others, but she wrote all the speeches given by any of these members and all the letters to the editor. She arranged all the forums and acted as a one-person gang behind the facade of a quasi-group of protesters.) Nevertheless, because of their lively participation in the group's discussions, the separate views they bring, and the vague nature of their decisions, persons in an informal group are more likely to wrangle before they reach an acceptable decision. They prefer to have face-to-face conversations with target persons, on the assumption that a mutually agreeable plan of action could be found. If they get nowhere by using a gentle method, however, and if they run into too much opposition or resistance, they are not opposed to using stronger means to win what they want.

7. The fixed hierarchical structure of a formal group is liable to arouse competitive interpersonal relations among members. The disciplined way of life causes each member to wonder whether others' gains will preclude his or her own. Therefore, an individual in a formal unit makes sure that his or her wants are not being overlooked. In a formal group, the potential for rivalry among members is enhanced by the possibility that one can move to a higher-status level of the organization's hierarchy. An individual who attains a superior position can make sure that his or her own desires receive favorable attention. In a formal group, therefore, members are more likely to be suspicious of the intentions of their associates, to be sensitive to power differences among participants, and to have their interpersonal relations soured by competition.

Within an informal group, by contrast, members tend to have compatible general needs that are best met through teamwork. Gains for oneself are less important than gains for the group, outsiders, society at large, or nature. In this kind of unit, members are aware of their mutual interests and their equality. There is trust among them, and they are ready to help one another. They communicate openly, and they listen to separate views during a group discussion. Each believes that his or her ideas are welcome, and each is willing to find agreement in the differences among ideas.

8. Because of their tendency to work for narrow goals, members of formal groups are not likely to find other units willing to join forces with them. If their problem concerns many people (for example, improved collection of garbage, fuller support for mothers on welfare, or control of rents), a formal organization of allies may be formed, bringing together representatives from several local organizations to create a continuing community council. This is the kind of entity sponsored by Saul Alinsky in Chicago and in the disadvantaged neighborhoods of other cities. Within an informal group, by contrast, objectives and methods of action tend to be looser, so that alliances may be developed through recruitment of neighbors or solicitation of help from sympathetic organizations. A small cell (composed of persons interested in the care of the environment, for instance) forms alliances when it mounts a demonstration

that requires the effort of many persons. After such an activity is completed, the alliances are dissolved (Douglas and Wildavsky, 1982).

9. The degree of formality or informality in an organization can be changed, as necessary. It seems probable that shifts will more often be away from informality and toward formality, for several reasons. Because formal groups are more tightly controlled and more closely planned, it is perhaps harder for managers or members of such bodies to loosen connections among members or to modify procedures, for members will fear that disorder could follow from such changes. Participants in an informal group, however, work in easily modified ways and therefore are probably more willing to change their approach when that seems wise.

We can assume that those in a formal body are not going to drop their pressuring methods in favor of permissive ones should their group fail to influence target persons. Rather, they probably will exert even stronger pressures and in so doing will make their group's structure even more controlled and formal. If aggressive methods continue to fail, they may try problem solving, bargaining, or litigation, which may lead them to make their unit more informal.

In an informal group, members tend to employ nonconstraining methods and probably recognize that it takes time for these to be successful. Should such gentle methods fail, they may either drop the whole issue or move toward more coercive means. They are more willing to do the latter if they are angered by the reactions of target persons to the proposals that change agents have put before them. If the agents turn to the use of pressuring methods, they develop a more formal group structure (for the reasons noted earlier). Thus, formal groups become even more formal when they fail; informal groups, too, become more formal when they fail.

This shift toward greater formality probably occurs because both kinds of groups fail more often than they succeed. Target persons tend to oppose or resist the suggestions of change agents more than they accept them. Citizens more commonly give their support to established decision makers than to reformers. Target persons are more eager to please their veteran supporters than a newly formed set of dissidents. Finally, social activists prefer difficult goals to easy ones.

Summary

The qualities peculiar to a particular group are called the properties of that body. Three conditions have an influence on the properties of the groups that interest us.

1. The properties of a social action group are those that the leaders think it needs to influence target persons and meet its goals.
2. The properties of a group for social action may be formal, informal, or in between.
3. The more that change agents plan to use constraining methods, the more they build the properties of a formal group into their organization. The more that agents of change plan to use nonconstraining methods, the more they develop the properties of an informal group.

If agents of change want to encourage target persons to make up their own minds about what to do, they create an informal body. If they intend to put pressure on target persons by leaving them minimal choice on these matters, the change agents favor a more formal organization. The method of the group determines the formality of its structure.

Regardless of whether members use constraining or nonconstraining methods, and regardless of whether a group is formal or informal, groups engaged in social action tend to be similar in a number of ways. Such a group is relatively small and is composed of members from a limited geographical area who know the group's purpose well and strongly support it. Participants recognize that their group's goal will be difficult to attain and that it will demand unusual actions of them, yet they feel that it is a just aim and must be achieved. They are more interested in local issues than in converting neighbors to beliefs that have become fashionable.

Formal and informal groups differ with respect to nine kinds of properties (discussed in detail in this chapter). These differences arise because members favor different approaches toward influencing target persons. When members change the structure of a group (often after a group action has failed), they are likely to make their group more formal.

5

‎ز‎ا‎ز‎ا‎ز‎ا‎ز‎ا‎ز‎ا‎ز‎ا‎ز‎ا‎ز‎ا‎ز‎ا‎ز‎ا‎ز‎ا‎ز‎ا‎ر‎

Preparing Groups
for Action

Once developers have organized a group and developed suitable properties for it, they arouse members' interest in doing what needs to be done. They create this stimulated state by describing the satisfactions members will derive from being in and working with the group. The organizers assume that persons who are thus gratified by their membership will be more attracted to the unit and more committed to its goals (Cartwright and Zander, 1968). By causing members to become involved in the work of their unit, the organizers increase their own ability, and the members', to influence one another's behavior and beliefs and make one another more eager for action.

A *motive* is a person's disposition to strive for a certain kind of satisfaction. One who is so disposed has the capacity to be satisfied by attainment of a given incentive. Members of a group for social action may have any of four kinds of motivation. The first is the usual self-oriented motive. The other three are less familiar because they are unorthodox ways of accounting for the desires of

69

persons in a group for social change. We must examine these three so that we can identify sources of lively energy (beyond the satisfaction of selfish wishes) that members put into their efforts for the group.

Self-Oriented Motives

When a *self-oriented* motive is aroused, an individual is interested in benefiting himself or herself and seeks situations that provide such personal satisfactions as purity of soul, excitement, admiration, power to influence, relief from tension, expert information, pride in achievement, or elimination of worry. Participants in an activist group may want to settle individual complaints. A number of persons, for instance, join forces because they all feel that they have been treated unfairly by a powerful body—say, the board of education. If they present a united front, they can make an influential appeal to the decision makers for the change they desire—to buy safer school buses, perhaps. A person may also join an organization composed of activists who each have different personal motives. Members feel, however, that they can satisfy their separate wants through collaboration. For instance, they urge the board to begin night classes for adults, while each member has in mind a different subject for study.

A group composed of persons with dissimilar aims may develop just one personal motive, which is to be the same for each of them: more self-confidence in dealing with authorities, more self-esteem, more intelligent voting in elections, or more love of beauty. Members may also encourage one another to create their own singular motives; each member agrees to assist colleagues in satisfying these special desires. Community councils, self-help groups, and workshops for training community leaders are groups of this kind.

The sort of action bodies that we hear about most often are those in which members want something strictly for themselves. This type of entity, I suspect, is more common than those whose members have more social motives. In a study of purposes among three hundred associations, I observed that two-thirds were devoted to helping their own members, and only one-third were interested in benefiting nonmembers or society as a whole (Zander, 1971,

1985). In a laboratory experiment, participants took part in a simple task. At one time, they worked for their own gain; at another time, they worked for the group's gain. They were asked whether they next preferred to work for their own good or for that of the group. In either case, the reward they could earn and their activity would be the same. Over two-thirds preferred to work for themselves alone (Zander, 1971). Students of society claim that citizens take care of their own wants more often than they help others. Bellah and others (1985) provide anecdotes, based on conversations with all kinds of people, that illustrate an alleged rise in the incidence of individualism or self-centeredness among modern Americans.

Desire for Group Success

A second kind of motivation arises when members will be satisfied by their group's achievement even though they will not benefit personally. They feel pride for the whole team, not for separate members, and are pleased about what the unit accomplishes. Such group-oriented pride is heightened if observers outside the group laud the unit as a single entity and use its name, not those of individual members, in doing so. When members' satisfaction is due to the accomplishment by their unit as a whole, participants want the group to perform well in the future, are proud of it if it succeeds, and are embarrassed for it if it fails. They think of the group as a single achieving whole, and they learn to feel what we can call a *desire for group success*. This kind of motivation is termed a desire, rather than a motive, because it is not an enduring disposition of members that, if aroused, can be activated in all places and at all times; rather, it is a product of members' experiences in their specific organization. Members may feel quite differently about other bodies to which they belong. The desire for group success acts similarly to a self-oriented motive except that the focus of concern is the group's fate, not the individual's. This desire is commonly at work in athletic teams, sales departments, assembly lines, community fund-raising organizations, and other bodies where the unit's score is an indicator of how well it has performed and where this output is attributed to the efforts of the unit as an entity. The sources and effects of a group-oriented desire are discussed by Zander (1971, 1977, 1985).

Desire to Benefit Others

A third kind of motivation for those in a social action group is the *desire to benefit others*. It is the capacity of members to be satisfied when their efforts help persons inside their unit or outside it. While acting in accord with this desire, members voluntarily assist specific others, without anticipating rewards for themselves beyond the satisfaction they will derive from being helpful. If the activists incur costs (energy, time, money, stress) in order to provide this service to others, they expect no compensation from those who have been helped or from anyone else. This desire is aroused when organizers of a group learn that specific persons need assistance and cannot help themselves. Agents of change who are touched by deprivation among the needy ones form a group to provide what the disadvantaged persons need. A desire to benefit others can be as strong as or even stronger than a motive to benefit oneself. Think of the mother who keeps house for the good of family members, the minister who aids his flock beyond the call of duty, the Red Cross volunteer assisting in an emergency, the docent in a museum who helps visitors see what they might otherwise overlook, or the "pink lady" volunteering her help in a hospital.

Desire to Improve Conditions in the Community

A fourth kind of motivation is the *desire to improve conditions in the community*. Some innovators may be aware of the need for a given reform in the environment and may have the capacity to be satisfied if an improved state of affairs is attained there. Examples of better states that innovators may wish to establish are fiscal stability in government, safety of citizens from floods, access to concerts by visiting artists, or planting of shade trees along city streets. This prime satisfaction may arise in change agents when they develop a new and desirable state of affairs in natural settings or man-made structures or in provision of services for unspecified citizens.

Any or all of these four kinds of motivation may determine the behavior of members. One kind of motivation may be aroused alone, or a combination may be active simultaneously. All are additive—that is, when several are aroused, the stronger the motive or desire of any type, the stronger the resultant impulse to take action. Nevertheless, the objectives that will satisfy each motive or desire among a combination must be reasonably similar before the effect of one will supplement rather than interfere with another. If an individual wants objective A but the group as a whole chooses objective B, then the strength of the impulse to move toward either A or B is less for that individual than it would have been if both member and group had agreed on an objective. Likewise, the motivation and desire of members to benefit themselves, their group, others, or the community can combine to create a stronger effect than any single motivation or desire would have had alone. One kind of motivation may be considerably stronger than others. In such a case, the strongest one has the greatest effect on the behavior of a person and on that of the group.

Typical incentives for members of action groups have been described by Wandersman and others (1987) as a result of their study of neighborhood organizations. They observe that some incentives (called *benefits* by the authors) are personal—solution of a specific problem, accomplishment of personal goals, achievement of material rewards, increases in status, and development of stronger political influence, for example. Other incentives are relevant to relations with other group members. These include contributing to others, knowing more about community problems, providing a useful service to the town, becoming more responsible, and developing friendships with colleagues. Such incentives are plainly more attractive if their value exceeds their costs. (The effort required to participate, time, financial expense, and the neglect of family matters are all examples of cost.)

Getting Members to Move Toward Their Group's Objective

The more value people place on their unit's goal, the harder they will work on its behalf. They also judge whether the goal will repay the effort and whether the group can succeed. Thus, we assume that the vigor of a change agent's efforts on behalf of a group is influenced by the strength of his or her motivation, and its strength in turn is due to the combination of three conditions (Zander, 1971, 1985): (1) the strength of the relevant motive or desire, or the capacity to achieve satisfaction from attainment of a specific incentive or goal (this is similar for each of the four kinds of motivation already discussed); (2) the value of the incentive, or the perceived likelihood that attainment of the incentive will provide the satisfaction that the member seeks (members place greater value on incentives whose attainment promises more satisfaction); and, (3) the perceived probability of success, or the member's confidence that the group can reach its objective.

Consider an example of the origins of these three conditions among members of an action group who wished to benefit both themselves and outsiders. The unit was developed in a neighborhood where several houses had been robbed, and each resident feared that his or her home might be next. The robbers not only got away with valuable things but also injured the owners, and had repeated such deeds in several places. Neighbors recognized that many among them were scared *(their motives for security were aroused)*; everyone would feel better if the neighbors could prevent such crimes. A few persons got together to plan a watch patrol for an area of twelve city blocks. Members planned to monitor the streets on foot or in cars, night and day, to look for suspicious persons or signs. When any were seen, the observers would call the police. The objective of the group *(the members' common incentive)* was to prevent more robberies in that area and to catch anyone who did break and enter. The watchers assumed that citizens would feel more secure because of this patrol and that residents who were not directly taking part in the activity would also feel safer. There was little doubt that this objective was important to the watchers and to their neighbors because of the relief that its accomplishment would provide *(the incentive had high value)*. The goal, moreover, seemed attainable *(the probability of success was good)* because publicity given to the watch patrol would deter potential thieves from practicing their profession in that neighborhood. Patrols of this kind had worked well elsewhere, the police welcomed such surveillance by residents and were ready to come quickly when called, and patrollers were interested in performing a service that would benefit themselves and others. Although each person took his or her turn on patrol alone, all watchers benefited, as did the neighbors who did not walk a beat. The patrolling took time and effort and was boring, yet these costs were outweighed by the value of what all were doing for the good of themselves and others.

The patrolling body continued for several years and unintentionally became the model for similar units in other parts of town and in neighboring cities. The group did not reach its objective in the first six months or even in the second six months, but the number of robberies decreased. Persons in the patrol decided, however, that occasional evaluation of their work was not providing clear enough feedback on how well the unit was doing. This perception was reinforced by the patrollers' realization that they could also have been watching for undesirable conditions that were not robberies, such as vandalism, excessive noise, flooding of sewers, roaming dogs or rats, and unsightly disposal of waste. They agreed to evaluate their progress and to set new goals each month concerning a number of such matters and report their findings to proper agencies other than the police department. The appropriate city officials accepted this plan and welcomed the opportunity to help residents help themselves. The group's goals were now more specific, in terms of time span, and broader, in terms of the number of areas covered. Members could regularly judge how well they were performing in several respects by comparing their recent scores with those obtained in earlier periods. They could also rate how well they were doing in comparison with other patrol bodies similar to their own.

The participants soon developed a wish to improve their scores and do better than the patrols in nearby towns. When they began to aspire to higher scores and to set harder goals than they previously had worked for, they generated in themselves a *desire for group success*. This urge was focused on the work of the group as a unit—on the score that the whole group earned, not only on personal security (which had been the initial motive of participants). It was a strong desire because the members owned a lively interest in having their unit do well. Accordingly, they set a goal that they believed would bring them success *(their incentive for the group as a whole);* and this goal, we presume, was attractive to them *(the value of the incentive was great).* They were confident of achieving the group's goal *(their perceived probability of success was high)* because that objective was close to scores they had attained as a group in the past; it was harder but not too much harder. Furthermore, even if they were not able to stop all thievery, they could still succeed in the other areas that they now had under surveillance. If they failed in some respects, they could succeed in others. Thus, they seldom needed to think of their unit as a complete failure (Zander, 1977).

Now take an example of a wholly self-oriented motive that was gratified (and modified) through organizational action. The prime mover was an amateur musician. He liked to play the French horn but had no opportunity to do so because he needed other musicians to bow or blow along with him, and there was no musical group in town. His *personal motive* (to make music) was sharply aroused when he learned that members of the city council regretted the lack of a musical organization that could play at ceremonial and joyful occasions. This news converted the horn player into an organizer. He saw an opportunity to fulfill his desire to play the horn. He and other music-loving friends polled persons who could play instruments and invited them to help form an orchestra. Before long, the pollster had enough artists to form an ensemble, and so they asked the city to make them its official orchestra. Within months, they received financial support from the city, as well as a paid director, a place to rehearse, and a new bandstand.

The initial *motive* in this illustration was the horn player's desire to make music. His *objective,* the means for satisfaction of that motive, was to form an orchestra. This was a strong *incentive* because, if attained, it clearly would provide the satisfaction he sought. The *chances of successfully organizing* a unit of musicians were hard for him to estimate at the outset, but they became clearer as instrumentalists like himself joined the cause and as city officials lent a hand. The motives of the organizer, his incentive, and his perceived probablity of success were evident. It seemed likely, moreover, that the collection of musicians would soon develop a *desire for the success of the group* as a unit, *group goals* that could satisfy this desire (once they were attained), and *confidence in the chances of reaching the goals they had set for the band.* The output of the music makers would be the work of the entire ensemble. The orchestra became a performing and goal-setting entity and became known as such in the community. The members had desires for it that they valued, even if these were not the same ones they had for themselves as individuals. They could be expected eventually to develop a desire to please their listeners.

In these two examples, group members were working to fulfill self-oriented motives, a desire to help others, or both. Now consider an instance in which those involved were aroused primarily by a desire to benefit others, with no accompanying intent to satisfy themselves at all.

A group of northern white college students moved to a southern town during the 1960s to work toward elimination of discrimination against blacks in the use of such public facilities as toilets, drinking fountains, restaurants, buses, and shops. Their eventual aim was to remove such discrimination wherever it was found. The first subgoal set by the group was to make the lunch counter at a ten-cent store available to people of all races. Attainment of this objective was valued because it would give the cause some attention, provide a service that black people prized, and remove a small part of the stigma suffered by black people under those restrictions. The agents of change recognized that success, in this instance, would be a beginning step; it would provide some satisfaction, but not much. As they began planning how to influence the manager of the store, they felt that they had little chance of success. They did not succeed in their first attempts, in which white students and black citizens staged a sit-in at the lunch counter, because they were forced to leave. Thereafter, they deliberately chose methods that would provoke the police to arrest them, thus encouraging bystanders to provide support. Their eventual success in opening the lunch counter to black customers was due as much to the help they received from observers as to the boldness of their actions. From that experience, they developed confidence to move on to changes needed in the bus station. The white students clearly got no personal gain from this activity beyond the satisfaction they derived through helping the disadvantaged group.

Other groups with altruistic desires help provide shelters or food for the homeless, patrols on snowy ski trails, fighters against forest fires, or aid to immigrants. A related kind of motivation among members is the desire to help the community. That people in town may be pleased by reforms is not the main goal. The improvements that reformers advocate may also be to protect the "rights" of a natural setting, by caring for neglected forests, conserving open areas, cleaning lakes that are too polluted to nurture fish, planting in parks that are barren of flowers, or saving an ancient oak tree. Because members need public support for these tasks, they take up conditions in the community that they believe will most interest the target persons.

Managers Make Members Ready to Take Action

The readiness of members to act and the strength of their effort on behalf of their group's purpose are determined by the combined effect of the three factors we have been considering: the strength of the motive (or desire) multiplied by the strength of the objective (or incentive) multiplied by the perceived probability (or confidence) that the group will be able to attain its objective. As each of these three factors is stronger, the tendency of members to do what the group wants increases. The same kind of multiplicative result can be created for each of the four kinds of motives or desires. The total effect of these motives and desires describes the amount of arousal in a given member at any one time. Group developers and leaders try to make this sum as large as possible—that is, they try to increase the strength of the three factors for any of the four kinds of motivation.

How is the strength of the three factors increased among members of a social change group? The process is the same, generally speaking, for each of the four classes of motivation, and so we need not consider each separately (Zander, 1971, 1985).

Increasing the Strength of a Motive or Desire. A motive or desire, as we have noted, is the disposition to be satisfied by the attainment of a certain incentive. Managers of a group increase the strength of a motive or desire among colleagues in either of two ways: by finding out what will satisfy members and then making that form of satisfaction more vital to them, or by instructing them in the usefulness of having specific wants that they may not possess.

The simplest (but not the most reliable) way of discovering the motives of members is to ask them what brings them satisfaction. The members discuss and recall satisfying actions of this group or other units. They are asked why these particular outcomes were important, how they can now be attained, and how their value can be increased. In effect, this discussion is an analysis, in which members examine the value of certain kinds of satisfaction. They recall that in the past they have achieved gratification by reaching specific objectives; therefore, they can hope to do the same in the future, if they wish. They name this kind of satisfaction: pride in community, greater power for their group in community affairs, better care for the poor, more public approval for themselves, or less noise from traffic.

One unit whose members discovered the value of a motive that they initially had not had in mind met to consider ways of improving the flow of auto traffic in town. During their meetings, the conferees came to realize that what they really wanted was to limit growth of their community. They wanted, if they could, to prevent persons from moving into the city and to forestall further construction of buildings there. Those aspirations were not realistic, but there were many things that could be done to slow the town's expansion. The members developed group objectives (incentives) that went well beyond their original personal motive (to free up the movement of automobiles).

If, in order to learn what their motives are, we ask persons what kinds of events will be satisfying to them, the respondents may not be sure how to answer; they may not be aware of such things. If we want to identify the motives of others, we may do better by observing their behavior in meetings and noting what excites them and why. We do not initiate a direct discussion of their motivation; rather, we infer members' motives from what aims appear to make them most enthusiastic in their talk and actions. When this information is in hand, an observer reports to members what end seems to interest them the most. This desire is given a name that indicates its nature and importance. Naming also strengthens the desire's hold on participants. Through observation, a monitor can discover hidden motives among members and can bring these to light, so that members can decide what to want. Consultants who advise groups frequently find that they cannot suggest ways for a body to proceed until its members have chosen group objectives, and these goals in turn cannot be delineated until members' personal motives are identified.

Organizers may believe that none of these motives or desires is appropriate to the task at hand. When that is the case, managers try to inculcate new and useful wants in participants. They provide pep talks, slogans, memoranda about what needs to be done, or ceremonies in which the efforts of members are praised. The emphasis is on teaching them what a motive or desire is, demonstrating the nature of the concept, and showing that one or another in particular is worthy of members' adoption—that a specific source of satisfaction is worthwhile. Those who supervise groups try to increase the strength of motives in other ways, such as by doing the following things:

- helping members understand the differences between a motive or desire and an objective, the value of the group's goal, and the probability of attaining it
- choosing sound aims for the group, along with plans for work, so that members can attain their aims (satisfaction arouses a taste for more)
- making sure that members understand the sources of their satisfaction and the consequences of a particular outcome for the group
- helping the organization develop a clear objective (incentive) because members usually develop a stronger motive, as well as better means to satisfy it, if the group's objective is measurable and attainable
- indicating to members how and why membership in the group can be a source of satisfaction for various motives
- making clear to each member that his or her efforts help the group to satisfy all participants
- being willing to modify or discard aims that cannot be attained to a satisfactory degree

- identifying the obstacles that prevent fulfillment of the members' motives and helping members overcome the obstacles

In sum, managers can identify and strengthen the motives that are pertinent to the efforts of a given group for social action. They do it all the time, even when they are not aware of what they are doing.

Increasing the Value of an Incentive. The value of an incentive (the objective for a person or a group) increases as members gain more confidence that achieving it will provide satisfaction. Managers of a group therefore try to make members see that attainment of the objective will be gratifying. They point out that the amount of energy members exert toward attaining a goal results both from the strength of their motive and from their confidence that the group will be able to reach its goal.

Participants in a group that is seeking change may perceive little likelihood of actually doing so because the conditions they wish to bring about are so different from conditions in the present. They cannot believe that this gap can be closed, and so they see little value in trying to change things. Such discouragement is common, according to Boulding (1988), in groups that want to preserve peace in the world. Therefore, Boulding has helped dispirited peace-seeking bodies develop more confidence in their work by leading them through a series of questions and actions in which they picture the world as they want it to be and think of ways to make it that way. The questions and exercises she employs (reworded somewhat, to suit our purposes) include the following:

1. What is the best possible improvement you can imagine in this community? (This query stimulates the respondents to draw up a wish list for the future. It asks them to hope rather than fear or let themselves be dragged down by mere realism.)
2. What past efforts to change things in this town have turned out well? (The results of this exercise suggest that good events in the past may be like those yet to be experienced—the future, like the past, can be improved!)

3. Imagine what the community will be like after the desired
    change is made.
4. Share these imagined futures with others, in groups of two or
    three persons. Try to achieve a consensus or single view of the
    best future in this town.
5. What kinds of changes in the local social structure had to be
    made in order to help this imagined state of affairs work well?
    (This and the following two topics are also discussed in small
    groups.)
6. Looking backwards, how were these imagined changes
    achieved? What probably had to be done to bring them about?
7. In light of the answers to the previous questions, what can we
    do in the present to bring our desired future into being?

It is not uncommon for members of a change group to concentrate wholly on the value of their objective or incentive, ignoring
both the strength of a relevant motive and the probability of achieving the goal. Perhaps they do this because it is easier to comprehend
the value of the end state than to understand the other two factors.
In support of this notion, several scholars have remarked that people do not always respond rationally when asked to estimate the
probabilities of favorable or unfavorable outcomes for a given activity (Douglas and Wildavsky, 1982; Nisbett and Ross, 1980; Kahneman and Tversky, 1979; Tversky and Kahneman, 1978). People tend
to play down the chances of poor results when deciding what to aim
for and how to get there. It is not surprising, then, that they may
give the value of the goal the most attention. They commit themselves to work toward it, regardless of their motives or the perceived
probability of attaining the goal.

Some students of organizations assume that this commitment
of members explains by itself why participants work hard for their
group or for themselves. These writers generally pay no attention to
the value of motives or to the perceived probabilities of success.
They concentrate instead on the promise that persons make to work
toward a particular outcome for themselves or their group. If someone pledges to carry out this work, however, then the value of doing
so (the value of the incentive) is necessarily high. The term *commit-*

ment simply connotes (for me) the presence of an attractive incentive.

The major feature of any commitment is that people bind themselves to behave in a stated way *when and if* they take action. They do not promise to take action. Dictionaries define commitment as an obligation or pledge to carry out some action or policy or to give support to some policy or person. Kiesler (1971) conceives of a commitment as the pledging or binding of oneself to a course of action. Commitment is a property of a person that can vary in strength; an individual may be more or less committed to a given behavior. A commitment, Kiesler says, is important in one's way of life because one tries to keep one's attitudes consistent with one's commitments, and one changes one or the other (usually the attitude, since the commitment is stronger) to maintain a desirable consistency. Kiesler (1971) has studied the impact of commitment on individual behavior in a program of research. He reports that committed people recognize that they are responsible for their own actions, and thus they try to keep themselves on a steady path. If they violate their commitments, people conclude that their promises to themselves are weak and should be strengthened, or that the content of their pledges was unwise and should be changed.

Kanter (1972) studied the nature of commitment in communes and utopias. In this kind of organization, she believes, a commitment is directed toward doing what the organization needs, so that it can function well and provide what the members were seeking when they joined it. She writes (Kanter, 1972, p. 66) that commitment "refers to the willingness of people to do what will maintain the group because it provides what they need. . . . Commitment links self-interest to social requirements. A person is committed . . . to the extent that he sees it as expressing or fulfilling some fundamental part of himself; he is committed to the degree that he can no longer meet his needs elsewhere." A commune changes a person, while little attention is paid to conditions outside.

Wilson (1973) defines commitment to a social movement as the willingness of participants to give their energy and loyalty to a body. Commitment demands the surrender of self, energy, and resources to the common good. Commitment is stronger as members agree to work for the cause rather than according to their own personal inclinations. A commitment leaves open how a committed person is to be moved to activity, but it provides a standard against which the behavior of a committed person can be judged.

How do groups for social action get members to make commitments to the group goals? A variety of methods are employed. The most common is a discussion among members, in which alternative objectives are considered and evaluated. Members choose among these, basing their choices on whether attainment of the chosen objectives suits the values of members and whether social support will be available when members work toward these objectives (Zander, 1971, 1985). When members decide on the group's goal, they thereby promise to abide by the standard set for the body. This is a public agreement, whereby all persons pledge, in effect, to value the group's objective. The more important the group is to them and the more they wish to remain members of it, the more they stick to this decision and press one another to do so (Cartwright and Zander, 1968).

An individual adheres more closely to a commitment, according to Kiesler (1971), if this avowal concerns behavior that is important to the person, is repeated often, and is not reversible, and if the promiser takes the pledge of his or her own volition. A commitment to oneself alone is especially strong, Kiesler believes, because such a promise usually is about personal matters under one's own control. One who commits oneself to do as a group requests, however, obeys that oath more fully by joining the body, staying with it for a long time, and not being pressed to remain. For Kiesler, clearly, a commitment to a group is greater if the promiser tries to be a good member of a group that is attractive to him or her.

Members of a commune are required to believe certain things and behave in particular ways. Some of the procedures used in communes to create such commitments can be employed in community groups as well. First of all, the entity is separated from other groups. Within this isolated body, officials use special methods to shape the members' values and actions (Kanter, 1972). In one of these procedures, called *sacrifice,* a participant is asked to give up valued behaviors or objects, on the assumption that the strength of his or her desire to remain within the entity increases once the individual has agreed to abandon precious possessions for the cause. Another mechanism, labeled *renunciation*, requires a participant to renounce all relationships with persons outside the commune, in order to heighten closeness with those on the inside. The members are told to shun contacts with friends, relatives, and other non-members and are forbidden to leave the grounds. A third procedure is the creation of *harmony*. Participants are asked to sing and dance jointly, share their possessions, work on common tasks, join group meetings, engage in rituals, and encourage the belief that people beyond the fence are enemies.

The commitment of members to a group, as some see it, wholly governs the behavior of those who have promised the group to obey its demands. Gerlach and Hine (1970) have examined the ways in which new members of groups for black power become committed. These authors say that commitment to such a body results in devotion, dedication, and intense fanaticism for its creed. For Gerlach and Hine, the signs of a committed person are a one-track mind, strong convictions, an unwillingness to consider con-trasting views, and a capacity for taking risks in order to move toward the objectives of the body to which they are pledged. These beliefs make them militant, radical, and prepared to act as though they have information and insights that nonmembers do not have. The commitment is to something greater than oneself.

Commitment, as Gerlach and Hine conceive it, is a psychoso-cial state that comes about after people change their view of them-selves from submissive to active and have engaged in overt and public acts that make it impossible for them to revert to their pre-vious way of life. Conversion, the result of a bridge-burning act, is the culmination of several steps that a person takes while being transformed from an outsider into an activist. At first, as a bystander who is sympathetic to black people's ambition to have greater influ-ence in the community, one tries to learn about the basic assump-tions and valued ideas of the group. One is invited to join, to take part in planning, and to consider methods that members could use toward the group's objective. One joins, and one's involvement in the group grows as one expresses one's ideas in meetings. Because they have a part in the planning, neophytes become willing to take part in group activities, even if doing so exposes them to the negative reactions of persons who are opposed to giving black citizens a stronger voice in local affairs. The new members take part in demonstrations or rallies, doing things they have never done before and thereby changing their demeanor from passive to active. They are converted from being submissive students of an issue to being active supporters. They are part of the group and feel that they belong. They are fully committed and demonstrate this to themselves by engaging in public behavior that conforms to their new beliefs. Their commitment means that they place high value on the goals of the group.

Effects of Commitment. When one makes a commitment, one is more likely to keep it than not; thus, it is a source of control over one's behavior. This is one of the consequences that Kiesler (1971) reports from his research. People who commit themselves to certain actions or beliefs are also less likely to change these than are people who are not committed to those ideas, and committed individuals' reflections or attitudes about the content of their commitments are also less changeable than their thoughts or feelings about matters to which they are not committed. Kiesler (1971, p. 30) concludes that "the degree of commitment tells us how closely some behavior is tied to the self and how easy it is to dispense with it if that is necessary." A committed person resists pressures to behave in ways that do not agree with his or her pledge.

Employees who work side by side develop a loyalty to that body and thus tend to become committed to its ways and objectives. This is what happens in the quality circles within manufacturing firms in Japan. The members of these work groups are allowed by management to set their own goals and their own work procedures. As a result, according to Zander (1983), they work for their groups, not for themselves. Walton (1980) has compared groups of highly committed and weakly committed employees. He remarks that teams in which workers are more committed tend to have supervisors who believe that commitment is necessary for good performance. The committed groups do in fact perform well. Their employees are more comfortable with the tools and procedures they use, are more contented, and learn their jobs more rapidly. In such formal organizations (doubtless more enduring than community groups for social action), commitment to the value of a unit's goals clearly has useful effects. Knoke and Wood (1981) report that persons who are more committed to their groups do more to help those units survive by providing time, money, leadership, and help from outside sources.

Moreland and Levine (1980) have observed several consequences in groups where members are fully committed. These are acceptance of the group's goals (called *consensus*), favorable affective ties to other members (called *cohesiveness*), willingness to exert effort in behalf of the group and to fulfill the expectations of associates (called *control*), and desire to maintain membership in the group (called *continuance*). They also suggest that commitment can be a two-way proposition. A member may become committed to the group, and the group may become committed to the member. The commitment in each direction is stronger as the value of each to the other is greater. Clearly, a committed person values the actions and ends that he or she promises to work toward.

Helping Members Perceive That Chances of Group Success Are Good. From the foregoing, we see that the value of a group's objective helps members become involved in work toward that goal. But this objective must also be seen as attainable, I assume, before members will take any action. Therefore, leaders try to increase members' confidence in achieving the objective they value. More precisely, leaders strengthen members' perceptions of the probability of successfully working toward the goal. Much of what managers do is directed toward keeping up the morale of subordinates by helping them believe that they can accomplish the group's goal. Thus, they help members set realistic objectives for their organization. These objectives ought not to be too easy, since the accomplishment of simple ends is seldom very satisfying, nor should the goals be too hard, for then the group probably will fail. A goal should be a bit more difficult than the goals that the group can usually attain with reasonable effort, and it should be somewhat harder than a goal that has been achieved recently (if the group has had previous experience). This is a *challenging* group goal. It typically arouses more enthusiasm among members than do goals that are either easier or harder (Zander, 1971).

Members will perceive their group's objective to be more achievable if it is measurable—that is, if members know precisely what evidence they must possess before they can say that they have reached their goal. Thus, if a goal is measurable, members can see whether they are reaching it and whether they are succeeding. A group's objective must also be attainable. Members must be able to see what procedures they have to follow in order to attain the goal. If the group's objective cannot be made measurable or attainable, then leaders of the group often turn to subgoals that are. These smaller goals may have little or no relevance to the major objectives of the group. They are attractive simply because they are measurable and attainable. Such small objectives are most commonly invented when the broad purposes of a group are fuzzy and abstract, as in bodies guided by ideological, religious, or political beliefs (Kweit and Kweit, 1971; Zander, 1985).

Members' estimates of the chances that their group will succeed are also affected by their views about the change they wish to see made. If they view the current situation as harboring serious deprivation for themselves, and if they see it as stable, continuing, and difficult to modify, then they are less willing to take action. This pessimism will be reinforced, moreover, if they begin to feel sad about quite unrelated matters and to perceive that things are bad all over. For example, a town lost its only large company, and many citizens lost their jobs. Thereafter, the city received an increasing number of complaints about the schools, the library, the swimming pool, and potholes in the streets.

Members are less willing to take action if they view unfavorable conditions as their own fault (Seligman, 1975; Trotter, 1987). To immunize participants against self-blame, group officers help them realize that the situation they want to improve can be modified. The leaders do this by pointing to the successes of comparable groups that have worked on similar matters. They also teach members to see the issue as an isolated problem, as neither a cause nor an effect of other difficulties in the town, and they stress that the problem is not due to the actions of the change agents themselves.

To bolster members' faith that they can succeed, leaders must also provide them with the necessary resources. These include equipment, tools, space, personnel, training, and funds. Members of most groups for social action would benefit from training in procedures for solving problems and implementing preferred solutions. Members may also need instruction in how to raise funds, collect and analyze information, make their group attractive to recruits, and mount an influential program. Members can also be encouraged by asking counselors what to do and how to do it. Some advisers of organizations require the units to pay them in advance because the gathering of these funds as a first project strengthens the group and makes participants more willing to accept the individuals whose advice they are paying for (Lancourt, 1979).

More than persons in other kinds of bodies, a group of change agents needs support from bystanders because observers can influence the views of target persons about proposals for reform. Therefore, agents of change try to win the approval of citizens. They also seek such support for another reason—the activists may be able to recruit new members from among bystanders who wish them well. Despite their need for confidence in the group, members may strive to reach a goal even when they doubt that they can. This is the desperate try by a disadvantaged team whose members are strongly motivated and feel that the goal is important enough for them to make their move against poor odds.

Arousing Members to Take Action

We have considered the things that leaders do in order to get participants ready to act. When group members are thus prepared, they must be triggered to move. The main issues are simple. What actions will we take? Who will do what? When do we start?

An ideal decision about what steps to take leads members toward the group's objective, but such an ideal is not always chosen because the goal may be too vague, too unrealistic, too difficult, or too costly to serve as a valid criterion for selecting a course of action. Instead, a given method is selected because it seems possible and represents an activity that members feel they can carry off well. It allows members an opportunity to do something, even if it merely means that they show their anger (one of the favorite emotions within such groups) (Brill, 1971).

Once the method for action is selected, jobs are assigned to members, and the kind of properties that the group needs are de-fined and developed. A date is set for commencing the operation. Necessary supplies, speeches, signs, symbols, and other resources are assembled, and persons with special roles are briefed, trained, and rehearsed. Walking through the action and being critiqued by coaches help these actors gain confidence that they can do what is expected of them.

On the appointed day, they act. In subsequent weeks, their morale and enthusiasm are maintained through reviews of how well the group has performed. Objectives or methods are changed, as necessary, and the planning steps described in this chapter are re-peated. The members' enthusiasm usually does not last long, espe-cially if things go slowly or go wrong. (We will return to such matters in Chapter Nine.)

Summary

A member of a group that is planning to work toward a local change may be driven by any of the four kinds of motivation de-scribed in the foregoing pages. The willingness of members to par-ticipate in their group's activities is determined by the strength of their motivations. Motivational strength results from a combina-tion of three factors: the weight of the motive or desire, the weight of the incentive or objective, and the perceived probability that the incentive or objective can be achieved.

Organizers of a group increase members' readiness to act by heightening the value of each of these three factors. Managers use many procedures to arouse enthusiasm among members, and each is intended to enhance the impact of one or all of the three factors that determine motivational strength. When a member makes a promise (called a *commitment*) to behave or think in a given way, he or she agrees to take the relevant objective seriously and to view its ac-complishment as a valuable thing to do. A committed member may give little weight to the strength of a motivation or to the probabil-ity of successfully accomplishing the objective. Closely tied to moti-vation is the kind of method that the members decide to use in taking action. We are ready now to consider procedures that agents of social change employ in their efforts to influence target persons.

6

~~~~~~

Permissive Methods
Used by Groups

Agents of change must decide which procedure they will use in trying to influence target persons. Ordinarily, they employ some familiar method—a parade, demonstration, rally, speech, workshop, conference, letter to the editor, handbill, brochure, bargaining session, lawsuit, or threat. Rosener (1978) describes thirty-nine methods used by local groups for social action. What groups choose among such possibilities depends on what they think will work, what they are capable of doing well, and the kinds of responses they believe target persons will have to different kinds of advocacy. They also ask themselves several questions. Shall we try to influence target persons by encouraging their freedom of choice in responding to our proposal? Or shall we assume that they have power we cannot alter to settle things on their own? Shall we use methods that place constraint on target persons, or ones that put little or no pressure on them? In this and the next chapter, we consider a number of methods for social action. I have ordered these under eleven categories. (In Chapter Eight, we will examine why one method rather than another is chosen.) Each category has a place at some point along a scale depicting the degree of help or pressure that change agents intend to offer target persons. These categories are listed here in descending order, from methods most likely to encourage autonomy among target persons to those that are least likely to enhance autonomy. In relations with target persons, agents of change may do the following things:

- hold back from contacts with decision makers, discuss the issue among themselves, and use civil disobedience
- provide models of desired behavior
- provide expert information to the whole community or only to decision makers, diffuse that knowledge widely, and give advice
- negotiate with target persons
- engage in a problem-solving process with them
- employ the help of a legitimate institution or third party to mediate, arbitrate, elect, petition, or judge
- provide nurturance or assistance to needy persons or target persons
- persuade target persons through debates or propaganda
- bargain with target persons
- reward target persons
- coerce target persons, interfere with their work, damage their property, threaten them with harm, or seize hostages

These categories are not equidistant on the scale from low to high constraint. Their sequence suggests, however, that methods of social action vary, from being quite permissive at one extreme to being very coercive at the other—sources of stimulation and assistance versus sources of pressure and threat. Any method can be more or less constraining according to the way it is used. Civil disobedience, for example, can be a weak form of withdrawal, on the one hand, or a kind of aggression, on the other. Members may move from one point on the scale to another. They may use several different methods at the same moment.

Some of these methods can be used sensibly only if a number of people join in. This is often the main reason why agents of change form a group. They want to use a given procedure, and they recognize that many persons must work together if they are to do so effectively. Mechanisms that require collaboration among more than a few individuals include attention-getting activities, such as rallies, mass meetings, street theater, exhibits, conferences, or circulation of handbills; organized efforts to diffuse information through informal channels; gathering of signatures on petitions and presentation of them to legislators; provision of nurturance to people in need; and coercion of officials (blocking their proceedings, taking hostages, or harming property and people). Other kinds of methods either can be used by individuals working alone or cannot be used as effectively by persons acting in concert. These include making speeches, writing letters to the editor, teaching, serving as a consultant, or conducting a lawsuit. Even when an activist works alone, he or she appreciates the support of bystanders, who provide him or her with ideas, encouragement, and less solitary forms of action. We are interested here in the methods that groups use, regardless of whether those methods need many hands or only a few.

For each of these eleven kinds of methods, we take up four topics: examples of procedures within this category, why activists choose this method (that is, what change agents think it will do for them), the effects of this method on target persons, and how agents of change make the method most effective. (The latter issue is treated more fully in Chapter Nine, where we will consider, in general terms, how change agents strengthen their social power.)

As we examine these eleven methods, we will observe that members have special intentions when they choose each one. Several of these intentions are worth noting briefly at the outset. Reformers who use constraining methods usually want a specific result from target persons and try to make sure they get just that, even if they must monitor the behavior of target persons to be certain. Activists will watch for signs that a target person intends to behave as he or she is being pressed to do. They will observe the target person's apparent motives, goals, and procedures, as well as his or her way of interacting. Innovators hope, ideally, to influence all of the factors just mentioned.

For constraining methods to be well used, the activists must know whether target persons have changed in desirable ways, so that the reformers can bring forth additional incentives, such as rewards, threats, or harmful actions, if those are necessary, and let up on these if they succeed in changing the target persons. In short, they must follow up, measure, monitor, or spy on target persons to see if events are turning out as the innovators wish. Change agents who use nonconstraining methods, in contrast, want a situation improved in whatever way makes sense to the target persons. The initiators therefore provide ideas and information, so that the listeners can choose the course they think will work best. The activists are interested in the responses of decision makers and are willing to accept a result quite different from one they may have favored at first, as long as it seems satisfactory to all concerned.

Decisions makers who are subjected to constraint (by rewards, propaganda, kidnapping, threats, or harm), in contrast to those who are not pushed in these ways, often try to make it appear that they are doing what they have been asked to do, even when they are not. They cover up any rejecting feelings (or behaviors) in order to diminish the likelihood that the activists will place more pressure on them. They want to get the reward or avoid the penalty. It follows that agents of change who use constraining methods can be more effective in modifying the overt behavior of target persons (such as their statements, decisions, actions, and procedures) than in changing their covert beliefs, feelings, or attitudes because visible behaviors can be reliably monitored, while ideas or attitudes cannot. Activists can keep pushing target persons to change their public behavior, but they cannot apply effective pressure to the latters' hidden feelings or beliefs because they cannot (in ordinary community life) accurately know what the targeted individuals have inside their heads. It seems reasonable, then, that constraining methods will change visible actions but not hidden ones, while nonconstraining procedures will stimulate a change in either the behaviors or beliefs of target persons (Cartwright, 1959; Cartwright and Zander, 1968).

Because nonconstraining methods offer a choice to target persons, the latter, when exposed to these soft procedures, are not likely to be entirely upset by the efforts of the change agents. Constraining methods, by contrast, tend to generate anger or fear among those who are exposed to them because the recipients feel that the style of the change agents is repulsive and demeaning (see Chapters Nine and Ten). Users of constraining methods, by comparison with users of nonconstraining ones, also differ in how carefully they select the persons they intend to influence. Those who employ constraining methods select exactly whom they wish to change, and in what ways, so that they can closely monitor the reactions of those people. Users of nonconstraining mechanisms, however, are less certain of exactly what they want and from whom, and so they appeal to as many persons in the community as they can. They have no need to conduct surveillance of persons they would like to influence; indeed, they probably could not do so if they wanted to.

Finally, it is likely that some methods are out of bounds for agents of change in most American communities—for instance, declaring that God is on one's own side (but has forsaken one's rivals), as religious fundamentalists claim today in Nicaragua and Honduras; using extreme violence against individuals; conducting a coup d'état; or creating a commission of experts to settle matters that require trained judgment. In this chapter, we consider the first five of the eleven methods for social action.

Agents of Change Keep to Themselves

Probably the most frequent course taken by persons interested in a change is to do nothing except, perhaps, talk among themselves in order to gain peace of mind. They keep their distance from target persons because they hesitate to make a direct contact with them and believe that they may approach such persons in the future, that someone else will try to influence the decision makers more effectively, or that the group's ideas eventually will become known to those persons and stimulate them to take action. The issue at hand may be so complicated that the would-be change agents expend their energy trying to understand it and planning what changes they eventually may advocate. Increased insight into the source of a problem is often so relieving that they no longer are concerned about acting on it. Talk is cheap—and easier than action. Examples of talk groups are not hard to find. In Beijing, in the 1970s, students created discussion circles, sitting on the pavement outside the Forbidden City. They talked about what was wrong with the way the country and the city were being run and posted statements about these topics on a wall nearby. They invited visiting journalists to speak to them and asked questions about the ways of governing in the visitors' lands (Fraser, 1980). The discussants did not try to confer with Chinese officials (that was too dangerous), but the groups were noticed by authorities and were soon suppressed. More recently, such discussion groups formed again and made loud demands. Their calls for changes in the government eventually were ruthlessly stopped by the Chinese army. Sometimes mere talk is seen to be dangerous by powerful persons.

Other forms of passivity are notable among individuals who hope to foster innovations. For example, parents in a midwestern city decide to make no more proposals to the board of education or observe its meetings until the board has different members; in the meantime, they discuss among themselves how to improve the local schools. People with AIDS chain themselves to the doors of city hall and refuse to leave until the city provides better services for persons suffering from this syndrome. Communes, utopias, monasteries, and secret societies are often interested in reform, yet their members stay away from target persons. Other agents of change courteously disobey laws or do not cooperate with local authorities, thereby engaging in civil disobedience. Although such action *is* civil, it often is used to provoke target persons into repressive moves, which then earn the disobedient ones support from bystanders. Civil disobedience can also be a way of exerting coercive pressure on officials, which we shall examine later. The common denominator among these procedures, we see, is that participants intend to have an impact by standing to one side and by exerting no direct pressure on target persons.

A few other ways of withdrawing should be noted, even though these are seldom used publicly today. One is to accept fate and not complain, as did the Stoics in ancient Athens. Another is to avoid worry or anxiety by remaining calm and distant from troubles of the day, ignoring them. An additional means is to pay attention to otherworldy issues, to fret over ideals, morals, and abstractions that drift far above practicality. A final method is to move out of town. All such modes soothe their users, so that they are not bothered by and do not need to take action on issues that others find troublesome.

Why is it useful to keep one's distance? An obvious reason is that individuals interested in sponsoring a change believe that they ought not to deal with those they hope will help. They may fear retribution if they make their ideas known to official persons or try to persuade them. Thus, they use an indirect procedure—for example, one in which many persons obey regulations but do so very slowly, to make it clear that they think the rules are onerous. They reason that they cannot be arrested while they are obeying these laws. Furthermore, in the case of civil disobedience, if many persons disobey simultaneously, only a few of the total number can be caught. Agents of change may also avoid talking with those whom they hope to reform because they feel that those persons are evil and that any association with them will be bad (Douglas and Wildavsky, 1982). For instance, small cells of persons concerned with pollution of the environment in Maine refused to meet with managers of the companies they blamed for damage to their surroundings; doing so, they said, would be equivalent to bargaining with the enemy.

Another reason agents of change adopt a passive method is that they do not want to be visible and do not want their behavior to be disapproved by their neighbors. This was a problem for people living in a town where mild actions to prevent the creation of a toxic dump nearby were ridiculed by observers. Change agents may also avoid face-to-face meetings with target persons because they fear that the latter will think such contacts are a sign of weakness. They may not be sure their idea is sound or that it will be taken seriously by decision makers. Sometimes innovators do not present their case because they prefer to think of the target persons as angry and wish to benefit from the stimulus that a hostile relationship provides for their own efforts. Labor unions, managers, neighborhood improvement associations, and hate societies often prosper when their mere existence generates hostility among outsiders. Finally, a group that wants things modified may take no action because members' wishes have been ignored previously and they doubt that they can now persuade those who paid no attention in the past. Familiar instances of timid persons who quietly wish for changes are immigrants from Asian countries, members of self-help societies, Native Americans on reservations, homeless persons, and children who secretly wish that the city would build a swimming pool in their neighborhood. They choose to hold back; talk among themselves is all they dare.

What are the effects of such withdrawal? Most commonly, nothing. The target persons either hear no news about the inturned unit, ignore what they do learn about its wishes, decide its members are too unimportant to deserve attention, do not get a comprehensible presentation of the unit's thoughts, or postpone a response until they are asked for one by the reformers. If target persons know that the agents are aggrieved or deprived, they may develop feelings of guilt if they recognize that they themselves are responsible for the others' complaints. They may recognize, moreover, that the deprived persons feel timid about presenting their problem and would welcome support for their cause. For instance, male managers of a bank that had no females in administrative positions were embarrassed when they learned that women employees were privately discussing how they could start a bank on their own, where some of them could then become officials. As a result, the male managers decided to promote some of the women. The sit-ins conducted by black students in restaurants, libraries, swimming pools, and other public places were effective in good part because the participants created feelings of guilt among target persons and observers through their quiet, courteous, and well-dressed appearance while rudely being refused service in those places. The students felt righteous, moreover, when they realized they had made the refusers feel guilty. They believed that this guilt meant that the target persons were now aware that the reformers had been wronged. The innovators hoped the embarrassed ones regretted their actions and were ripe for changing their ways. What they needed to do, the actors thought, was to keep the guilt alive until the decision makers were ready to change conditions.

How can this method be used most effectively? As already indicated, it helps to make target persons feel that they are to blame for the deprivation of the others. The passive ones encourage these feelings of guilt by behaving in ways that reveal their deprivation while showing no anger or aggression that could cause target persons to see them as troublemakers. They do not complain publicly or blame the target persons aloud. They show no hostility when arrested during a sit-in; they go limp in response to being arrested by policemen. They do not respond when verbally attacked by authorities. They hold silent vigils in public places, prominently praying for the protection of those they want to influence, or starving until death arrives in order to press for public consideration of an unpleasant condition that is being ignored. If officials blame the deprived people for their condition ("the homeless prefer to live on the street"), the power holders reduce their feelings of guilt. Accordingly, it is necessary that members of a dissident group not negotiate with those they wish to influence, since such talks may assuage the superiors' sense of self-blame or help them find a reason to accuse persons or causes other than themselves.

The leaders of a passive group watch for signs of low morale among their members because a drop in confidence may occur if participants become impatient and discouraged over the apparent lack of progress while they talk among themselves, disobey civilly, and wait. The reformers want to do something, to see signs that they are moving forward, and neither of these indicators may develop if members stick strictly to their passive plan. Wise leaders and members face the possibility that such reduced motivation may occur among participants, and so they discuss how they can handle their dismay. The discussants consider what they hope to accomplish, the chances of gaining that end, and why they have chosen to be passive. Most of all, they remind themselves that use of a patient procedure requires a groupwide decision in which all participants have a say. They need to commit themselves to the goal and the method, promise one another to abide by their plan, and press those who stray from this pledge to get back in line. Effective passive programs need the support of many persons.

In summary, change agents sometimes influence target persons even though they do not meet with them. They adopt stand-aside methods because they dislike interacting with the target persons or fear the consequences of doing so. Users of this approach try to generate guilt in decision makers and develop deep faith in the correctness of their own goals. Passive procedures are most effective if the receivers are made to feel responsible for the state of affairs that agents of change deplore and if members of the group for social action keep up their confidence while waiting for decision makers to take action.

Agents of Change Serve as Models of Correct Behavior

Agents of change may stimulate the interest of target persons simply by showing how things could be done better. The initiators do not talk to those they hope to influence because they assume that the decision makers will hear about or see the demonstration, that this ideal model will intrigue them, and that it will inspire them to copy that behavior or to ask subordinates to do so. For instance, a group of persons may wish to improve the appearance of local parks. They get permission to plant flowers and bushes in one of the parks, and they furnish the plants and labor themselves. They thereby provide an exhibit for the city's leaders, showing what the town could have in other places. Modeling can be seen in efforts to furnish temporary housing for the homeless, to run a voluntary leisure-time program in an urban neighborhood, or to provide tours of well-run farms to agriculturists. Encouraging observers to learn from models is the basis of the federal Model Cities program, of the reports provided to all local financial campaigns of the United Fund (showing how much each town has collected in recent years), and of excursions for city officials to examine methods of traffic control in other communities.

Sometimes persons or places unknowingly serve as models. We see examples of this when the dress, speech, mannerisms, or bad habits of popular individuals are copied by watchers. Familiar personal models are sports stars, lifeguards, politicians, coaches, ministers, movie actors, music makers, or drug dealers. Occasionally these persons become aware that they are models and decide to become sources of good influence. Witness the professional basketball player (barred from the sport because he used dope) who speaks to groups of young people about the dangers of illegal drugs, or the former white-collar criminal who now teaches ethics. Likewise, officials of a town may copy procedures they observe being used in other communities, such as carpooling, hiring of handicapped persons, flex-time traffic regulations, use of a community coordinating council, or pollution controls. It is not uncommon for a locale to become an active source of influence after it has served as a passive model and the modelers realize that its practices are worthy of emulation. For example, fifty years ago, officials in several counties of southwestern Michigan welcomed visitors from far away to examine their demonstration programs in rural public health (financed in good part by the Kellogg Foundation). A group of black persons succeeded in getting restrictions abolished against the use of public facilities by members of their race and became a model of how such a unit could be used in other places (Gerlach and Hine, 1970).

Why do agents of change sponsor models or serve as exemplars themselves? First, it is a comfortable way of exercising influence. It seldom involves embarassing moves or requires skills beyond their ability. Second, it is a wise method to use when replicable cases are available, access to them is easy to obtain, and the persons to be influenced are looking for ideas and are prepared to be interested in a good demonstration. Ripeness for being so influenced can be induced, of course, if envy is generated among target persons when they are shown how well other communities have handled problems like those at home. Influencers may make sure that the target persons see and hear about a model and will take care that it is presented to them in an attractive way. Third, agents of change who provide imitable models usually believe in the value of having those who are to be changed make their own decisions without being pressured. In other words, the influencers hold that calm consideration of an example allows target persons to decide whether the model is a good one and whether they wish to copy it at home. If they decide to, they are more likely to put this idea into practice than if they had been urged to do so by reformers. A model of a good practice does not influence target persons unless they see it, and they will be intrigued by a demonstration only if they think it is a potential solution for a current problem. They will be comfortable evaluating the model because they are free either to pay attention to it or to ignore it.

How can a model be most effective? Ordinarily, if the exemplars are individuals, their existence must be known to those who will be influenced, and their example must be attractive to observers. Well-known or popular people are often asked to serve as models. It helps if many among the general public approve of the model and mention their positive feelings to the target persons. Those who provide a model must make sure that it is visible, that its appealing features are understood, and that target persons approve of it.

In summary, target persons can be influenced if it is possible for them to imitate the practices or products of models. For agents of change, the main value of modeling is that persons whom they would like to influence convince themselves to copy the model. Those who provide a model offer target persons maximum freedom to make this choice.

Agents of Change Provide Information

Members of some social action groups simply supply information to target persons and to anyone else who will look or listen. They do not try to persuade or inflame listeners with propaganda; they merely impart new knowledge. They assume that these ideas will show target persons that things are ripe for change, or that the information provides a sensible answer to a question that is before citizens of the community. Those who distribute this information take it for granted that some members of the audience are interested (or could be) in the issue at hand and are looking for thoughts that will help them understand it better.

Dispensers of information use any of three different approaches. The first is to distribute ideas through the use of mass media or attention-catching means for reaching listeners. The second is to use planned diffusion of knowledge, with the help of people who learn ways to change certain practices and agree to teach these to others. The third is to counsel those who ask for help in their efforts to develop an innovation of some kind.

Planned Distribution. An endless variety of methods is used by activists to put the facts before people in the community. These include advertisements in newspapers, billboards, classes, conferences, conventions, demonstrations, displays, exhibits, letters to the editor, handbills, mailed brochures, mass meetings, newspaper stories, outdoor rallies, parades, public hearings, speeches to clubs, street theater, workshops, and appearances on television news programs. These procedures differ in the kinds of resources, skills, management, and personnel they require; they are alike in that each of them provides a given message to numerous potential listeners, only some of whom will pay attention to it.

Members of a group for social action who prefer procedures like these do so for several reasons. First, the providers believe that the community wants such special knowledge and that they are experts (more or less) in the matter. This reason is clearly behind letters to the editor, in which readers attempt to make corrections to a previous news story or to expose what is behind a public report issued by a self-appointed task force that has been studying an issue of local concern. Second, the dispensers of information assume that their knowledge will be viewed as reliable and unbiased because they are experienced students of the problem. Third, it is desirable to reach as many persons as possible with these ideas because the recipients have votes and a vested interest in the ideas under discussion and will make their opinions known, or because the organization needs the help of many persons. Fourth, this is a safe form of citizen action because it requires no face-to-face confrontation with target persons (whom activists may wish to talk about, but not to). It is an anonymous method (or can be), and the procedures to be employed are plain enough, even though they demand some skill, which can be bought. This method is preferred by agents of change who want to provide reliable data to those who must solve a current problem. It is not the method used by those who wish to persuade target persons to make one specific change and no other. Of course, any means of dispensing information may cease dealing with facts and become a way to persuade or coerce; we shall take up such methods later on.

We know from research that most persons who are exposed to knowledge dispensed by initiators ignore that information. Two kinds of individuals are likely, however, to pay attention and even be influenced by this method: those who are looking for an answer to a problem and find it in the data provided, or those who already have ideas on the matter and discover in the information a confirmation of views they already possess ("I thought so!"). People who have never dealt with the issue and thus have no preordained ideas about it may become interested if the style of the presenters is particularly agreeable and trustworthy. In general, the mere provision of factual information is more likely to have an impact if it speaks to a need of the listeners and if it suggests a means whereby that need can be fulfilled. As a case in point, if traffic is very bad at rush hour on the main crosstown avenue, dispensers of information about the management of traffic will induce interest among drivers if they emphasize the need for smoother flow of autos and if they suggest ways of improving things. The desires of listeners are aroused, and they are shown how to satisfy those desires.

The message is most effective if it is addressed to people who have a certain curiosity; their motives are easily aroused. The dispensers of information must also assemble the resources they need, such as money, space, equipment, and writers who can present the message well. Because information spreading requires the collaboration of many persons, the activists devote considerable effort to rehearsing before they begin to circulate their story. They realize that their facts must be correct and well presented. Finally, their information is more telling if it proposes an objective (the kind of change needed) in clear terms, indicates what must be done to reach that end, suggests a plan of action, and assures target persons that many citizens are interested in attaining the goal and that these persons will help in efforts to reach it.

In sum, factual information is publicly presented by agents of change because they have important ideas and want to make them available to those who need to know, or because facts about the problem will arouse interest among many who are exposed to them. In this situation, the way to make information most effective is to make it useful and satisfying to listeners.

Planned Diffusion. In this procedure, valued knowledge is spread among members of a target population. Initially, a subset of these people is instructed, and these persons then dispense this wisdom to neighbors and friends. An example is the providing of information to a selected group of farmers about the proper use of a fertilizer that will increase their yield of corn. Members of this primary group agree to tell their neighbors. In other instances, one person from each department of a large organization is told how to use a new program on a computer and is asked to give this information to co-workers, doctors demonstrate a surgical method to local colleagues that they learned in a recent course at the state university, or preachers teach assistants how to spread the word from house to house.

Rogers (1983) describes how ideas are formally diffused among farmers. The process begins after the trainer selects a set of agriculturists in the neighborhood and teaches them a new procedure. This group meets several times, to learn both the theoretical and the practical sides of the innovation. (As we shall see, success of the diffusion method depends heavily on the attributes of the people chosen for this initial set.) The newly trained farmers then employ what they have learned in their own work (if they wish to do so) and make the results of this innovation visible to neighbors by leaving a part of each field untreated. This demonstration provides a small-scale controlled experiment. The effects of the new method, as well as of its absence, can be seen by neighbors as they pass these plots. The owner of the spread on which the innovation has been introduced welcomes questions raised by passersby. Such casual modeling and discussion of the new practice are the main parts of the diffusion process. By means of informal, over-the-fence conversations among farmers, the information is radiated. The growers can find their own way to use the new method at home, if the demonstration before their eyes interests them, or they can ignore it. The consequences of the procedure are later reported and discussed in meetings of planters in that area.

The diffusion method is chosen for several reasons. Its use depends on the fact that practical and not widely known new knowledge has become available in a given field of interest. Ordinarily this information is the result of professional experience or research in medicine, agriculture, education, government, social welfare, or manufacturing. Agents of change think that these ideas will be helpful to persons who do not yet have them. Moreover, there is a specific population of persons who are eager to learn about the new procedure. Experts in the advanced learning are available and willing to teach what they know. A primary corps of first learners is available. When the time comes, these people are taught to serve as demonstrators on their own farms. Finally, the teacher sees this as a superior way to teach. Students learn by do-ing—that is, they learn by trying to improve conditions in their own activities, by themselves, with help available if they need it. Learners are also inspired to take up a new way when they see the good effects of the new practice in a colleague's efforts. Friends help friends to improve, but only if asked; nobody presses anybody.

Aside from providing an opportunity to learn a new practice, what effects does this educational procedure have on those who take part in it? Some find it anxiety-provoking because they feel that they are too much on their own and without a "cookbook" to guide them in the future. They want clear and unequivocal answers, not ideas to be used experimentally. In contrast, widespread acceptance of an innovation among many neighbors may lead everyone to de-velop a strict standard of good or required behavior on the matter, one that all are expected to obey. Those who do not are pressured to get back in line, on pain of being treated as deviants if they do not. Such pressure toward uniformity is especially hard for a nonconfor-mist to resist if he or she wishes to be liked and accepted as a member of the target persons' community in the future (Cartwright and Zander, 1968).

Rogers (1973) observes that farmers who more readily adopt the new ideas are different from those who do not. The contrasting characteristics of adopters and nonadopters suggest the kinds of differences that may also exist among takers and refusers in other fields of endeavor. Agriculturists who adopt the innovations more quickly, by comparison with those who drag their feet, have more formal education, a higher social standing in the community, and bigger farms. Such qualities make them more likely to be influen-tial among their neighbors on questions of good agricultural prac-tice. In addition, those who more rapidly adopt the proposed changes do more reading, associate with fellow farmers more often, have more contacts with the expert teachers, have neighbors or friends who are also in the initial group of trainees, see greater value in the proposed innovation, are generally more amenable to making changes in how they run their business, and are persons whose opinions have weight with their neighbors.

Rogers (1983) has examined the sequence of moves that a change agent typically makes when encouraging adoption of a new practice. The initial agent of change needs to do the following things:

- help potential adopters become aware that their current practices are not wholly satisfactory and that they need to be changed
- tell people about new practices available to meet their needs and about where they can learn these better procedures if they wish to do so
- help listeners identify the causes of problems in their own situations
- assist people in defining the best solutions for their particular difficulties
- get people to commit themselves to the use of a procedure that appears to be a remedy for their situation
- aid committed persons in their efforts to translate this new plan into action
- follow up with each individual in later months, to be sure that the new practice is working and to help him or her establish a continuing routine
- achieve a clear termination of the relationship between teacher and student and leave the changers on their own when they are confident that they can handle the new method

To take these steps effectively, Rogers (1983) suggests several things. It is helpful if carefully selected people are invited to the beginning session. They ought to be comfortable with new ideas, better educated than most, willing to try new methods, influential among colleagues, and naturally friendly and sociable. Persons with these attributes, as we have noted, are more willing to adopt new methods and to discuss them with others who are curious about the results.

The process of planned diffusion works best, Rogers says, if new practices are accepted by persons who have influence in the neighborhood, and these holders of power are more likely to adopt new ideas if doing so does not cause them to lose power, status, money, or any special benefits that they derive from their current ways of doing business. The people with greater power in the area therefore act as gatekeepers, who prevent threatening innovations from entering the neighborhood and who welcome new practices in farming that promise to help everyone. When a farmer with power adopts a given practice, it is less likely to be resisted or opposed by other farmers than if the innovation were put in place by an ordinary member of the community. Rogers adds a caveat, however. The latter observation does not hold true if there is a crisis, such as an economic depression, a drought, a storm, or some other emergency. In such a situation, persons who are low in the status hierarchy can be successful in selling their ideas if they are able to sway neighbors on emotional grounds or if they have some special talent or solution for handling that condition. They can even overcome the opposition of the people who ordinarily are the most powerful. The impact of this tyro decreases, however, as soon as the practices he or she advocates are accepted and established. Thereafter, the regular holders of power again take over. It is probable, in light of these observations, that planned diffusion is useful for spreading procedures or beliefs widely among many persons who are free to accept or reject them, but it seldom can change the minds of influential individuals who make decisions for the community and who oppose the proposed new practice.

Our consideration of planned diffusion has concentrated on persons who raise plants and animals because the method has been used most often among such people and studied in those settings. Diffusion has also been employed in other situations, of course— medicine, education, automobile repair, carpentry, insurance sales, and computer operation. Generally speaking, the reasons for using this method, the separate phases to be followed, its effects on people, and the conditions that make it most effective should be applicable to settings other than agriculture. Such a hunch awaits examination, however. Can a process of diffusion be useful when a parents' club tries to convince the city council that more money should be spent on recreation and playgrounds? It could be if the parents used the diffusion process to spread their idea to neighborhoods of the city by starting a few summer playgrounds with the help of volunteers, leaving other parts of the town without such an amenity. A successful demonstration would eventually reach the eyes and ears of those on the city council, or members of an official group in the community (such as the planning commission) could be used as the set of persons who are first taught a new method and who are then invited to communicate this procedure to others. In so doing, they will doubtless become interested in the innovation. Suppose that they learn new criteria for zoning neighborhoods, so that the value of property in the town will remain high. Thereafter, they take these ideas to different parts of the city, so that they can be taught to property developers and real-estate appraisers.

Counseling Target Persons. Instead of dispensing knowledge to a public that has not asked for it, or coaching persons who then spread the information to their colleagues, agents of change may be asked to serve as advisers to target persons. They provide counsel on matters in which they are experts, or they help advisees decide among themselves what might be best for them. In so doing, counselors foster a readiness among target persons to modify their ways of operating. For example, a department of recreation asks citizens to work out a new plan for leisure-time activities among older people. The police ask for advice from residents of a housing project on how the tenants can help reduce the sale of illicit drugs in the area. Mothers and fathers suggest to school officials that they jointly prepare a set of standards for adolescent behavior in and out of school. Such sets of ordinary citizens are advisory bodies. Some organize themselves; others are appointed by those who want advice (Kweit and Kweit, 1971; Langton, 1978). (Appointed units are of less interest to us at the moment.)

One problem for advisers who have ideas to offer is to get themselves asked for help. To be known and used, counselors must advertise—not literally, by means of a television spot or a newspaper spread, but by letting target persons know they are available to provide counsel on a particular issue because of their experience or expertise in the matter. For example, a set of citizens in a small city offered to help the city council collect data and ideas for controlling the deer that were ravaging gardens and parks in the town. Another group regularly attended meetings of the welfare board and spoke on issues of concern when time was made available for citizens' comments. This procedure was used by some members of the League of Women Voters, who sat in the audience during meetings of the county commissioners. The observers became so knowledgeable about the business of the board that commissioners often asked them for their opinions or requested them to check with other members of the league to see what those women thought about a given issue. Clearly, the women gave influential advice, without making it obvious that they had intended to do so.

Citizens can become advisers to decision makers by holding hearings on a lively issue, reporting results of these forums to officials who are faced with that issue, and making it known to target persons that they will gather more data on the matter if asked. A team may also study what has been written on a hot problem and prepare a statement containing recommendations. It is not uncommon for an individual to tell officials that he or she will study a topic and come up with options to be considered as solutions. Agents of change convert themselves into consultants, in sum, by making themselves useful and by indicating that they are prepared to continue.

They have to decide, however, what role they intend to play. Are they to be experts, who have reliable answers? Coaches on how to work toward a solution? Demonstrators of what could be done differently? Counselors on how to think in more broad-minded terms? Commentators on the opinions, attitudes, and beliefs of the target persons? Questions like these are proposed in Lippitt, Watson, and Westley (1958). Those authors describe the phases that counselors move through when providing advice on how to introduce changes in a social entity:

1. The client system discovers the need for help, sometimes with stimulation from the change agent.
2. The helping relationship is established and defined.
3. The problem is identified and clarified.
4. Alternative solutions are examined; change goals or intentions are established.
5. Efforts are made to introduce a realistic change.
6. This solution is generalized and stabilized.
7. The helping relationship ends or a different type of continuous relationship is defined [Lippitt, Watson, and Westley, 1958, p. 123].

Why do agents of change choose to counsel target persons? Several situations make counseling look like a good approach—for instance, when the issue facing the advisees is complex and not easy for anyone to define or understand. The advisers may have no clear or compelling answer to urge on the listeners, and so they suggest that the matter needs a problem-solving approach, and they offer to help in the use of this process. They become more willing to offer their own ideas, however, if they believe that their expertise is superior to what other advisers can provide. An agent of change may also bring an open mind to a conference of target persons, without advocating a favorite point of view, and offer a variety of alternative solutions.

Persons who ask to be counseled may fear that the advisers have biases, and so they examine the offered ideas to make sure that these are useful and not merely attractive. The advisees usually have incomplete knowledge about the issue at hand. As a consequence, they become dependent on advice givers when they request help. Dependent persons are, by definition, easily influenced by anyone on whom they depend, and so they must guard against accepting unsound advice. If the counselor leads a problem-solving discussion among counselees instead of advising them, he or she may irritate discussants because the latter are being asked to find answers inside their own heads. If they had known how to solve the problem, they say to themselves, they would not have turned to a counselor. Target persons can evaluate stated advice by setting up a task force to appraise it, seeking a second opinion, or postponing action until they are confident that the counsel is wise.

A counselor usually tries to prevent advisees from opposing his or her suggestions; there is no point in generating opposition among counselees unless one intends to inspire a lively discussion and little else. Experienced counselors know that their advice may be more useful if they concentrate their comments on ways of defining the problem. In so doing, they note and define concepts that are pertinent to the phenomena under discussion. By providing names for these concepts, along with descriptions of their sources and effects, counselors give advisees terms to use in analyzing what is going on and in thinking about what can be improved. A counselor provides advisees with ways to think about their situation, along with information on how to deal with the issue at hand.

An effective counselor recognizes that persons being counseled may resist advice for reasons that are not the counselor's fault. A likely cause of counselees' resistance is an unwillingness to admit to themselves (and to observers) that they need help and are unable to solve their problems on their own. Another is fear of failure or awkwardness if they try to install a new procedure in their organization. Moreover, they may dread the uncertain consequences of change, even before they attempt a new procedure. A further cause is pessimism among counselees about how well they can carry out a revision because they have failed in the past on a similar activity. Still another source of resistance is fear of embarrassment over the counseled group's actions or of disparagement by those who think that the innovation is not sensible. Finally, target persons resist if they lack effective means of making decisions or implementing new ideas. They dislike working on a change when they do not know how to carry it off well.

Counselors can help reduce resistance among advisees. First, they try to determine the nature of target persons' anger or fear through observations, individual interviews, or discussions with the group. They describe to the advisees signs of uneasiness noted in them and demonstrate how anxieties interfere with the interaction between counselor and counselees. Counselors also help participants overcome these feelings by showing them how the effects of these attitudes can be controlled. Finally, they help members overcome their feelings of resistance. (We shall return to a consideration of resistance in Chapters Nine and Ten.)

In summary, persons who wish to introduce an innovation may do so by giving relevant information to target persons, or to constituents of those people, by using regular communications media, employing methods for distributing knowledge or arousing interest, teaching selected individuals who thereupon diffuse what they have learned, or serving as counselors to individuals who are considering whether and how to introduce an innovation. Generally speaking, each of these methods helps receivers judge what and how to improve things while feeling under no external pressure to do so.

Agents of Change Negotiate with Target Persons

Suppose a group that wants better shelters for street people meets with the local board for social welfare, to talk about that problem. Those in each party (reformers and members of the board) try to learn and understand what the others know about the situation, and they attempt to reach a common point of view. They discuss their feelings about places currently being used by homeless people and what they think is acceptable or regrettable about conditions facing persons without homes, but they do not try to decide what ought to be done to solve the problem. Such a discussion is called a *negotiating session*. It is a process of conferring in which participants work to reach a common comprehension of the facts involved in a particular state of affairs. The meeting may be preliminary to a decision or solution, but the negotiation itself is not intended to settle matters (beyond, perhaps, agreeing on definitions of the issues).

An example of a negotiation would be a conference attended by members of a neighborhood improvement association and by those on the city's planning commission. The topics for discussion are the noise caused by traffic on a major highway and the effects it has on nearby residents. They talk about who is bothered most, in what ways and at what hours, and about what citizens can do about the noise. They consider how other towns have deflected and dampened such clamor by erecting solid walls near the shoulder of the freeway, and they discuss how well these have worked. They agree that the issue merits further attention, and the city officials offer to measure the amount of sound precisely, in decibels, for several days, along that stretch of the highway. They decide to meet again soon. The agents of change feel relieved because the problem has been brought before persons who have responsibility for such issues.

A comparable set of negotiators composes a committee of representatives from each of six cities in one county. They meet to consider problems arising from an increase in traffic among their towns because drivers who wish to avoid crowded expressways move along two-lane back roads that were not designed to carry as many cars as they now must. Much of the talk in the committee concerns what each town is planning to do to ease traffic jams; motorists from each community cause problems for the others. They agree that someday they must develop a sensible joint solution, once they understand what that could be. They currently have no power to act as a body, only to understand one another's approaches to their common problem. They may be able to help rather than hinder one another as a result of these meetings.

Why do discussants negotiate? There are several reasons. One, already implied, is that members of separate bodies know or suspect that they see things differently and that it is necessary, because of their close relationship, to meet and clear the air. They want to get the facts straight and tell one another how they view things. Another reason is that the issues involved are complex, emotionally involving, and new to people on both sides. Therefore, it is useful to talk about them, so that everyone will realize how others perceive things and feel about these matters. Negotiation is the method of choice, moreover, when misunderstanding is liable to develop between citizens and target persons and both sides want to avoid it. Negotiation is also useful when other methods have failed and participants need to understand why. Negotiating can be a subtle way of applying pressure toward changing things when target persons are clearly responsible for alleviating unfavorable features of the matter under discussion. The innovators say that they merely want to discuss the matter, but they hope the discussion will cause target persons to realize that they have been neglecting the issue.

The major consequence of using this procedure is that each side learns the other's opinions and attitudes. This in itself is reassuring and often so satisfying that the parties feel they need do nothing more about the issue, but if people are deeply disturbed by the problem, it is unlikely that mere sharing of information will slow them down or that participants will listen closely to one another. In such an instance, the mood is more likely to be one in which participants want to persuade, not merely to understand. Other, pressure-laden methods may then be tried. In fact, discussions about barriers to constructive interaction commonly stall once these differences are defined; people are hurt, insulted, or angered by the opinions that others express.

To negotiate effectively, participants come to the meeting

with clearly defined ideas about what they know, believe, and feel. These ideas help them recognize that their views are not always the same as those expressed by persons on the other side, and they can see what the differences are. These ideas also help participants identify the questions they wish to ask. As in solving a problem, negotiating requires participants to be objective in expressing their views and in trying to understand those of others. Members may agree to disagree on some matters. In a negotiating session, the atmosphere is free and open, and any topic is fair game. The only restrictions on interaction are those that members set ahead of time, in order to ensure an orderly process.

Several procedures are useful in a negotiation. They are the kinds of steps that a problem-solving group uses to prepare participants for choosing a solution from among a number of alternatives. These devices help people bring up the matters that they wish to discuss, without fear of retribution. In one approach, participants are divided into small groups. Members from both sides are assigned in equal numbers to each subgroup, and each unit is given a separate question to consider. On completion of the brief discussion (a half-hour or so), a spokesperson for each body tells the whole conference what his or her unit has considered and what understandings or opinions it has reached. The contrasts among these reports provide material for further conferring. Reporters from each small set may also be brought together to participate in a panel discussion on the central issue. The subgroups may take up a number of topics. What is useful about the practice under discussion, and what ought to be changed? What points have been omitted so far in the give-and-take? Why do different sides have contrasting beliefs? What have other communities done when faced with a problem like the one before us?

In another practice, called *brainstorming,* conferring proceeds under special rules. This procedure is helpful when new ideas are needed; therefore, discussants should be able to talk freely. Criticism of any suggestions made by others is prohibited. Free thinking and wild notions are welcome. The more ideas, the better. Combinations or modifications of others' proposals are in order. The two prime aims in brainstorming are to defer any judgment of what discussants say and to develop a greater number of suggestions, since greater quantity begets better quality (Osborn, 1957; Zander, 1982).

An additional method for enhancing sound discussion is known as the *nominal group technique*. Here, participants take advantage of the fact that people become more productive when working on an individual task in the presence of others. Participants sit at a conference table and write as many answers as they can to several questions. Oral interaction is prohibited. What is the real problem, as you see it? What are its causes? What can be done about it? Answers to these questions are listed on a blackboard, with no identification of who wrote which. Face-to-face discussion of one item at a time follows and leads to views on which all can agree (Delbecq and Van de Ven, 1975).

When participants are inhibited about participating publicly because they do not want to make their opinions known, the *Delphi method* is useful. In this approach, each negotiator is asked to write his or her opinions and predictions about the topic. The results are given to a coordinator, who sorts the main ideas into a number of categories. This list is returned to the respondents, who are then asked to comment, pro or con, on each category of answers. These responses are again summarized and returned for remarks, until a set of fairly common beliefs emerges and the appraisals of each idea are summarized in writing. With these data in hand, the negotiators proceed in the usual fashion (Delbecq and Van De Ven, 1975; Zander, 1982). In Japan, negotiation is sometimes conducted silently (and not face to face). One discussant prepares a draft that describes differing views on a topic. This draft is circulated among the participants as many times as necessary. Each person makes anonymous changes on each draft until no more changes are made by anyone. A variation on this approach is to have one person interview each of those who are to attend a negotiating session. The views of all members are summarized anonymously at the outset of the meeting. The differences can then be discussed; agreements can be ignored (Vogel, 1975; Zander, 1982).

To sum up, a group of responsible citizens may wish to understand the views and feelings of other persons, without intending to press at once toward a change in practice or a decision on what ought to be done to improve things. The citizens try to reach a shared understanding of facts and opinions on a specific state of affairs, a process called *negotiating*. Ordinarily, the effect of such talk is calming, both for agents of change and for target persons. To promote such a calming atmosphere, discussants may use special techniques, which make it possible for interaction to flow freely and for feelings and facts to be objectively presented. Negotiating arouses interest in the issue under discussion and causes participants to want a say in what can be done about it. They move, in short, toward making the negotiation into a problem-solving activity because they have already laid much of the groundwork for solving the problem.

Agents of Change and Target Persons Engage in Problem Solving

In problem solving, persons from two or more parties work together to find an answer. Neither side intends (overtly, at least) to make sure that its point of view is taken as the final outcome, although persons from both sides wish to have a say and to influence one another while working toward a sound product. Their joint goal is to find a wise solution, even if this creates a disadvantage for some at the conference table. Deutsch (1973) calls this approach *constructive problem solving*. When agents of change try to get target persons to participate in a problem-solving discussion, the reformers usually are aspiring to participate as equals with those they hope to join in discussion. If target persons have considerable social power, however, they probably will not be willing to take part in a problem-solving procedure simply because activists ask them to do so. If the target persons agree to take part in such an activity, they admit thereby that things need improvement, that they (the target persons) are incompetent, and that they do not have answers to obvious problems. Sometimes target persons adopt a process of problem solving after a conflict has developed between themselves and the agents of change, and it becomes evident that they must relax and discuss the matter more sensibly if they hope to resolve their disagreements. (We consider problem solving to resolve a conflict in Chapter Nine; at the moment, we are interested in its use as a means to work with change agents toward a sensible conclusion.) To understand the process of problem solving, we first must note a few separable concepts.

A *problem,* for agents of change and target persons, is a specific situation to which members of both parties must respond if they are to achieve satisfactory movement toward their objectives. Participants face a *dilemma* if they have no effective response to the problem. In a *joint problem-solving* process, members of both sides identify alternative ways of dealing with the situation and then select the most satisfactory course from among these. A *solution* is a response that alters the specific situation, so that it no longer causes a dilemma. *Decision making* is the selection of a preferred solution from among available alternatives. Problem solving moves through several phases: describing the problem that requires a response and stating why a response is necessary, identifying a number of possible solutions, deciding on the best solution from among these alternatives, and taking action to implement the decision.

A problem-solving process begins when an issue is put before a target group and its members respond by considering whether the matter is worthy of discussion and whether they want to work on it. There is a division of labor here. The initiators describe the problem; the target persons decide whether they want to spend time on it. If the latter say that it is not an important issue or is not worthy of attention, the topic is probably dropped right there, and no problem solving ensues. To prevent stalling by target persons, activists come to a meeting equipped with evidence showing that the state of affairs they deplore has adverse consequences for many persons, or that a golden opportunity exists to improve the current state of affairs. Unsatisfactory conditions will continue if the condition under complaint is ignored.

When change agents present a problem for discussion, they explain the significance of the issue, without revealing their feelings about the difficulty or their preferred solution; a slanted introduction of a topic can lead to biased comments by participants. It is difficult, however, for change agents to declare that they have no vested interest in the problem being presented. The fact that they bring up the issue, when it is not always their place to do so, suggests that they have strong feelings about the matter. Therefore, wise initiators put more emphasis on describing the unfavorable consequences of the situation that they deplore than on presenting a solution that they favor. They stress, in brief, that the topic is worthy of attention and that they do not have a ready or favorite answer.

Obviously, it is important that the bone of contention be described clearly by those who present it because conferees commonly start talking once a topic has been offered. Unless the issue is clear, however, the comments of different people do not cohere, and each is speaking on a different matter. It is hard enough to keep a group of problem solvers on a given topic, whether it is clear or not; it is doubly difficult if the question is muddy. What is more, an unclear statement cannot easily be clarified during a discussion because too many voices bring forth too many interpretations of it. The problem is being raised by change agents, and so they are the ones who must define it precisely.

Even though reformers and target persons may agree that a given issue is worthy of discussion, they nevertheless may feel that it is unwise to talk about it because certain of its characteristics (such as too many parts, excessive heterogeneity among these parts, or vagueness of the central issues) make it difficult to handle. Participants may decide to pass the problem along to a subgroup or to a set of experts who are asked to consider the matter and to provide advice on how to remedy it, or separate bodies may be given different aspects of the point at issue. This approach was used to solve a controversial problem in a Texas town. The problem concerned the kind and size of bullets that members of the local police force should carry. One group considered the ethics that were most salient in the subject under discussion. Another unit reviewed data on the effects that bullets of different sizes have on the human body. A third entity integrated the conclusions of the two other groups and made final recommendations for action (Hammond and Adelman, 1976).

Once the problem and its ramifications have been clearly stated, participants begin to list things that could be done to resolve the question. The value of the group's joint problem solving depends, obviously, on the quality of the ideas offered during this time of listing. A wise answer is more likely to be found if there are many alternatives from which to choose. There will be more and better suggestions if participants are free to offer ideas and if the favorable or adverse effects of each proposal are thoroughly explored.

When a participant proposes a possible answer during a problem-solving conference, conferees begin to test whether the suggested approach provides a resolution. They consider how complete an answer it promises and what side effects it may have if it becomes the chosen course. More specifically, they ponder a number of questions. What gains or losses will agents of change, target persons, and others get from this approach? How much will participants approve of their own groups after selecting this solution? What will the rest of the community think of the target persons?

A difficulty that dogs every decision-making body is that discussants cannot confidently answer such questions because they cannot foresee what will happen and what the consequences of a given decision will be. Officials, particularly those who have been elected, have to keep in mind the need to act as they think their constituents would want them to. They may also be constrained by legal requirements that prohibit their kind of body from choosing a course different from the one they are now following (Funk, 1982). When they describe these legal limitations, they may be suspected of making excuses so that they can avoid making an improvement.

If none of the available alternatives is truly appealing or legitimate, and if no one can think of a better answer, the discussants try to find the proposal that is the least objectionable. They put a good face on this weak choice by inventing arguments in favor of it, after the fact. This form of rationalization is called *bolstering*. It involves listing the good consequences that may follow from the decision while minimizing unfavorable results, exaggerating the need for action right away, minimizing the interests of persons outside the group, and playing down discussants' responsibility for the effects of their action (Janis and Mann, 1977).

Why is the problem-solving method used? The most important reason is that agents of change and target persons alike value rational behavior and know how to act in a problem-solving conference. They are sure that they can handle the procedure well. Another reason is that persons on opposing sides are not a threat to one another. They can speak to the issue in logical ways and will not need to defend themselves from retribution if the decision is not pleasing. Calm consideration of pros and cons comes about when conferees are open-minded. They are willing to seek the best answer and to accept what they find, even if it is not what they initially were seeking. Of course, problem solving is useful only if a problem for which there is no obvious answer can be identified and precisely described. Some problems cannot be understood or solved at the moment, and it helps if these are identified clearly as matters that are not yet ripe for change.

The primary effect of a decision is satisfaction, at least for some. If those on both sides welcome the result, and if they have worked with reasonable harmony, then the decision is likely to be implemented. It is important for target persons to like the content and process of such conferences because it is they who typically decide whether a decision will be followed by action or by inaction.

A problem-solving meeting demands special skills. We have seen some of these; others are also notable. If participants strive too hard to keep things harmonious during a meeting, they may be putting aside good sense. They choose the solution that will keep members compatible, rather than the one that is most sensible. Janis (1972) believes that certain kinds of behavior contribute to such ineffectiveness. First, discussants consider only a few solutions and ignore other alternatives. Second, they fail to examine the adverse consequences that will follow their preferred course of action. Third, they too quickly drop alternatives that appear unsatisfactory at first mention. Fourth, they make little effort to get the advice of experts. Fifth, they fail to set up fall-back procedures in case the preferred idea does not work out. Five techniques that help to prevent such groupthink are asking each member to critically evaluate all alternatives, requesting each participant to discuss the content of the group's deliberations with associates outside the group and to report on these findings, assigning the role of devil's advocate to one member, examining the views of persons whose ideas are known to conflict with those of group members, and (once a decision has been made) having participants consider any remaining doubts at a later meeting.

A meeting of change agents and target persons may run into difficulty when the latter have more influence than the former. A problem arises because the higher-status persons tend to talk more often with one another and not with the lower-status participants. Individuals with little social power talk less and most often address their remarks to superordinates, not to their peers. Even so, higher-ranking people usually think that lower-status people talk too much. The result is that most oral messages in such a meeting go in one direction—upward. This pattern cuts the innovators out of much of the regular give-and-take, and they react by speaking only when spoken to (Zander, 1982). A change agent will find it useful to point out any such imbalance in participation, to address remarks to all members, to ask powerful persons to give greater consideration to remarks from activists, and to address more comments to them. If this does not work, the initiators and the officials may meet in separate groups and in different rooms, on the assumption that all will talk more freely in these more comfortable sessions. The members of each group send representatives to the meetings of the other side, to summarize each group's current thinking until both sides become willing to be in the same room, share their ideas, and work toward an acceptable solution. It helps to keep a problem-solving discussion among change agents and target persons small because talk is more equal in a small group than in a large one. Members can be made more ready to participate if special procedures are followed (such as brainstorming, nominal groups, or the Delphi technique).

The effects of certain issues in a community can cause controversy. These issues may include water pollution, acid rain, disposal of toxic wastes, use of animals in research, poisonous gases, noise from traffic, asbestos in ceilings, erosion of farmers' fields, and use of nuclear energy. Many such problems cannot be settled by talk among the uninformed; experts have to be called in. Nevertheless, experts may not make their technical advice simple enough to understand, and unsophisticated advisees may be timid about asking questions. When dealing with matters like these, citizens must come up with methods that make it possible for decision makers to understand the facts and the consequences of alternative courses. In such a case, it often helps if discussants temporarily make the problem-solving process itself a topic for consideration, so that discussants feel free to talk openly about how well the conference is proceeding and can suggest ways of improving their methods. Toward this end, some groups use observers who sit to one side, taking no part in the discussion and making notes on the nature of the interaction (not on what is good or bad about it), so that these data are in hand when improvement of the problem-solving method comes up for discussion (Zander, 1982). Moreover, objective observation gives members rational insights into what kinds of behavior make for constructive problem solving.

It goes without saying that problem solving requires mostly harmonious relations and mutual respect among members. Interpersonal cooperation is enhanced under several conditions. Participants should feel that every discussant is trying to protect others' rights. Conferees should favor a goal that will bring satisfaction to all. Everyone should agree on most basic matters, such as facts, feelings, values, and sources of the problem. Persons on both sides of the issue should indicate that they will respect whatever decision is reached, and no one should try to blame others for the problem being considered (Deutsch, 1973).

To sum up, agents of change and target persons may agree to act as a single problem-solving unit. The issue discussed is the one brought forward by individuals who see a need for reform. Because persons on both sides have vested interests in a solution to the problem, special care and skill are needed among all participants to create and run an effective problem-solving discussion.

Summary

Initiators of change sometimes want a situation improved in whatever way makes most sense to the persons they are trying to influence. In such cases, initiators provide ideas and information to those individuals or discuss with them sound ways of dealing with the problem. The reformers may act as models, circulate ideas, provide advice, negotiate with target persons, or try to create a problem-solving situation. These are methods in which reformers place no restraint on decision makers' motives, plans, decisions, or acts.

Because these methods provide freedom of choice to target persons, the latter are not likely to offer resistance. They become willing to consider changes that they could make in their beliefs and behavior. Target persons then act because of their faith in their own plans, not to get their own way, earn a reward, or avoid reprisals.

In the next chapter, we shall consider additional methods used in social action. As we move through that chapter, we shall see how the methods become increasingly strict ways of limiting the choices and motives available to target persons.

7

~~~~~~~~~~~~~~~~~~~~~~~~~~~~~~~~~~~~~

Pressuring Methods
Used by Groups

We turn now to the remaining six methods, which agents of change are likely to use when they are sure of the ends they seek and wish to induce target persons to accept and work toward those goals. In the sequence of procedures we examine here, the activists increasingly employ incentives that are desirable (or repulsive) to the target persons in order to get them to change things.

Change Agents Seek the Help of Legitimate Third Parties

Persons who wish to develop acceptance for an idea may realize that they are being ignored by those they hope to influence. The advocates, because they feel that their goal is just, turn to a method that will earn their cause due attention. They employ one of the procedures available in every community to help persons with grievances confront those whom they want to reach. These are *legitimate* methods in the sense that residents of the area have established and approved of them, often by passing laws. The common denominator among these approaches is that a third party (or its stand-in) is asked for judicious help through the use of formal rules, the presence of mediators, or both.

Consider examples in which the third party is represented by, let us say, a set of rules. Take the guidelines prepared by a city planning commission, which citizens in the community are to follow if they wish to bring business before the board. These regulations require that would-be speakers request permission in writing to take the floor, describe the topic of their comments, and promise to talk no longer than five minutes. They are not allowed to speak at a meeting of the board unless they adhere to these rules. Persons who wish to prove that there is a need in the town for a new bus line may circulate a petition among neighbors, asking them to sign it if they approve of the idea. To make these petitions valid, the individuals circulating them have to follow requirements concerning signers' age, place of residence, and length of residence. Likewise, if reformers want to apply pressure on state legislators to pass a law on conservation of water, they must obtain the required number of signatures and present these to the legislators. Comparable procedures are to be used if they wish to place the name of a candidate on the ballot.

At other times, reformers may try to bolster their case by getting target persons to agree that they will accept the help of a mediator. This official is to keep the discussion between presenters and listeners flowing smoothly. He or she may function in accord with rules that discussants develop ahead of time or in line with rules that have the weight of state or local law. Management and labor, for instance, can create their own procedural plans before a bargaining session begins and pledge to abide by the outcome of this process. In so doing, they also must conform to general laws governing mediation of labor-management disputes. An arbitrator provides the same help as a mediator but also has the right to reach a decision, hand it down, and require that it be obeyed by all concerned. This process is called *binding arbitration*. Members of elected boards in public agencies are usually prohibited from submitting to binding arbitration, since they are legally beholden to the people who elected them, not to an arbitrator.

Another kind of third party is a judge in a court of law. Agents of change may request an injunction from the court to stop a practice that they think should be restricted, such as dumping toxic waste in a river, running machinery before it has been inspected for safety, or harassing homeless people who try to get a hearing before the social services commission. An increasingly common technique used by groups that have been created to complain about the negligence of companies is to sue a firm, provided that the plaintiffs can show they have been hurt by the actions of those they bring to court. For example, Meier (1987) reports that over six hundred suits were filed against businesses by citizens before 1987 in matters of environmental control. Although companies that have been sued have protested these suits, saying they were frivolous, were in support of the plaintiffs' pet projects, or were forms of extortion, the number of suits is expected to continue rising, along with the stakes involved. The Clean Water Act, passed recently by Congress, provides for daily fines of $10,000 to $25,000 for each violation. Before this legislation existed, similar complaints were directed to local, state, or federal government in an effort to make officials enforce laws already on the books. More recently, the emphasis has shifted to the polluters themselves, usually manufacturers, because the new law now allows that shift. Sometimes a company forestalls a lawsuit by promising to clean up its act and making a contribution to the organization that brings the complaint. This practice keeps the firm out of court, saves the expense of hiring lawyers, costs less than what a jury might award the plaintiffs, and allows the firm to claim that it has made a tax-deductible contribution to a nonprofit agency. Other companies have reached agreements whereby they put sums of money aside that must be handed over if they break the law again. Such suits and agreements provide a way for citizens to have a useful part in ensuring that laws are well enforced.

The use of a legitimate method by agents of change requires that certain general conditions be present. Clearly, rules must exist before the process begins, whether these are created by officials of the larger community and have a regular place in a legal code or are developed by activists themselves. These regulations, by solemn pledge on both sides, are to be obeyed in implementing both the discussion and the content of the final agreement. The legitimacy of the rules may also derive from contracts, tradition, or custom. The important point is that all participants promise to abide by the regulations. Legitimate methods, to be used well, ordinarily require knowledge and skill. People must understand them and be able to follow where they lead. In many instances, complainants hire a person trained in the law who puts their case forward, for a fee, in court. Such moves require money, patience, and plenty of time, since the wheels of justice grind slowly. Above all, complainants must have a good case; otherwise, it is a waste of resources to appeal to a third party for help.

Why are legitimate procedures used? They are usually employed because other methods have failed, and the innovators are not able to get a reasonable hearing from target persons about changes they wish to propose. The innovators may also have been heard by target persons, who then keep the complainants waiting too long. A request by change agents is considerably more potent if they ask that an accepted rule be obeyed than if they press for a change on the grounds of logic or preference (Frank, 1944). A legitimate method is also useful if agents of change do not trust the target persons and want a disinterested entity involved in the discussion, to keep the talks fair and aboveboard. The reason labor-management bargaining sessions use a mediator or an arbitrator, for example, is that neither side is confident that its counterpart is telling the truth. Many formal organizations are governed by laws that state whether and how changes can be made in the way they operate. Funk (1982) describes a number of these regulations and their effects.

The main reason for using a legitimate approach is that (in principle, at least) the issue is settled once and for all. After an agreement is reached, there should be no more pressuring, on the one hand, and no more opposing or resisting, on the other (unless the verdict is appealed). Participants must obey the decision. There is also a reasonable chance that justice will prevail. The method offers an opportunity for change agents to have an impact that they might otherwise never achieve, provided that they have a good case.

The effects of using such processes are noteworthy. As mentioned, participants come away feeling that the matter is settled. Everyone must abide by the outcome, whether it is palatable or not.

Furthermore, the decision provides criteria for determining what is proper behavior, and these criteria can be used later to assess how closely participants are sticking to the rules. The use of a mediator or a referee may have other good consequences (Deutsch, 1973). A mediator can help participants face up to the issue and understand it, including some aspects of it that are hidden or embarrassing to reveal. He or she can help bargaining move along by providing favorable circumstances, devices, tools, or tricks that allow participants to reach a full understanding of the issue. In so doing, he or she can assist all parties by correcting misperceptions that they develop about one another's statements. A mediator can establish rules for courteous interaction, so that discussants show respect for one another. He or she can help determine which ideas are worthy of consideration as possible solutions and which ones are unlikely to lead anywhere. A mediator can press leaders to promise that they will abide by the decision, whatever it is. He or she makes the final agreement palatable to all, so that no one will regret the outcome, and helps make the decision acceptable to bystanders who have a vested interest in this discussion. Although the issue is settled, there may be a residue of hard feelings among those who lose. Persons recall things said during the process that were derogatory or unfair. The winners, for their part, may feel that they have not gained everything they wanted.

How is a third party used most effectively? The agents of change should have a good case and be able to demonstrate that the matter under discussion is a source of a serious deprivation for them and others or that it offers an opportunity for improving a current state of affairs. When taking a suit to court, moreover, they hire a lawyer to guide them through the legal system, and they furnish that person with effective witnesses, data, money, and encouragement. Finally, agents of change who use a third party need to be persistent and patient. A third party (or strict rules) can slow progress. Target persons may also stall or employ tactics that embarrass agents of change, so that the latter give up the fight.

To sum up, a number of issue-settling procedures are legitimate because they have been approved by citizens in the community as ways to judge the validity of complaints and to get relief from these. Such methods ordinarily require participants to abide by the outcome. They are unlike some other methods often used by agents of change who are trying to influence target persons. They are based on strict regulations, and participants must abide by these rules. They require knowledge of the process before they can be used wisely. They demand that participants have a good case, and they require time, patience, money, and expert help. The value of these procedures is that they usually solve the problem once and for all, unless the decision fosters anger and a desire for retribution among those who did not get their way.

Reformers Nurture Persons in Need

Some groups are created to improve conditions for persons outside the unit. They may describe to officials the situation facing disadvantaged individuals and tell these listeners what ought to be done for the needy ones, or they may develop a demonstration of a helpful service, with a view toward inspiring decision makers to support a similar program in the future. We are interested here in the altruistic acts of change agents and how these can influence target persons. This display of nurturance is, in a way, another example of modeling. We are taking it up here as a separate method, however, because reformers who demonstrate how to care for needy persons may plan to improve things for others with no help from neighbors, or they may wish to show decision makers how to be caring persons. The deprived individuals may become target persons themselves if they are urged to help in plans and actions for the nurturance of their disadvantaged colleagues, or citizens at large may become target persons if they are pressed for money and labor to support the helping program. Finally, a model activity to care for the deprived takes much energy, time, and compassion. Persons who create a model must feel deeply that what they are doing is important; it is not simply a temporary, interest-arousing process.

The kinds of demonstrations that helping persons develop are well known. They provide resources to persons who need them, such as food, clothing, shelter, or money. They care for personal needs of individuals through educating, healing, reforming, or saving their souls. They provide emergency assistance in case of a fire, flood, storm, or accident. To provide such nurturance quickly or frequently, they may form enduring organizations whose members are trained to do what is needed.

The motivation of members in these groups is to benefit disadvantaged persons, without receiving any payment themselves other than the satisfaction of helping deprived ones. This help is provided either by the innovators or by the target persons who agree to furnish care for those in need of it (Bar-Tal, 1976; Macaulay and Berkowitz, 1970). The reformers also help decision makers by showing them how they can better provide a particular kind of nurturance. It is not always easy for reformers to interest officials in offering a new service. If the officials agree to a change, they are admitting, in effect, that they have not been operating as wisely or compassionately as they should, and the implementation of a new plan reveals this. The target persons also may believe that individuals who require help are lazy, greedy, or unwilling to take care of themselves and therefore do not deserve to be nurtured. Caring programs, moreover, cost money and have a way of becoming more expensive once they are under way.

Activities to help others are complicated and require their initiators to have sufficient good will, patience, know-how, and resources to accomplish what they set out to do. Why do agents of change choose to provide nurturing? The most obvious reason is that deprived persons appear unable to improve their situation on their own. They do not have the knowledge, tools, or money to get the kinds of services they need. What is more, the deprived often do not ask for help because they do not want to be obligated to benefactors, are embarassed to admit that they cannot help themselves, or do not think that they can get the kind of aid they need. The helpers, for their part, prefer to be kindly volunteers in these efforts because they prize the satisfaction they derive from helping. Their cause is also more convincing to target persons if they do not accept payment for the services they provide.

What are the consequences of such an approach? If the disadvantaged persons value the help given to them, they will be grateful but at the same time will feel obligated to those who provide it. Because of this, they may refuse further assistance or accept as little as possible, for fear that they will be expected to reciprocate but will be unable to. Sometimes the help of reformers is not welcomed by those to whom it is offered because it creates a burden for the receivers, who must agree to be saved, give up past beliefs, or take care of a "gift horse." Not uncommonly, the effort of do-gooders is more bother than it seems to be worth, yet those who provide assistance feel good about themselves. They are proud of their efforts, even when the outcome is not all they had hoped for.

Several conditions cause such a demonstration to be more effective in the sense that the disadvantaged are actually assisted or the target persons agree to sponsor further assistance. Helping behavior is more likely to succeed if the innovators derive satisfaction from aiding disadvantaged persons. Thus, they examine what deprived persons need and plan what they should do to meet those needs. In a successful nurturing group, members provide help in ways that do not make the assisted persons feels incompetent or dependent on their helpers. If the initiators intend to rescue people who are in an emergency, they practice how to perform this mission speedily and work to improve their operation. The reformers make sure that official persons know about the demonstration, learn what favorable outcomes it provides, and recognize that such services need wider and continuing support from the community.

To summarize, agents of change may influence decision makers by providing or demonstrating services that help individuals who cannot help themselves. Initiators of nurturing expect no reward other than the satisfaction they derive from knowing that deprived persons have been assisted. They intend their appeal or demonstration to persuade target persons to provide continuing support for such a program.

Activists Persuade Target Persons

Ordinarily, persuasion is a more constraining method for exerting influence than we have considered so far. It is a deliberate effort by activists to control the beliefs or behavior of target persons. Persuaders direct their words to persons who can implement an innovation (the makers of decisions), to those who can help influence the former (the public at large), or to both. Any of the methods for providing information (discussed in Chapter Six) may be used in persuading, but the content of persuasive comments is intentionally one-sided. The users of persuasive methods intend to convince listeners that no views or actions other than the ones being advocated are acceptable. Ordinarily, the change that persuaders want will benefit them more than the listeners, even when they claim otherwise. Accordingly, persuaders do not closely consider contrary statements or arguments made by the other side, since doing so could tempt listeners to welcome such ideas and lead them to favor the wrong notions. Persuaders try to restrict the number of decisions available to members of the audience by telling them that if they continue on their present course or choose a way that is different from the plan being advocated, there will be unfavorable consequences. The target persons will move onto a wrong path or will miss opportunities to take a correct one. Persuasion is often a way of warning people about the dire consequences of incorrect behavior or beliefs, or it can be a means for giving people a chance to go straight. It also can arouse desires among target persons to avoid unwanted side effects or to achieve gains from behaving as they are being pressed to do. Target persons are urged to act on the basis of the bad effects that will ensue if the proposed change is not made, or they are induced to seize the chance to make proper moves. In all cases, activists believe that they know best, and they sell their point of view strongly.

Some forms of forceful persuasion are tolerated by everyone. Politicians in the midst of campaigns or in debates over new laws are allowed to present their own points of view and to disparage those of their opponents (as long as they do it honestly). Lawyers understandably plead the cases of their clients in biased terms. A neighborhood association is not likely to consider both points of view, the city's and its own. Persuaders push their self-serving views using posters, manifestoes, proclamations, speeches, rallies, or cartoons. In all of these methods, the issue is described in a narrow way; it is not presented in terms of a full account.

Because persuasion is essentially an effort to convince, persuaders depend on facts that are inherently compelling. For instance, a group was formed by a couple whose daughter had died of a blood disease after being given an antibiotic in Spain for a sore throat. The drug was made in the United States. Once popular, it had long been prohibited for most uses by the Food and Drug Administration because of its side effects. Nevertheless, the manufacturer continued to sell it, without proper warnings, in other countries. Members of the action group asked friends who were planning to travel abroad to buy this drug and bring it home with its package insert intact. After collecting sixty of these foreign-language inserts, the members had them translated into English. They took them to officers of the company (a local firm) and showed them that none of the protocols mentioned the precautions against its use that are required in the United States. The officials of the firm thereupon changed the wording of the package insert for all countries. The company had previously hidden these facts about the dishonest instructions in packages sold abroad. Once the facts were exposed, they could no longer be covered up. In the absence of such data, and without the implicit threat that these could be made public, earlier attempts to persuade the firm to stop dumping this drug improperly in other countries had failed.

Ardent persuaders may have hirelings who accompany them and help them develop vocal and supportive audiences wherever they go. Officials in ancient Rome, as an illustration, had claques that threatened individuals who did not applaud the leader when he appeared. Members of the German National Socialist (Nazi) Party encouraged participation in rallies through similar means.

When people use persuasion to appeal to listeners' emotions—by shading the truth, exaggerating the unfavorableness of conditions, or arousing fears or greed—they are using *propaganda*. Thum and Thum (1972) describe the following devices that propagandists employ to change the beliefs and feelings of listeners:

- generating fears of what could happen if a change is not made
- appealing to listeners' desires to be more fashionable, influential, or higher in status
- distracting the audience by emphasizing one thing in order to hide another (for example, the propagandists sidetrack criticism of themselves by accusing their critics of being disloyal, or by stressing a topic that is not pertinent to the issue at hand)
- engaging in distorted logic while emphasizing the rationality of the statements being made ("Everyone knows that . . .")

- oversimplifying issues by presenting complicated problems in terms of slogans or stereotypes
- using loaded words to describe the opposition (*lazy, greedy, stingy, unpatriotic*)
- deceiving by offering untruths as facts

Propagandists press their views by making sure that only a small part of a controversial question gets a full hearing. Bailey (1983, p. 125), a student of aggressive persuasion, writes that the demands of persuaders "are peremptory; . . . [they] assert truths that they present as inescapable, defying argument, so essentially true that they are beyond the need for corroborating evidence." The users of such self-centered arguments recognize that these are biased but defend their style by saying that they are supporting what is right, or that they have deliberately chosen to make an emotional appeal because an objective method will not sway listeners from their mistaken beliefs.

How do reformers justify an attempt to persuade? They declare that they are disadvantaged because of things that the target persons do. Thus, they try to convince listeners to change in ways that will benefit the speakers. Persuasion is less likely to be used when benefits of a change will go to receivers instead of initiators. Those who try to persuade may also do so because they have a definite point of view that they want to advocate with all their hearts. Moscovici (1976) says that a firm commitment to a particular stand is often a stronger source of attempts to persuade than is the amount of social power that agents of change hold with respect to target persons. When change agents have little social power in a community, Moscovici's notion may be correct, but when activists have adequate power to influence target persons through social action, I suspect that this generalization may not hold.

Reformers try to persuade (without using propaganda) if they are confident that they can argue their case well. They have the necessary skills, resources, and assistance to support their argument effectively. Gamson (1975) has studied the methods used in a number of large, dissident social movements. According to Gamson, protesters employ persuasion more than any other device when they are sure that they can correctly predict what the target persons will do in response to a request for change and when they know that the individuals to whom they are appealing have the same long-range goals as they themselves do. This finding of Gamson's suggests that reformers will be less likely to use persuasion if they think their chances of convincing their listeners are slim.

Those who engage in aggressive persuasion justify their style, both to themselves and to those who have a stake in the change, by asserting that their cause is important and right, and so any method is suitable as long as it works. Examples of rationalizing a pushy approach are provided by Douglas and Wildavsky (1982), who studied small sets of activists as they worked to reduce the amount of pollution in the environment. The members of these cells believed that society is evil because it is dominated by organizations that belong to a conspiracy to corrupt and spoil the countryside. The agents of change could not tolerate this wickedness, and they sought to root it out. They urged citizens to join a local protest cell and to condemn companies that were spoiling the environment. The most effective way to combat the activities of a firm, members of these units believed, was to use hostile propaganda in describing how and why officials in the business were allowing the wastes of their firm to spoil nature. This use of assertive rhetoric was justified, they said, because the enemy industrialists were willfully evil; aggressive persuasion was acceptable when it was a way to make target persons engage in problem solving, and persons under the bombast of strong propaganda eventually would become willing to talk, in order to stop the flow of negative pronouncements about them.

How do target persons respond to persuasion? Their reaction is often argumentative. They may also develop fear, greed, anxiety, anger, revulsion, or passivity, according to the content of the persuaders' remarks, the style of their delivery, and how committed the decision makers are to the programs that reformers want to change. When target persons have intense reactions, they are unlikely to discuss the issue in a rational manner because they become rattled. To keep cool also suggests that they are yielding to pressure. Decision makers will try to oppose the ideas being pressed on them by persuaders if they recognize that the speakers are using distorted and one-sided arguments in support of their proposal. They will resist the notions proposed if the presentation is wholly self-centered and if the advocates will not listen to responses. Persons who are recipients of strong persuasion commonly respond by using exactly the same tactic with the change agents. The results are an escalation in the pace of interaction and a keen effort by those in both parties to win the argument. (We consider the effects of such escalation in Chapters Eight and Nine.)

Persuaders use special rhetorical devices to be effective. Broadly speaking, they try to prevent the development of opposition or resistance among listeners. They attempt to have their ideas dominate communication channels, so that other notions are less likely to get a fair hearing, and they do not respond to anything that listeners offer as a rebuttal. Deutsch (1973) suggests several aspects of a strategy for effective persuading. First, one makes the proposal clear to listeners, so that they will know what is expected of them. Clarity eliminates any opposition that could be ascribed to misunderstanding of or ambiguity in one's request. Next, one states, in sympathetic terms, that members of the audience will probably have problems in accepting the ideas being offered, and that one will help the receivers overcome these difficulties. Third, one demonstrates how the listeners will benefit if they do what one proposes, and one cites as many gains as possible. Fourth, one points out that others in the community will benefit from the change. Fifth, one states flatly that one intends to make the target persons change their ways and will help them implement the improvements being urged. Finally, one shows the listeners how everyone's objectives will be compromised if the proposed modifications are not made soon.

Bailey (1983) believes that the effectiveness of persuasion depends on the wise use of passion. He uses this term to cover emotional behavior (hostile, friendly, allied, or rivalrous), and he says that passion is stronger than rationality in interpersonal relations because people tend to defend their views in passionate ways, and doing so makes them immune to rational arguments. Rational activity also has a weaker impact on receivers because it causes people to doubt, penetrate, and criticize, rather than yield. A rational process, moreover, deals with ideas that are not wholly comprehensible because they are usually loaded with discordant information. Bailey says that one cannot sensibly ask whether an argument advanced by a persuader is valid or invalid, nor can one test it by the rules of logic. One can only ask whether the argument is effective because it has changed listeners' minds. Rationality requires training to be used well, but anyone can use passion skillfully. Thus, it is easier to use passion than rationality. Given these contrasts between rational and emotional interaction, Bailey suggests styles of speaking that make passionate persuasion more effective:

1. Present yourselves as moral persons with good reputations.
2. Demonstrate that your group of change agents has many friendly ties with members of the audience.
3. Show that you speak with authority because of your experience, knowledge, and training, and because of the sound values underlying your proposal.
4. Remind the audience of coming danger if a change is not made. Cite forebodings and warnings of future events that cannot be ignored. Recall the threat inherent in the actions of certain powerful persons, but do not ridicule these.
5. Focus on the feelings and nature of the listeners, not on their deeds. Persons can be praised or condemned more tellingly than their acts can be.
6. Use models, exhibits, or vivid examples that make your point easy to understand.

A speaker who hopes to persuade listeners can be more effective, of course, if members of the audience already agree in good part with what he or she says and are aroused by the assertiveness of the style he or she employs. As an illustration, fundamentalist preachers excite the faithful each Sunday to renew their beliefs and fears about matters that they already accept. Rosenblatt (1985, p. 102) describes how Louis Farrakhan, speaking at Madison Square Garden, had the audience with him from the outset as he delivered a sermon urging them to be haters: "But the crowd were not only predisposed to Farrakhan, they seemed to be ahead of him, rising to his message so eagerly it was hard to tell if the incitement preceded the response. Farrakhan's male guards, who sat lined up on chairs facing forward on the stage, were trained to leap to attention whenever the audience went wild, as if creating a sudden row of exclamation points. The drill suggested that the audience must have been bursting to express its hatred all along. It seemed so. Farrakhan may be a second-rate demagogue, but he has some first-rate hate to play with." This hatred was directed toward Jews who are merchants or landlords in black neighborhoods of New York City. Rosenblatt suggests that anti-Semitism may be a way of fostering an alliance with white gentiles.

Persuaders who use emotion-laden arguments are said to be extremists because they exaggerate and mislead. Even so, their right to speak is usually protected in our society. Bollinger (1987) recalls two arguments made to justify free speech in America and proposes a third. The first is that impediments should not be placed on freedom of speech because the best test of an idea's truthfulness is whether it gets itself accepted in the competition among all the views on the matter at issue. The second is that protection of the democratic process requires legal walls to be built around the right to speak; to be certain that valuable ideas are protected, extreme ones must be protected as well. Bollinger's third argument is that people learn about the views of their neighbors and about how to make democracy function well by being tolerant of extremists. Thus, tolerance is a social skill, an ability to compromise, which citizens cultivate by making social discourse an arena where any and all ideas may be proposed. By doing so, people learn to practice a self-restraint that has great dividends. In accord with Bollinger's view, extremist change agents should be told by target persons that their notions are tolerated for the benefit of the democratic process, not because there is any inherent value in them. The moral of the story is that wise social change groups encourage their listeners (and their own members) to support freedom of speech.

In summary, when activists wish to modify the beliefs or behavior of target persons directly, they may try to be persuasive. Persuaders usually are more interested in earning benefits for them-selves than in helping listeners, yet they try to increase the weight of their argument by assuring members of the audience that they will gain from making the proposed transformation, or they emphasize the unfavorable consequences of allowing things to continue as they are, using distorted and emotion-arousing appeals to back up their claims. When persuasion is wholly couched in affect-laden terms, it is called *propaganda*. Persuasion works well in getting target persons to modify matters under their control, unless target persons discover that the reformers are seeking to benefit from a dishonest appeal at their expense. Passionate propaganda is probably more persuasive than mere facts.

Agents of Change Bargain with Target Persons

Suppose that individuals advocating a change tell listeners that they are willing to eliminate some parts of their request if the listeners will drop their objections to other parts. The approached persons, in turn, offer to adopt some of the suggestions made by the agents of change, if the latter will alter some of the ideas they have brought to the conference. This process, in which persons on each side give some things and gain others, is called *bargaining*. Members of a new neighborhood association, for instance, say they will stop making a plea for new sidewalks if the city will promise to pave their streets. Participants ostensibly work toward a solution that is equally valuable to persons in both parties. Often, however, one side gains more and yields less than the other; it obtains a better bargain. As another instance, members of both parties refuse to change their initial stand, so that the bargaining stalls and becomes an empty exercise.

Why do agents of change try to bargain with target persons? In most cases, they do so because they believe that the others are willing to think about modifying their practices in some way, may give up something during a bargaining discussion, or may make a deal with the innovators. Bargaining often develops after other methods fail. Those on each side feel that they can have some control over their rivals by making attractive offers and counteroffers. Reformers are also likely to try bargaining if they believe that they have enough power to influence the acts of target persons and are not merely weak pleaders. They may have this power because there are many members in their group of change agents, they represent an official body that is known to be powerful, they have sponsored frequent and influential media campaigns urging the decision makers to introduce changes, or they have been coercive toward target persons to make them willing to bargain.

Change seekers may also want to bargain because they recognize that they have something the target persons covet, such as votes, funds, expertise, community support, or labor; therefore, bargaining is sensible for all concerned. The proposers may perceive that their ideas can be improved through the discussion involved in bargaining because the process gets target persons thinking about changes they may be willing to make, or agents of change may bargain because they believe that they can get their own way, without giving up much.

The consequences of bargaining depend in good part on the content of the bargain. Participants may hit on a mutually agreeable plan that satisfies those on both sides, or those in one party may be pleased because they have won what they wanted, while members of the other party are dissatisfied because they have lost on a point they value. If this loss is great enough, the losers may become angry and force the winners to defend themselves against their wrath. It is not uncommon for bargaining to deteriorate into conflict, in which persons on each side try to coerce the other side, rather than make concessions. After a bargaining session, the winners feel satisfied with themselves and rest contented, but the losers examine, evaluate, and improve on their argument, so that they can bargain better in the future. In the long run, losers are indirectly helped because they must overhaul their case and their strategy. Winners, however, may not see the need to engage in such self-appraisal and passively rest on their laurels (Zander, 1982).

When is bargaining most effective? Consider the circumstances needed if the outcome is to be equally satisfying to change agents and target persons alike. Both sides must be fairly equal in their ability to influence the other; otherwise, those with the greater influence will listen little, talk a lot, and push the matter in ways that suit themselves. Effective two-way bargaining also requires members on one side to make an offer to compromise—to give in on some matter, in the hope that those on the other side will do likewise. The initial offer is something that the providers know or hope the others want. A responding offer will likewise be on a matter that is probably desirable to the others. Ideally, then, the sacrifice and the satisfaction should be equal on both sides. There is a danger in making the first offer, however, because persons on the other side may see this as a sign of weakness and believe that those making the first offer are giving in. The ones who receive the original compromise may accept it but make no counterproposal, since they are now ahead of the game.

It helps for people on both sides to have a clear understanding of what people on the other side want and to be able to satisfy this desire amply during the bargaining session. Neither side should offer anything that is considerably more valuable than what the other side can give, since doing so makes it appear that the offer is a bribe.

Pruitt (1972) describes several ways for bargainers to be sure that concessions are equal. One is to make a small unilateral concession, with the statement that no further offer will be made until the target individuals advance something in return. Another is to propose an exchange of concessions; persons on one side say that they are ready to concede on a given point, if those on the other side will also make a concession. It helps to make this proposition through an intermediary, whose offer can be disowned if the other side is not interested, or to call in a mediator who talks with those on both sides and thus opens communication on issues that have been avoided.

If bargainers approach a session as though it were a contest that they intend to win, their tactics are different. To come out ahead, they must gain more and give up less than the others do. Accordingly, the would-be winners make sure that they know the preferences of the persons with whom they are bargaining, know what the others are offering, top that offer, and emphasize that this will be the last chance for a settlement. Initial stakes of a truly competitive bargainer are set high, so that the respondents will feel compelled to bargain, for fear of losing if they do not. Demands stated in strong terms at the outset lead those on the other side to recognize that they cannot hope to get all they want from such hard bargainers, and so they keep their own aspirations low.

Strong bargainers tend to become assertive, in order to bolster their stand. Assertive tactics are described by Bailey (1983):

1.   Make a frontal attack on the premises and values of those on the other side. Urge them to abandon their views, on the grounds

that they are not convincing. Display raw emotion, to create fear or shame in the others, or to play upon their pity and compassion. Ask the listeners if they can bear the consequences that will follow from an unfair bargain.

2.   Argue on grounds that are prized by all concerned, such as democratic values, the need for equality, or the golden rule.

3.   Appeal to the importance of using reason and logic, and to the value of an open mind that considers both sides of an issue.

4.   Remind listeners that they have a duty toward others who will be affected by the agreement being formed.

5.   Appeal to the other side's cunning self-interest. Be smart; look after yourself first. This is especially useful when past obligations can be invoked, and when others can be pressed to undertake new obligations or can be invited to enter into a special deal.

6.   Appeal to the mutual interdependence among the persons involved, and stress that each side needs the other.

If people on one side hope to benefit more as a result of bargaining, they cannot let themselves give in to threats, pressure, or other forms of coercion, and they cannot let differences escalate in such a way that those on both sides will not listen to the give-and-take while a conflict grows. The winner in a bargaining session wants to prevail without generating resistance that may interfere with easy access to the gains.

In summary, while bargaining over a proposed change, members of two units holding incompatible views try through discussion to reach a mutually agreeable decision by giving up some things in order to gain others. Agents of change usually are not able to get target persons into a bargaining relationship unless they have power fairly equal to that of the persons they hope to influence. To reach an agreement that pleases both sides, participants must be ready to compromise. To win, those on one side make the other side see that it cannot get what it wants while ignoring their desires. In the long run, it is better if each side wins equally.

Agents of Change Reward Target Persons

People working for reform may try to make their proposals

acceptable to target persons by offering to reward them if they do as they are asked. Such rewards include having their pictures in the newspaper; receiving public praise, medals, plaques, statues, or banquets in their honor; having streets named after them; or receiving a day of celebration for the new development. Target persons will reject such benefits, however, if they see them as bribes, payoffs, inadequate prizes, or illegitimate offers. Sometimes rewards are given to target persons after they have behaved in an admirable fashion, with an eye toward teaching them to continue their good efforts.

Apparently, a reward promised in order to induce a particular action is not always taken to be a bribe, if the offer is made for a good cause. For example, when staff members of a government agency and a private foundation told townsfolk that they would be given a grant if they planned ways to improve social services in their community and followed procedures prescribed by the granters, the offer was accepted without guilt (Marris and Rein, 1967). It is not unusual for an official body in a community to offer rewards to groups of citizens. For instance, police patrols are often increased if neighbors requesting such protection help by monitoring their own streets.

The reasons behind the use of rewards are well known. Persons who want to influence specific others sense that those others are uninterested, and so they offer a reward to arouse their enthusiasm (Gamson, 1975). The offer may be made as part of a proposal for change, in which case it will be provided only if the decision makers actually do introduce the innovation; or the reward may be used as a reinforcement for approved past behavior, and the recipients are led to understand that they will be rewarded again if they repeat their good actions. One advantage of publicly rewarding target persons is that bystanders see certain actions rewarded and assume that anyone else (themselves, for instance) who behaves in the same fashion will also be rewarded.

What are the consequences of receiving a reward? We know from research that a person who gets a reward is grateful toward those who provide it, but not if the reward is seen to be payment for services agreed on and rendered or deserved for some other reason. In such a case, the gain is not a reward; it is a payment ("I had it coming"). A reward will not be effective if it is not valued by the receiver. Moreover, if the same reward is offered repeatedly, its value falls, and it is no longer satisfying. Those who are rewarded many times eventually raise their price and want more for the same amount of service.

Persons who move into action solely because of an offered reward are ordinarily motivated only to earn the reward, not to carry out an action that is valuable or sensible in its own right. The reward, not the change, is the incentive. When this is the case, people do only what is necessary to get the reward. They behave in the ways requested by the reward giver. They make these actions visible, so that the agent of change knows that their behavior deserves to be rewarded. The agent of change keeps an eye on the target persons, to be sure that they do the things that warrant the prize. Because target persons' overt acts can be observed, rewards are useful ways to encourage behavioral innovations. If a reformer seeks transformation of the beliefs or attitudes of the target persons, however, it is difficult to determine whether they have in fact made such changes. People can say that they have revised their thinking in order to win a reward when actually they have not. The point is that rewards are more effective in changing target persons' overt actions than in changing their covert beliefs.

Agents of change can be expected to use rewards in several ways to enhance their influence over target persons. They make sure that the object or event they offer as a reward is valued by target persons, since a reward is not a reward unless the receivers believe it is. They make sure that the persons being rewarded know why they have won approval, so that the awarded behavior will be repeated. They make sure that bestowal of the reward is made public, so that it will provide a lesson to bystanders. They make sure that the reward is not offered in such a way that it is taken as a bribe, since such offers are demeaning, unethical, and often ineffective. They take care to have plenty of rewards available, so that their supply does not run out. They do not offer the same reward repeatedly. They recognize that by using rewards they can influence overt behavior better than hidden feelings, ideas, or beliefs.

In summary, change agents try to influence the behavior of target persons by providing events or objects that the latter value, on the assumption that rewards will stimulate target persons' interest in creating a change. The persons who benefit feel grateful toward the providers of the reward, unless the receivers do not place much value on the reward or feel that they have earned it as payment for their efforts.

Agents of Change Coerce Target Persons

Activists become coercive when they intend to constrain freedom of choice among persons they wish to influence. In using coercion, change agents threaten to punish target persons if they do not do what they are asked to do or do not stop behaving in undesirable ways. The coercers inflict a penalty or punishment on the ones being coerced, until the latter change their behavior. There is no limit to the ways in which reformers can be coercive. For example, citizens interfere with a session of the city council by interrupting unwanted speakers. Workers employed downtown block access to the city's parking structure after the city raises rates on streetside parking meters. Homeless squatters build shacks on university property, to make their deprivation visible. Parents threaten the school board with recall if the board does not fire the football coach. Students raid a building where animals are housed for use in medical research. A neighborhood organization stops making contributions to the town's United Fund because the local athletic club was not given a grant that it requested. A nuclear power plant is set on fire by activists opposed to such sources of electricity. Bus drivers run late because of alleged discrimination by the traffic commission in the hiring of homosexual women.

We shall consider three types of coercive action here. First, activists interfere with efforts of target persons, so that the latter cannot do their regular work. Second, they physically limit the freedom of target persons or hostages. Third, they threaten harm or inflict it on target persons, other individuals, or things of value. But first, a few comments on the nature of coercion.

Any coercive act places constraints on the behavior of those toward whom it is directed. The threatened penalty is repulsive, and in order to avoid this punishment, the persons being coerced do what is asked of them. The driver obeys a traffic cop. A university's board of regents stops talking when students crowd its meeting room to shout insults. Constraints are stronger as the proffered punishments are more undesirable. If the target persons see the penalty as not repellent (or not likely to occur), they will pay little attention to coercive demands. Like rewarding, coercion changes overt behavior more effectively than it changes covert beliefs, since visible actions can be monitored by the coercer, but ideas and attitudes cannot. Therefore, those who use coercion typically spy on persons they put under pressure, to make sure that punishment is promptly delivered when it is deserved. As we shall see in Chapters Nine and Ten, the threat of coercion, its actual use, and the subsequent surveillance put on persons who have been pressed to change generate poor interpersonal relations between the agents of change and the target persons. These in themselves become a separate cause for concern.

We get an insight into how often activists use coercion from the study done by Gamson (1975). Gamson examined the strategies employed by a number of protest movements. Most of these bodies had hundreds or thousands of members, and so they are not replicas of the units we have been considering. Nevertheless, much of what they did took place in community settings, and so Gamson's findings are not wholly irrelevant to our purpose. Gamson looked for two kinds of success in the work of these groups. One kind is the community's *acceptance of the change agents' group* (that is, the unit was seen as a set of spokespersons who represented legitimate interests). The activists were therefore respected and given attention. The other kind of success is what Gamson calls *attainment of new advantages* (that is, the group achieved its objectives to some degree or won other valued outcomes). Thus, the unit won respect as a group, accomplished something worthwhile, or both. The organizations in Gamson's sample had similar rates of success in winning acceptance (47 percent) and in achieving new advantages (49 percent). Gamson was interested in two ways of protesting. One way limited the freedom of target persons and included instances of strikes, boycotts, vituperation, discrediting of antagonists, or restricting the moves of those being pressed. The other way was more violent and included harmful attacks or threats to persons or property. The freedom-limiting behavior was used by 42 percent of the groups, and violence was used by 25 percent. The larger the organization, the more its members were likely to engage in violence; the smaller the group, the more likely it was to be the recipient of violence. We shall review more of Gamson's results later.

Blocking the Progress of Target Persons Toward Their Goals. In some methods of coercion, activists set out to make it difficult for target persons to conduct their regular business or achieve their normal objectives. The blockers say (or shout) that they will continue their obstruction until they get their way. I can think of five different blocking maneuvers.

In one form, called a *sit-in,* participants seek services in a place where they have been forbidden to enter. They remain until they are forced to leave. For example, black students walk into restaurants, libraries, or bus stations that they are not supposed to use. Workers slow their actions to a snail's pace, so that production is reduced to a trickle. Dissidents stand or sit on a highway, so that trucks and cars cannot move into a nuclear power plant or remove weapons from a munitions depot.

In a second way of creating a barrier, agents of change interfere with the business of target persons. They strike, walk out, sabotage machinery, or take over a meeting and allow only their own members to talk.

In a third type of blocking maneuver, reformers interfere with the work of persons in an organization whose practices they wish to change. They attend the meetings of a decision-making body, such as a city council or a board of education, and prevent business as usual by making loud comments (from the audience), seizing the microphone, occupying all the seats in the hall, refusing to be quiet, making it impossible for speakers (on the wrong side of the issue) to be heard, or bringing along a brass band.

Alinsky (1971) urges members of inner-city neighborhood community councils to make their grievances known to governmental officials in no uncertain terms. He says, "Our concern is with the tactic of taking; how the have-nots can take power from the haves" (Alinsky, 1971, p. 126). He provides a set of rules (actually, they are maxims) for what he calls *power tactics.* He means, in our terms, successful coercion of decision makers through interference with their meetings. Alinsky's list of rules includes the following: "Power is not only what you have but what the enemy thinks you have" (p. 127); "Make the enemy live up to their own book of rules" (p. 128); "Ridicule is man's most potent weapon" (p. 128); "Keep the pressure on" (p. 128); "The threat is usually more terrifying than the thing itself" (p. 128); and "The price of a successful attack is a constructive alternative" (p. 130).

The leaders of an organization of tenants in a housing project created a rent strike, refusing to pay what they owed until their apartments were rehabilitated. Brill (1971), in a book-length description of this strike, says that central members prevented the eviction of tenants for nonpayment of their rent by threatening to create a riot if nonpayers were forced to move out of the housing project. This threat worked so well that they used it repeatedly thereafter.

A fourth form of blockage is a *boycott,* in which dissatisfied persons agree to buy nothing from or provide no services to individuals who are responsible for an unpleasant state of affairs. Familiar examples are refusals to shop in certain stores, ride local buses, or work for particular bosses.

A fifth form of blocking maneuver is a hostile demonstration, in which disadvantaged persons reveal the depth of their displeasure by breaking windows, vandalizing furniture, or destroying equipment used by target persons.

The common feature of these five blocking moves is that reformers willfully create barriers that interfere with the productivity of those they want to influence. Why do activists use such approaches? They use them mostly because these are ways of getting attention from individuals who are ignoring the demands made by the change agents. Blocking actions force the affected people to pay attention to ideas that they prefer to ignore (Carter, 1973). These methods also allow activists to indicate clearly that they are angry and dissatisfied and want a change. Change agents use barrier-producing procedures if they know how target persons work and can therefore see how to block their work. They also hope to create confusion, which arises out of the obstructed persons' uncertainty about how to respond to the interventions. The target persons want to prevent interference with their work, but they also feel guilty if they do not provide a fair hearing to the reformers, and they become anxious if they provoke criticisms among bystanders who feel that the complainers have had too little (or too much) sympathetic attention.

The members of a group devoted to social action will be more ready to interrupt the work of target persons, according to Levitt (1973), if they feel and are willing to express moral outrage at the behavior of these decision makers. The change seekers are sure that their view is superior in its virtue to all others, and yet it is being ignored. They also are more inclined to intervene in the work of target persons if they want a solution to their troubles very soon but the officials are dragging their feet or are only pretending to give the matter consideration. The change seekers therefore feel that they can open the issue only by confronting the officials. They do not mind having their tactics or themselves disparaged, disapproved, criticized, or resented, and their courage to act is based on their faith in the cause they represent. Although their actions are a form of blackmail, they are prepared to use this method to get their way.

Robertson (1988) believes that protests are frequent in and around San Francisco because there are many universities in the area that create a ferment of ideas. There is a tradition of strong local unions, with an emphasis on group discipline and a "them against us" attitude. There is a variety of races, politics, ethnic bodies, and sexual preferences, which make conflict a regular part of life. Moreover, the climate allows year-round outdoor gatherings and demonstrations. Robertson remarks that many San Franciscans ally themselves to causes because they get a sense of identity from doing so and they enjoy rebelling against authority in outrageous ways. It is fun and provides excitement.

What effects do methods like these have on persons at the receiving end? Of course, they are seldom welcomed. To limit the length of the following discussion, I shall concentrate on procedures used in interrupting a meeting, since the psychology of such an action is typical of what happens in other ways and places. Furthermore, any blockage of work eventually must be settled at a conference table, where changers and target persons meet face to face. As we have remarked, blocking behavior is hard for recipients to handle. The aggressive recklessness that characterizes such behavior generates anger or defensiveness among target persons, as well as a temptation to respond in kind. The inclination to imitate the style of the interrupters is exacerbated if the ideas that the reformers propose are not useful. Indeed, it often happens that activists have no innovations at all to offer; they simply want to stop what is going on, to counter an operation that is responsible for their dissatisfaction. They block a meeting and demand that the program they dislike be cancelled, but they have no suggestions for a better way of doing things when they are asked what improvements they recommend. For example, college students want "irrelevant" teaching stopped, but they cannot say what ought to be taught or how, or interrupters make proposals, based on misinformation, about the organization they are attacking, and the target persons are embarrassed by trying to respond soberly to these far-out ideas.

A group of target persons whose members are prevented from working is faced with several alternatives: giving in to the interrupters and acceding to their demands, trying to reason with them, sitting and being reviled, or clearing the room. Any effort to suppress noisy confronters can backfire if bystanders are drawn into helping the suppressed persons and if these newcomers sharpen the aggressiveness of the activists. Then each side becomes increasingly hostile in response to the actions of the other. Under laws requiring that public organizations hold open meetings, it is not permissible to meet secretly and thereby dodge such interference. A likely resolution of this intervention is for the target persons to propose a meeting with the protesters, in order to engage in constructive problem solving. The target persons may be uneasy about proposing to do this, since past actions of the disrupters do not suggest that they will behave in ways necessary for a sensible session. Nevertheless, I believe that assertive interventionists can become calmly objective once they have an opportunity to present their case to target persons and can evaluate it against other proposals (see Lancourt, 1979).

How can barriers be used effectively? Consider two broadly different types of action: those in which change agents are disobedient (but their behavior is civil), and those in which the success of their intervention depends on a discourteous style. In civil disobedience, activists visibly violate customs or laws governing behavior, continue to do so when asked to desist, and respond to aggression against them with no hostility, since angry behavior could make them liable to assault and battery or generate public reaction against them. For example, a number of citizens occupied a mayor's office, refused to leave when asked, and went limp when dragged from the building. At the first opportunity, they reentered the office and began their vigil once more, singing, chanting, and smiling to those whose work was interrupted. Such group action requires members who have strong faith in their convictions, so that they can withstand criticism and attempts to repress them. They are civilly passive in order to demonstrate their moral strength and the faith they have in the rightness of their cause, not because they are weak and hesitant. Civil disobedience is more effective, as we noted earlier, if it generates feelings of guilt in target groups who ignore requests for relief. Reformers induce guilt by emphasizing the unfairness of the situation they wish to change. Their perseverance in the face of demands that they stop protesting increases guilt among target persons, and the reformers generate even more shame among target persons if they are forced to cease and desist. A demonstration of civil disobedience requires participants to engage in shared planning and to agree to stick to their plan. Passive resistance, as we saw earlier, may cause low morale among the resisters because their progress is bound to be slow. Therefore, managers of such a procedure repeatedly reassure members that their plan is a wise one, that their unit's success will be all they have hoped for, and that they are gradually winning their way, even though this may not yet appear to be the case. How to maintain morale among the courteously disobedient should be given more study.

Levitt (1973, p. 77) believes that the success of face-to-face confrontation depends on the use of "pushiness, jarring rhetoric, and sometimes outright violence." The actions are carefully staged, to get wide publicity at the expense of adversaries. This style of influence goes beyond mere persuasion because those who use it anticipate open disapproval of their methods and intend to ride roughshod over such criticism. The appearance of resistance among target persons is taken by the activists as evidence of the effect they desire to have. Levitt (1973) states that interrupters depend on exaggeration in word or deed. They overstate their case, sharpen the issue, and force listeners to respond. The confronters hammer away at only one or two issues and refuse to be drawn into discussing other topics. They express righteous anger and say repeatedly that the target persons are at fault. If and when members of the audience change their minds, they do so in order to stop this harassment.

Restricting Target Persons' Freedom of Movement. In this approach, change agents seize one or more persons and keep them isolated or under guard. They often take persons other than decision makers and declare that they will not set these victims free, or will harm them, if stated demands are not met by officials within a given period of time. The incentive presented to decision makers in order to make them act on these threats is to stop the suffering of the captured persons. In a related approach, activists may conduct a coup d'état, in which a band of militant persons captures key leaders in the governmental bureaucracy and forces them to do as they are told or replaces them with individuals who will act as ordered. Because this instructed subset occupies a central place in the organization, the remaining members follow the instructions issued by their usual superiors, and the administrative machinery continues to run as it always has (Luttwak, 1968).

Other examples of the use of physical restraint to force a change are noteworthy. The regents of a university are locked in their meeting room by students who are demanding that the school recruit a larger proportion of black, Asian, and Chicano students. Individuals whose behavior in the community does not suit self-appointed reformers are seized as a way of making them obey rules laid down by the vigilantes. Managers of a company are barred from their offices until they develop new methods for protecting workers from accidents. A well-known individual is taken as a hostage, so that the complaints of the kidnapers will be given wide notice. Trains, planes, or ships are hijacked, and passengers are kept under armed surveillance until the grievances of their kidnapers are resolved (or the aggressors themselves are apprehended).

Why do change agents adopt such methods? A major reason is that a small band can accomplish much in this way. It gets immediate attention from the news media, which make a wide audience available at no cost and describe the unsatisfactory state of affairs about which the hijackers are complaining. The hijackers thereby get a hearing from persons they otherwise could not reach, and sometimes they win sympathy from observers who have never heard of them or their cause. The act itself is a form of propaganda by deed, since it implies that the perpetrators have a good reason for taking such measures; they are asking for help in eliminating an entrenched deprivation.

Because hostage taking is illegal in most places, officials concerned with protecting public safety soon become involved. They must choose among stalling and saying nothing to the kidnapers, in the hope that the latter will decide that their attempt has failed; talking with the captors in ways that keep them calm; bargaining, in order to see what freedom for the hostages would cost; and attacking the place where the hostages are kept, in order to rescue them and arrest the criminals.

What conditions cause such hostile behavior to be successful? Gamson (1975) reports that the social movements he studied were more likely to attain at least some of their objectives through blocking, vituperation, or violence if they had strongly centralized (formal) supervision of their organizations, aimed to displace the leaders among target persons, and were not disposed to altruism. The writings of Hyams (1975), Laqueur (1979), and Luttwak (1968) suggest what takers of hostages usually have going for them. The actions are mounted by a small, well-drilled, closely directed group whose members have rehearsed their operation well. The small size of the unit makes it inconspicuous, hard to find, and not easy to identify. The squad works quickly and carries out actions that the actors know will stimulate outrage and repugnance among hostages and observers. Each member of the unit knows exactly what he or she is to do. Leadership is strong because the uncertain situation may make it necessary to revise the initially planned procedure after the operation begins. The squad's members are obedient and willing to do what they are told, no matter how repulsive these actions may be. They feel deeply about the importance of the group's objectives and are therefore willing to be fanatics.

Because publicity is necessary for the success of such an activity, participants are schooled in how to talk to reporters and how to state their demands clearly. The kidnapers are also trained in bargaining because a hostage-taking event involves oral give-and-take (at a distance) with police or other officials. Success often depends on the ability to drive a hard bargain, and so the kidnapers must be articulate, unflappable, aware of what they can and cannot concede, and apparently fearless. They learn the tricks of haggling, such as offering concessions at one time and cancelling them later, showing an iron fist at one moment and a velvet glove at another, changing their minds whenever an agreement is near, setting a deadline for action by target persons, and stalling for time when stalling is useful. Above all, they attempt to encourage sympathy among bystanders by making it appear they have been and are being treated unfairly. One problem for persons who use these methods is that there is no clear point at which to stop or give up. They are breaking the law, and so part or all of their energies are engaged in avoiding penalties.

A coup d'état (a type of activity not often used in democratic society) demands a precise set of circumstances if it is to be used effectively, according to Luttwak (1968). First, "The social and economic conditions of the target [organization] must be such as to confine political participation to a small fraction of the population" (p. 32). Second, "The influence of foreign powers in its life must be relatively limited" (p. 32). Third, "The target state must have a political center. If there are several centers these must be identifiable and must be politically, rather than ethnically, structured. If the state is controlled by a nonpolitically organized unit, the coup can only be made with its consent or neutrality" (p. 45). The strategy of a coup is controlled by two considerations: the need for speed, and the need to neutralize any opposing forces. Care is taken to avoid bloodshed (which can arouse resistance) during the coup. If there is a delay, the intentions of the rebels will become visible, and there may be enough time for opposition to be organized. If things move swiftly, however, enemies and friends alike will hold their fire, to see what leaders of the coup intend to do. (They learn this too late, after the new regime is already in command.)

Harming or Threatening to Harm. In the most extreme form of constraint, initiators inflict pain or damage on persons and objects, or they warn that they will do such things if their wishes are not met. Bombs are exploded in public places, citizens who have no relevance to the activists' grievance are injured, community leaders are harmed, informants are grilled or tortured, undesirable people are lynched, and prominent figures are assassinated or replaced by members of the opposition as part of a coup d'état. Threats are delivered through anonymous telephone calls, unsigned letters, burning crosses, or hostile graffiti. For example, a leader of organized crime and politics in China warns dissidents by depositing a black coffin in the living room of a misbehaver, or members of the Mafia deliver a dead fish to convey the same kind of message.

Brill (1971) tells how leaders of a rent strike at a city-owned housing project tried to frighten city officials into meeting the strike group's demands. They used planned behavior to show that they were powerful and angry. They all stared stonily at the mayor while refusing to answer questions (silent stubbornness was perceived to be a way of displaying strength), exaggerated the number of persons taking part in the strike, used military terms when addressing one another in a public meeting, boasted publicly about the effectiveness of their hostile acts, and showed up at bargaining sessions wearing African tribal costumes.

Actions like these are often said to be forms of terrorism because they terrify those who are harmed, are threatened with harm, or observe such events. The term *terrorism*, however, has different meanings among students of such behavior. Here are a few typical definitions; all describe terrorism as a *political* act. Terrorism is the "use of terror by political militants as a means of overthrowing a government in power, or of forcing that government to change its policies" (Hyams, 1975, p. 46). It is "the use of covert violence by a group for political ends and [it] is usually directed against a government, less often against another group, class, or party" (Laqueur, 1979, p. 79). It is "the use or threatened use of violence in behalf of a political or ideological cause" (Newhouse, 1985, p. 46). "Terrorism is the deliberate and systematic murder, maiming and menacing of the innocent to inspire fear for political ends" (Netanyahu, 1978, p. 48). Hitchens (1986) remarks that it is difficult to find a definition of terrorism that is not tautological or vacuous (the use of violence for political ends), a cliché (an attack on innocent men, women, and children), or a synonym for the actions of swarthy opponents of United States foreign policy. He reviews five recent books on terrorism and concludes that the term is essentially a cliché in search of a meaning. It is a handy label that obliterates the need for making distinctions among various kinds of violent acts employed to encourage social change. (A synonym in the urban drug culture of today is simply "criminal gang behavior.") This vague and emotionally loaded notion of terrorism has generated numerous misconceptions. Laqueur (1979, p. 219) lists several such beliefs: "Terrorism is a new and unprecedented phenomenon." (In fact, it has a long history in many parts of the world.) "Terrorism is used only by persons at the left end of the political spectrum." (In fact, dictatorships of the right always depend on it to ensure their power, and so do criminal leaders.) "Terrorism is employed by persons who have a legitimate grievance; removing the cause for the complaint will therefore eliminate the terrorism." (In fact, the complaints of terrorists are often hard to understand, impossible to remedy, or exceedingly self-centered.) "Terrorism is always effective." (In fact, it is useful only in limited circumstances, when a mass movement makes it part of a grand strategy or when it follows a political assassination.) "Terrorists are really human idealists and more intelligent than ordinary criminals who perform terrorist acts." (In fact, some of the worst horrors in history have been carried out by persons with strong ideals, and most of the successful terrorists of our time have the overt and full support of a specific religious group.) "Terrorism is used as a weapon only by the poor and weak." (In fact, many ardent terrorists are wealthy and powerful leaders.)

All in all, the term *terrorism* is too obscure and sweeping for our purposes. Its frequent use in daily discourse indicates that some agents of change choose to inflict deliberate harm on those they intend to influence. Fortunately, we seldom see such violent acts in American community groups engaged in social action except among (or between) criminal gangs, which use many of the methods that political terrorists use.

Why do activists plan to do harm to persons or objects? This question has many answers because reasons differ in different settings. One explanation points to the personal characteristics of those who use violent behavior or threats. Attempts to learn whether violence-prone people are similar in their personalities and different from the nonviolent have yielded few reliable or useful findings. It is evident, however, that harmdoers are most often young middle-class males (Laqueur, 1979). They frequently begin their careers by pressing for social change in legitimate ways, but because they are not successful with that approach, they turn to more extreme methods, assuming that doing damage to people or property will work. They know that hostile behavior will win the attention of the persons they hope to influence. Hyams (1975) asserts that agents of change use violence in order to weaken the status of local officials. Citizens observe that their leaders have not protected them from danger, and so they doubt the ability of the office holders and no longer want them in office.

Users of violence give other reasons for choosing an aggressive style. They think it will overcome the inertia of target persons and force them to attend to issues they have been avoiding. The aggressors also believe that this style will earn them the support of observers if their hostile actions are met with force. They assume that the products of modern technology make it easier to do harm without being caught. Examples of such products are plastic explosives, bombs that can be triggered at a distance, devices to interrupt or tap into enemy computers, poison darts, mind-altering drugs, and instruments that allow eavesdropping on private conversations over radio waves or telephone lines. In several parts of the world, and in some ethnic neighborhoods of the United States, a man who is wronged is disapproved of by his peers until he has had his revenge on the ones who offended him.

Doers of harm are skilled in rationalizing their behavior to themselves and to critics. Their usual argument is that the ends they seek are so valuable (fair, beneficial, overdue, correct) that they may properly use any method that will work (Pfaff, 1986). Any harm this procedure causes to target persons is a fair price, they think, for getting rid of a deplorable situation. The ends justify the means. As a variation on this theme, hostile change agents believe that the persons they are treating violently are so evil, wrong, and despicable that they have no rights. Such views have been expressed over the years by writers who support the infliction of pain as a method of introducing change.

Hyams (1975) reviews arguments expressed by philosophers of violence around the turn of the century, including Max Stirner. Writing in 1906, Stirner based his ideas on the necessity for ultraindividualistic behavior. Each person, he said, is alone against all others. A state or a government is not needed to provide for or protect a citizen. If an individual cannot get others to provide what he demands of them, he should take it by force. Faults in society are not due to the strength of the masters but to the weakness of the underlings. Each person must make his own way, depending on nobody else. (Where have we heard such ideas more recently?)

Nechayev (also cited by Hyams) advised individuals to transform themselves into ruthless egos dedicated to creating a revolution by creating fear in any who resist. First, revolutionaries are to assassinate all intelligent and important persons. They also must get rid of the would-be reformers because such persons may be successful in introducing desirable modifications and may thereby weaken people's interest in rebelling. Stupid and unimportant citizens should be left alone because their behavior warrants revolution and should visibly illustrate the need for reform. A more recent writer who offers comparable rationalizations is Fanon (1966), who declares that violence is "a cleansing force" that "frees the black from an inferiority complex, restores his self-respect, and invests his character with positive and creative qualities" (p. 73).

What effects do harmful actions have? They often intimidate target persons or cause them confusion about how to deal with such acts. Weak and hesitant responses occur if the persons under attack are not prepared to handle hostility or if they are not able to resist the change agents. They may unwillingly do what is asked, in order to keep the peace or avoid harm. They will not let themselves be so influenced, however, if they can deviate from the wishes of change agents without this deviance being detected. If the target persons are strong enough to ignore the activists' threats, they will meet aggression with their own aggression, which often encourages further and hotter hostility from the agents of change, and a cycle of escalation begins. The issue at hand is ignored because of anger and the desire on both sides to meet fire with fire.

Gamson (1975) found that participants in 25 percent of the protesting social movements he examined used violence against people. Movements that used violent behavior won about as much acceptance and respect as those that did not employ it, but violent actions allowed activists to accomplish more. Among groups that threatened to harm people, 75 percent gained their objectives and 25 percent did not. Among those that used civil methods, 53 percent reached their objectives and 47 percent did not. In Gamson's groups, violence paid off; it helped groups get the changes they sought.

We see, then, that violence can be successful as a stimulator of change. What may account for this success? Perhaps harmdoers prevent escalation of anger by indicating after an aggressive act that they are willing to negotiate or bargain with the target persons. Coercive activists often get their way simply because they have the power to use hostility in a telling fashion. They employ force to win and have enough control over future events to maintain the victory thereafter. The social changes introduced by criminal gangs or dictators are examples.

The most effective groups that use violent behavior are able to suppress quarrels among their own members. They avoid tiffs caused by anxiety over the commitment of their members to group values and objectives. Such conflict is kept under control because the members need one another for protection from the external threats that their groups face and that enhance group cohesion. Even so, several writers believe that most members of a violent team drop out sooner or later, unless they can keep up their enthusiasm for their cause. Leaders of violent gangs try to avoid having their units fall apart by assuring colleagues that they all have the same objectives and by preventing quarrels among participants over who is most faithful to group goals. One wonders how the dynamics of a ruthless, coercive group differ from those of an altruistic body. Do the two have similar problems in keeping the unit effective?

In summary, agents of change may threaten harm or do actual harm to individuals they want to influence, to observers, or to objects of value. They do these things in order to get the attention of target persons and the support, perhaps, of bystanders, and to create an incentive—a negative one—for change. These efforts may generate timid acceptance of their demands or aggressive counteractions. Even though most officials do not like to bargain with users of violence, they usually do. Activists who employ violent methods probably get their way as often as they fail.

Summary

When activists use constraining methods to try to influence target persons, target persons pay less attention to the quality of the ideas proposed by the initiators than to the incentives (to win a reward, or to avoid a penalty or punishment) that accompany the proposals. The receivers agree to introduce changes, in order to attain effects that they value or to avoid ones they dislike.

When they employ pressuring methods, activists realize that target persons may acquiesce in order to win a favorable response or avoid an unfavorable reaction. Thus, they try to determine whether target persons have really changed or are only pretending to have done so. The use of constraining methods requires close monitoring of target persons' behavior. If they do not want to change in the ways proposed by activists but do wish to win favorable reactions or avoid unfavorable responses, then they will pretend to have changed. Activists can monitor overt actions by target persons more reliably than covert shifts in target persons' beliefs, attitudes, or values. Therefore, activists who use constraining methods are often more effective in influencing the overt behavior of target persons than in changing their covert beliefs or feelings.

8

~~~~~~~~~~~~~~~~~~~~~~~~~~~~~~~~~~~~~

Selecting
the Appropriate Method
for Social Action

How do agents of change choose among the many methods of action available to them? Why do they choose one method over another? The answers to these questions cannot be simple because change seekers need to take many things into consideration before making a choice and because each situation calling for social action is different. Therefore, we shall consider some of the circumstances that can affect this decision. Before doing so, however, let us recall the situation faced by activists when they decide which method their group will use. The main ideas are these:

1. A number of persons (agents of change) wish to transform a given state of affairs in their community.
2. They realize that to bring this innovation about, they need the agreement and help of decision-making individuals in the town (target persons), and that they themselves must convince

these people or their constituents to sponsor the change, and perhaps help them to do so.

3. They work as a group because they believe that collaboration is more likely to be successful in influencing the targets.
4. The change they want to develop is their group's objective.
5. They can use any of a number of methods in trying to convince target persons that the change is necessary.
6. Some of these methods are more likely to be used for informing and advising target persons or requesting them to consider the issue. Different methods are employed for pressing the targets to make one specific decision and no other.

Determining a Course of Action

Which course of action the initiators pursue is determined, as I see it, by their answers to three questions, which they can hardly avoid. First, what will work best (that is, which method promises the greatest likelihood of success)? This estimate is tempered by the change agents' conjectures concerning how target persons feel about the issue brought before them, and by the change agents' judgments about what method they can use best. Second, what method most conforms to the values that they wish to follow while acting as agents of change? Third, what satisfactions can they derive from the experience itself of using a given method? In answering these questions, change agents must consider what approach will give them the most immediate relief. We now consider these matters more fully.

What Will Work Best? By the time change agents are ready to choose a method, they ordinarily know, clearly or vaguely, what end they intend to seek, and they assume that the success of their unit requires reasonable movement toward that goal. Such knowledge is not very helpful in choosing which tactic to employ, however, because any method of influencing, in principle, may be used to try to reach any kind of objective. The choice of method is more strongly guided, I would guess, by the activists' intentions concerning who is to benefit from the change and by their expectations about whether the target persons will favor or dislike the proposal put before them. To be more specific, reformers recognize at an early stage who is to benefit from the change: themselves, others, both themselves and others, or the community at large. This intention causes them to lean toward being either permissive (less constraining) or pressuring (more constraining) as they try to influence target persons.

Suppose, for instance, that they wish to gain an objective that will benefit themselves but no one else. In such a case, reformers will assign the most weight to their own desires and will want to pressure target persons to move in the desired direction and no other. They will probably prefer one or another of the constraining methods, unless the decision makers quickly agree to what the change agents request. In the latter instance, reformers will favor a nonconstraining method.

If, by contrast, reformers intend to benefit only parties outside their own group, they will devote most of their attention to the needs of those persons. When these others can be helped only through the good offices of the target persons, and when the target persons are not willing to assist in this cause, the reformers will probably put pressure on the decision makers by using one or more constraining methods, probably persuasion. Should agents of change want to aid both themselves and others, they will attend equally to the wishes of both groups and will prefer a method, such as negotiating, bargaining, or constructive problem solving, that can lead to actions that will satisfy both parties. In some instances, spokespersons for the other beneficiaries of the effort may join in this discussion as well.

In still other examples, the agents of change may wish to help the target persons by offering advice, information, or the results of investigations. Doubtless, reformers would not press such assistance on the decision makers if it were not welcome; therefore, they would avoid nonconstraining methods in such a situation.

Agents of change can do some things that will help them decide which method or combination of methods will work best. They make their choice by observing the targeted individuals in meetings, interviewing them, or talking with those who know them well, in order to learn how they operate and to judge how they might respond to an overture made by the activists. The following list describes scenarios for the behavior of target persons, as the agents of change may see them. In each case, a different influencing method may be appropriate. We proceed in sequence from encouraging to coercive methods:

1. Change agents themselves are disadvantaged. They expect that target persons will be sympathetic to their plight but they do not wish to ask for help. In such a situation, the agents of change simply wait and hope that the good will of the decision makers will make them feel that they should take steps to aid the disadvantaged change agents.

2. Agents of change learn that the target persons are also dissatisfied with the state of affairs that the activists wish to modify, and that these decision makers are seeking ideas about what improvements ought to be made. In this case, seekers of change may find (or illustrate) a model of what could be done, either through their own planning or by bringing before target persons a representative from a place that has dealt with the same problem.

3. Decision makers recognize that they are responsible for improving a bad situation and are looking for ideas about how to do this. They ask the agents of change for advice, ideas, or expert information, and the change agents provide it.

4. Target persons are not much interested in the issue bothering reformers because they are not well informed about it. Agents of change use whatever means they can to provide information about the issue to the target persons and the community at large. They write stories for newspapers or television programs, hold rallies, give speeches, stage exhibits, sponsor parades, or create demonstrations to present the facts.

5. Individuals for whom target persons are responsible are in need of housing, food, funds, or rescue. The agents of change provide nurturing and assistance directly to these needy people while hoping that the target persons will learn about this helping program and provide enduring financial assistance.

6. Target persons have plans for introducing changes similar to those desired by agents of change. The latter discuss the issue and negotiate with the decision makers, in order to be sure that all the persons involved are thinking alike.

7. Target persons and agents of change have similar objectives but do not agree on methods for gaining those ends. The reformers propose that both factions engage in a process of problem solving, in order to find a course of action that will satisfy both sides.

8. Activists believe that they cannot trust target persons to do what they say they will. The change agents therefore look for help from a legitimate third party, who will guide a process of mediation, binding arbitration, or use of the legal system.

9. Reformers believe that the only way to influence target persons is to persuade them, and so they mount an effort to convince the decision makers by means of debate, argument, or strong writings and speeches.

10. If efforts at persuasion do not work, the agents turn to the use of propaganda and emotion-laden ideas, including misinformation and distortion, in order to convince persons who have the ear of the target persons or who have the power to remove them from office.

11. Activists believe that target persons will be susceptible to influence if they are given a reward (praise, approval, titles, money). They offer a reward to encourage action by the target persons, or they provide it after the decision makers act as the agents of change desire. They give favors to get favors.

12. Target persons reject proposals by agents of change or ignore them. The change agents then force target persons to pay attention to their desires by interfering with the latter group's operations, through strikes, demonstrations, hostage taking, interruption of meetings, or other blocking procedures, until the desired change is delivered.

13. Target persons refuse to do what is asked of them. Agents of change therefore inflict injury directly on the refusers, or on bystanders or valued objects. They employ bombs, guns, coups d'état, or other kinds of violence to get their way.

Different views of beneficiaries and target persons call for different methods. Reformers consider additional matters when deciding which method to use. To increase their chances of success, for instance, the change agents try to prevent target persons from opposing a proposal—by casting it in terms that fit with past views and goals of the target persons, by demonstrating that the change will fit the target persons' traditions, values, ways of operating, or rules, and by claiming that it will help the target persons do better what they are already doing. They choose the style of presentation that they think will be the most convincing. If the target persons are formal in their procedures, the change agents behave in a formal way. If the target persons' procedures are relaxed, the change agents' style will be likewise. When meeting with groups whose members have much power, the activists will try to win the others' good will. When meeting with target persons who have little power, they will be forceful and brisk (Zander, 1982). It is also clear that change agents must assess similarities and differences when preparing to appear before groups of elected officials, city employees, supervisors of private agencies, businesspeople, or the voting public.

If they sense that the target persons are especially likely to resist direct constraints, the activists will try not to generate a negative emotional response among those they hope to influence. They are patient, rational, helpful, and informative, and they avoid propaganda, strong bargaining, and coercion. In short, the innovators use encouraging methods, rather than pressuring ones. Activists cannot confidently plan how to prevent resistance among target persons, however, until they actually make an attempt to influence them and discover whether their own behavior arouses an unfavorable reaction. In some instances, as we know, activists deliberately try to generate anger and rejection among target persons. They do this when they believe that their case would not receive a fair hearing if they were to use a more permissive method; they make matters unpleasant for the target persons, in order to make them ready to bargain.

Members of a group for social action consider other issues in deciding how to convince target persons. Early on, they ask themselves several questions. Have we solved such a problem in the past? How did we do it? If the group's own history is not helpful, its members learn how members of other groups have been able to influence the target persons, and they favor a method that has already worked.

Another consideration has to do with what members can do skillfully. Can they give speeches, reason clearly in arguments, write publicity, mount exhibits, bargain wisely, or threaten target persons? Do some of the members have the training needed for providing emergency care to individuals, preparing food for the homeless, fighting a fire or a flood, analyzing community finances, designing a flower garden, or counseling those in need of help? Do some members have the temperament to be poised on the witness stand, compassionate in nurturing, objective in problem solving, courageous in a demonstration, senseless in a riot, or ruthless in actions that are intended to harm people? The abilities of the members have much to do with the method they adopt. Some people will have had much experience in groups and meetings, and so they will participate in these with ease. Others need training and encouragement before they will risk activism. Naïve members prefer simpler methods—usually aggressive ones, I suspect.

Do group members have the necessary resources to use a given method? Some procedures cost more than others. Typically, social action turns out to be more expensive (in terms of money, energy, and emotional strain) than activists initially assume. Costly procedures include advertisements in the news media, exhibits, equipment for providing emergency care, mailings, hostage taking, and rallies. Necessary resources may be space, special training for personnel, medical supplies, books, or reports. Such resources are not necessary, however, for picketing, speaking before a body of decision makers, interrupting a meeting, or calling a conference of potential protesters. Priscoli (1978) gives a rough estimate of the comparative costs of different methods for social action.

A further question raised by activists is how long the procedure will take. Preference is given to methods that will be quickly effective, since a long wait reduces the enthusiasm of the innovators. Most groups become frustrated and lose their morale if their action takes too long. In addition, group leaders examine whether the details and step-by-step procedures to be followed are understood by members. Does each member know what he or she must do and how to do it? Are there clear processes for hiring a mediator, taking a case to court, getting a story published in the newspaper, obtaining a permit for a parade, or making a bomb? Leaders prefer actions that they know how to mount. To avoid disagreement, they probably favor methods that prescribe a clear division of labor among group members.

Will the Method Fit the Group's Values? Reformers avoid procedures that they believe are improper because such acts offend their beliefs about right and wrong. For example, they will not call names at a public meeting or throw rocks through windows if such actions violate their code of ethics. They will, in contrast, write a letter to an editor or participate in a strike if they feel that it is the duty of a citizen to help correct a situation in these ways.

The values of members influence whether they want to benefit only themselves, other persons, or both themselves and others. People who work to gratify only themselves probably have quite different values (in operation at the moment, anyway) from the values of those who work to satisfy others. Self-centered reformers may justify their selfishness by pointing to their strong faith in individual enterprise or in solving problems on one's own. Altruistic reformers may speak in favor of caring for others (the able should help the lame), or they may prefer cooperation among community groups and see value in jointly solving problems. Self-serving citizens would be more likely to use constraining methods and to justify their assertive style as necessary for taking care of themselves. Compassionate reformers would probably more often use nonconstraining methods, perhaps nurturing ones, to help others, but they would be prepared to take up coercive methods if softer procedures got no results.

Ordinarily, most activists prefer methods that will not offend bystanders, since they wish to win the sympathy and support of neighbors through their actions. In many cases, they hope to gain just that and little else. They will often avoid the use of procedures that expose them to ridicule or criticism. Participating in a parade, a picket line, or a demonstration, for example, may provoke public disapproval. Such an unfavorable reception occurred in a town that was next to a weapons-storage depot. A set of citizens in the community obtained signatures of local residents on petitions, which asked for relief from the actions of activists who had been protesting shipments of military supplies from that depot for many months. The protesters stood outside the gate of the depot day and night.

The townsfolk accused them of interfering with automobile traffic in the city and of littering. The petitioners submitted their plea for redress to the commissioners of the county, and they won. The protesters could continue their daily vigil, but they had to stay out of the street, remove the ugly shack they used in bad weather, and clean up after themselves daily.

Is the Method Satisfying? Change agents may select a method merely because the actions it requires are gratifying in themselves, even though the participants may have no definite notion of what their moves will accomplish. They may decide, for example, to shout derisive comments in the middle of a meeting, make threats, march in a parade, hold a rally, sponsor a silent vigil, call a meeting, or bomb an airport, without planning beyond these activities. They may do these things because they want relief from their anger, grief, or fear.

Weick (1979) proposes, as noted eralier, that members of some groups prefer at the very outset to choose a procedure, rather than a group goal. A method, once selected, helps members work together smoothly; later, when they analyze what they have done and why, they are better able to select an objective. Thus, members should first choose a method, Weick believes, because they get action under way, and the purpose of these actions will eventually become evident to them.

Why Members of Action Groups Choose Inappropriate Methods

An inappropriate method is one that does not help activists influence listeners because the reformers are not able to do what the procedure requires (write, speak, argue, vilify, charm, persuade), do not have the resources they need, or cause the target persons to become obstinate, opposed, or resistant. Why do reformers select methods that turn out to be ineffective?

One reason is that the people who choose the group's methods are not able to judge whether one procedure is better than another because their group's objectives are not clear enough to guide such an appraisal. If innovators are not sure what they want

to accomplish and why, they cannot plan how to reach their objective. When a group's end provides little guidance, moreover, separate ideas among members about the wisest plan of action will probably not fit together well; each person will pay most attention to ways of satisfying his or her personal interests because there is no criterion for evaluating what is useful for the body as a whole.

The success of change agents in influencing decision makers, as we have observed, depends on how correctly they estimate what ideas and style of delivery will be most acceptable to the target persons. For example, if the change seekers think that their listeners will appreciate background information, whereas the listeners actually want ideas about what steps they ought to take, the target persons will see the activists as too vague and unconvincing. As another example, the reformers may propose a solution when the officials want facts about the issue, so that they can choose their own answer in light of that information. In short, agents of change may take a wrong approach because they have not properly diagnosed what would best appeal to the target persons.

A further cause of choosing an inappropriate method is that agents of change become defensive, angry, or suspicious toward the behavior of the target persons. The reformers thereupon try to defend their honor, assuage their anger, or confirm their suspicions. Even though such emotions are legitimate reasons for trying to influence those who appear to cause them, they usually lead to behavior among change agents that makes the target persons want to defend themselves in turn, instead of trying to relieve the condition raised by the activists.

Another frequent reason for an unwise choice of method by agents of change is that they follow unsound procedures in reaching a decision. Perhaps participants are too eager to maintain good relations with one another, and so they fail to test ideas brought up in their meetings because doing so requires them to ask questions, criticize others' thinking, or disagree. Instead, they do what is most likely to be agreeable to all. They discuss only a few potential solutions and do not examine the consequences that may follow from these actions. They make no suggestions that might be controversial (Janis, 1972).

Some change agents talk more than others and therefore have

greater influence on their group's decisions, even though their ideas may not be the best ones (Zander, 1982). An imbalance in the spread of participation is not always bad, but it can be a source of difficulty if the method under discussion is one that affects many members, who all ought to have a say. The infrequent speakers may feel restrained because they do not understand the plan, are not interested in it, are afraid of making an observation that will be rejected, are intimidated by the difficulty of the role they are expected to take, or are awed by being in the presence of powerful persons. If an unbalanced meeting limits verbal participation in this way, a group's plan of action may turn out to be inappropriate (Zander, 1982).

When members of a group must deal with an emergency (such as a storm, fire, or flood), they are prone to make errors in choosing a course of action, either because time pressure makes them consider fewer options before they decide what to do or because decisions are made by persons who are not expert in handling a crisis. During such a critical period, moreover, information coming to the group may be of poor quality because messages provided in haste are either badly expressed or inadequately thought through. Under the anxiety created by stress, behavior tends to be less flexible and imaginative than it might otherwise be (Holsti, 1971). When members must hurry for reasons like these, the group's efforts are liable to be inefficient and less salient to its prime purposes.

Summary

Leaders of a group that is planning how to initiate a change choose among many methods for this action. In making a choice, they consider several things. What method will work best, in light of the group's objective and the nature of the target persons? To answer this question, they make a judgment about how much or little constraint they should use with the target persons, so that the latter will act. They make this judgment by observing whether the target persons are likely to be more interested in the substantive issue or in the incentive that agents of change offer. Activists choose the method that fits the target persons best.

They also select the procedure that they think they can per-

form most successfully—it has worked for others, the members are able to do what it requires, they have or can obtain the resources they need, it will be effective quickly, they know how to use it, and its effect can be reliably determined. They also favor a method that will not violate their values and whose use is itself attractive.

Activists may sometimes select a method that is inappropriate (meaning that it does not help them accomplish what they want) if their goals are too vague to guide a wise choice, if they have incorrect information about the target persons, or if they use unsound processes in trying to make this decision.

9

~~~~~~

Social Power
and Effective
Agents of Change

Agents of change, we are assuming, wish to influence target persons. They accomplish this aim when their actions change the others' behavior or beliefs. Those who cause such a change are said to have *power* over the ones they influence. Several features of the nature and use of social power are worthy of our notice (Cartwright, 1959; Cartwright and Zander, 1968; French and Raven, 1959).

Seekers of change who have power in their relations with target persons ordinarily are able to influence them only in specific matters, not in all. For example, they may induce members of a planning commission to act on a problem concerning traffic control or zoning, but they do not have this effect in a situation that involves conservation of open space or rules for managing parking structures. It follows that change agents' power is not effective in every case and every place. Moreover, persons with the power to affect the views of traffic commissioners may have no influence at all with members of the board of education.

Initiators who know they can influence specific target persons in specific matters may choose not to use their power at the moment; instead, they may keep it in abeyance until they need it. Thus, merely possessing a given sort of power does not mean that it will be used often or even at all. In addition, some persons with power to influence may not realize that they have it. We saw examples of this when we considered passive or withdrawn forms of social action, as well as the influence ascribed to people whom others imitate, without the models' realizing that they are influential. Some kinds of power come to persons simply because they are deeply interested or expert in a particular issue, even though they do not intend to be influential in that matter. An expert's power derives from the tendency of uninformed persons to ask the wise individual for information or advice. He or she has no influence (sadly enough) if no one knows that he or she is well informed or if no one listens to what he or she says.

Power is a two-way proposition. Persons seeking reforms may cause specific others to change in certain respects, and the reformers themselves may be influenced by the others in other matters. For example, in negotiations, bargaining, and problem solving, participants on each side recognize that others intend both to influence and to be influenced, to inform and to be informed. Thus, persons change their minds during a discussion and simultaneously change the beliefs of others. Target persons often develop more or less opposition and resistance, to protect themselves from being influenced and from being made uneasy by the style that the influencers employ. Much of what agents of change do when engaging in social action is therefore intended to avoid being put off by the opposition or resistance of target persons. The exercise of power in a give-and-take discussion can be seen as an ebb and flow, as a sparring match. In what follows, we cannot focus on the details of such actions and reactions; later we will consider such events in slower motion and in more analytical terms. For the moment, we shall concentrate on change agents. Later we shall attend to target persons.

The essence of social action is that advocates develop enough power in their relations with particular target persons to change their behavior or beliefs. Some groups of citizens may gain easy influence over a given set of target persons (on certain matters) because they have more favors to dispense or more expertise, resources, or confidence in their own views. These change agents are often community leaders who are already influential with many people in town. They may also have jobs that allow them to do work for community change during their regular working hours. Most other people find it harder to win as much influence as these community leaders because most others have fewer goods to give or use, are not as sure of themselves, and must use their leisure time to work for a cause. Most of us, unlike community leaders, have to earn any power we gain; it is seldom given to us (Perlman, 1978).

Motivational Bases of Influence

When activists ask target persons to help them toward a certain objective, why do the target persons go along? They may do so for any of several reasons. They think that doing so will win favorable publicity for their organization. They feel that not acting as they have been asked to do makes them seem narrow-minded and uncreative. They admire the way the activists operate and would like their own organization to be similar to the one the reformers run. They see in the proposed plan a duty that they should fulfill. They believe that they will enjoy the results of the suggested action. They perceive the proposal as an opportunity to help disadvantaged members of the community, or they become convinced that the proposal is sound and should be supported.

Speaking more generally, the reactions of target persons to change agents' influence attempt depend on how they see the consequences of accepting it or rejecting it. They will be more likely to adopt the proposed change if it is in their best interests to do so. They will not be attracted to it if it is liable to do them more harm than good, unless they intend to right a wrong that others have had to endure and, in so doing, to accept the costs.

Activists, for their part, intuitively recognize that targeted individuals in our society want to know what is in it for them if they make the transformation being proposed, and so activists frame their influence attempts in a way that they think will help the listeners in this respect. They try to arouse some motive or desire in the target persons, and they try to convince them that the suggested change will satisfy that desire. For instance, the members of a group for social action propose that steps be taken to improve the lives of the homeless. They present their case in a way that causes the listeners to care about the fate of the deprived persons ("Look at how they have to live!"), and they describe the satisfaction that the target persons will have after helping. They will be proud of their compassion, touched by the gratitude of the homeless, and feel much less guilty.

The general rule that agents of change seem to follow is this: *the stronger the motive or desire that change agents arouse among target persons, and the stronger the probability that this motive or desire will be satisfied through what the innovators propose, the more the agents of change will influence the target persons.* In accord with this rule, the wise activist strengthens a relevant motive or desire in target persons by making it seem important to them or by helping them recall the value they have placed on it in other situations. The wise activist also helps target persons see that attainment of the proposed objective will give them deep satisfaction. I suspect that not all agents of change operate as directly as these statements imply. Indeed, some groups are not able to adopt any strategy at all, let alone the ones to be discussed here.

As we saw in Chapters Six and Seven, members of a group for social action may intend, at one extreme, that targeted individuals make up their own minds about the benefits they can derive from adopting a change. At the other extreme, activists may hold that they themselves should develop as much control as possible over the matter. Consider, as illustrations, three different degrees of activeness and directness that agents of change can adopt to influence the motives of target persons.

Gently Active Approaches. Here, the agents describe (or demonstrate) the grievance (or opportunity for change) that the target persons ought to act on. They do not say what they think should be done to remedy matters, lay out an objective for a change attempt, or suggest an incentive for the target persons to attain. All such matters are left up to the decision makers, either because those persons know best what ought to be done or because the change agents believe that

the target persons will be much more committed to a specific
change if they reach that decision on their own. The initiators say
nothing, in this instance, about the motives or desires that target
persons can expect to satisfy as a result of introducing a given reform. The activists assume that the target persons will identify for
themselves what kinds of satisfaction will come from their moving
in a given direction. Methods that are likely to have such effects are
modeling, being passive or withdrawn, informing, and counseling.
All are nonconstraining procedures.

Moderately Active Approaches. With this degree of activeness, the initiators again describe the grievance or opportunity that
should arouse the attention of the target persons, but now they also
describe what they think can be done about it. They lay out an
objective for the change effort and speak in favor of it. They leave it
to the target persons, however, to decide what motive or desire they
may be able to satisfy by attaining that objective. Here, the methods
for social action are discussing, negotiating, problem solving, bargaining, or civilly trying to persuade.

Strongly Active Approaches. With this degree of activeness,
innovators forcefully describe what is wrong and demand relief at
once. They indicate exactly what must be done about the situation,
and they leave no room for a different solution. They prescribe
exactly what motive or desire should guide the behavior of the target
persons. The latter are pressed to see the value and satisfaction
inherent in such benefits as receiving a reward, gaining approval,
avoiding unfair propaganda, evading physical harm, or reducing
the threat of future penalties. The activists stress the value of one or
more of these incentives, by arousing greed for a reward or by demonstrating the repulsive effects of the punishments, penalties, and
pain that target persons will have to endure if they do not move as
they are being pushed to do. The target persons are convinced—not
because their action will be satisfying in itself, but because their
effort will win them external rewards or will ward off penalties.

We can note several things about the behavior of innovators
who use one or another of these three degrees of activeness. First, if

they use the gentlest degree and employ a nonconstraining method, the change itself is the incentive for the targeted persons, and they derive satisfaction from accomplishing it. If activists use the strongest degree and a constraining method, the major incentive for target persons (the prime source of the constraint) is the reward they will receive if they accomplish what is asked of them or the avoidance of a punishment they will have to endure should they fail to do. as they are told. The effect of a reward or a punishment usually wears thin over time. Therefore, a change is probably maintained more strongly by target persons if they have experienced gentle, nonconstraining methods at the hands of the innovators than if they have implemented the change after being exposed to constraining methods. The evidence is also rich that an internal incentive—one developed by the actors themselves, for themselves—evokes stronger maintenance of change than an external incentive does (Deci, 1975).

Second, change agents can suggest certain motives or desires for target persons to develop, can teach them to value these motives or desires, or can replace target persons' current motives or desires with new ones. Third, agents of change can provide incentives for the desires they arouse in listeners; these will be descriptions of a desirable change. Fourth, change agents are more likely to use nonconstraining methods when they have an opportunity to improve matters for others and are not claiming that they themselves are deprived or need to be benefited. Fifth, agents of change are more likely to use constraining methods when they believe that they themselves are unfairly deprived or that those they represent are.

Stimulating Target Persons to Take Action

In light of the foregoing ideas, we see that change agents' influence on decision makers depends on their ability to arouse compelling motives or desires. How do they do this? Let us examine several practical steps they can take to stimulate interest in a special situation among target persons.

At the outset, they make the grievance or opportunity for improving things known to target persons, to individuals who can influence the views of the target persons, or to both. Then the agents of change arouse a motive or desire that they know or suspect exists among the target persons (such as their desire for group achievement, wish to nurture disadvantaged citizens, eagerness to solve a problem, hope to remain in office, or wish to win approval from observers). To do this, change agents learn (or guess) what tendencies are arousable in the decision makers by observing them in action, talking with them about their satisfactions and frustrations, making tentative proposals to them and watching their reactions to these ideas, or asking other influential groups how they have aroused the decision makers. Change agents appeal to a salient motive or desire by describing the kind of satisfaction the target persons can expect to feel if they put the proposed change in place. They say, "You will feel proud of your organization for what it has accomplished," or "You will feel good about yourselves because you have helped persons who cannot help themselves," or "You will be pleased with the relief you feel after solving this problem," or "Your chances for reelection will be improved," or "You will win the approval of everyone in town." Once a relevant motive or desire has been aroused among target persons (or taught to them), innovators may elaborate on its value—or, more precisely, on the value of satisfying it. They stress how important it is for the target persons to be proud of their unit, to be altruistic, to be skilled solvers of problems, to be reelected, or to win approval for their services to the community.

Next, the agents of change show target persons the clear connections between their yearning for satisfaction and the action being requested of them. The activists emphasize that fulfillment of the objective will result in the kinds of favorable reaction that the target persons value, and they stress that the change being sought is not for the activists' benefit alone; target persons will also be satisfied. Then the activists encourage their listeners by emphasizing the likelihood that the latter will be able to make the change being proposed. The innovators build target persons' confidence in succeeding—by helping them obtain needed resources, sharing skills, outlining procedures, and bolstering the target persons' courage.

Finally, the activists call for action and an end to talk, study, and waiting. They press for a date when action is to begin, propose a schedule, and continue to urge change until it is completed. These are the things that reformers do when creating readiness to introduce a change. The innovators recognize, however, that pressure toward making a change is not enough; they also must counter forces that tend in the opposite direction. If reactive forces are not weakened, the push to change will result in greater uncertainty among the target persons, but not in an enduring change (Cartwright and Zander, 1968).

Conditions That Work Against Attempts to Influence

I believe that three kinds of circumstances slow effort to introduce a change. The members of the change group may lose interest in the plan, the target persons may oppose the plan after it has been explained to them, or the target persons may resist change agents' inducements. The effects of each condition are notable.

Loss of Interest. Change agents want satisfaction, and they work to attain it. It often happens, however, that they lose interest in trying to gain a favorable result. When this occurs, they no longer try to influence the target persons. The targets, in turn, also do not act because the activists give up. One reason why reformers lose their enthusiasm is that they become attracted to a desire different from the one they had at first. They decide, for example, that they want to win personal gains (a new sidewalk, paid for by the city) rather than solve a community problem (improved flow of traffic), or they want to get publicity for their group rather than be quietly proud of its unheralded achievements. If a new motive or desire becomes more attractive and the group's current goal is no longer a relevant incentive, the actors lose enthusiasm for that goal. My guess, however, is that a drop in enthusiasm is probably due less to a new desire than to a decrease in the value of the activists' objective. A goal becomes less attractive if reformers decide that they cannot influence the target persons to move toward it or if, on closer inspection, achievement of the initial objective will not provide what the change agents want. Increased police patrols, for instance, apparently are not going to reduce the use of illegal drugs. This kind of failure will tend to be more likely when changers propose a goal that is too difficult for target persons to achieve, when the goal is so vague that the decision makers cannot discern which path to take,

or when a proposed change is not connected to the original grievance. If agents of change cannot induce decision makers to improve
things, this failure may cause them to blame individual participants
or their group as a whole. Blaming soon generates strain among
members and a loss of efficiency in the group (Zander, 1982).

There is another way to account for the loss of spark among
activists. It is simply that they succeed. When decision makers do as
innovators have pressed them to do, the innovators relax. Their
objective is reached or soon will be. It is likely that more social
action groups fail than succeed in their attempts to influence target
persons. That is why a group's loss of interest in its objective is less
common after a victory than after a failure.

Opposition. Suppose that activists present a proposal for
change. The listeners ask questions and clearly say they oppose the
idea. The activists must overcome the others' lack of interest if they
are to have a chance of attaining their goal. To transform the beliefs
or behavior of target persons, they must counteract the targets' reasons for refusing to change their views. Otherwise, those reasons
will continue to be offered as opposition to the plan. Whenever
target persons yield to an influence attempt by change agents, they
must give up ideas and objectives they have previously prized
(Cartwright and Zander, 1968). The strength of their opposition
depends on three factors: the amount of difference between the
change proposed by the innovators and the views of the target persons; the degree of satisfaction that target persons derive from the
current state of affairs; and features in the change agents' plan that
are not attractive to the persons being influenced. In ordinary language, target persons will opppose a plan if it asks them to make
too great a change. They like things just as they are, or they see too
many unfavorable features in the proposed innovations. The innovators have to counter these three sources of opposition.

They overcome the first complaint, that the innovation is too
different from past practices, by making this claim appear not to be
true. They aver that the new plan at first appears quite different but
actually has many similarities with past practices, and they identify
these similarities. The proposed change, they say, is in effect a small
one. Any differences that do exist, moreover, are at the heart of the

new plan; they are invaluable, even if unusual. Activists meet the objection that past procedures have been satisfactory by pointing out ways in which this has not been the case and by explaining why satisfaction with prior practices could not have been great; the new change, when put in place, will provide more favorable outcomes.

The innovators try to prevent decision makers from fearing unpleasant side effects that might follow a change. To do this, they counter claims that target persons may make (for example, the new idea is too complex, too hard to implement, unlikely to work; it arouses anxiety, violates a tradition, damages the interests of many persons, or asks target persons to give up their rightful control over important activities).

Change seekers meet the opposition of target persons in other ways as well. They cite contrasting facts and give counterarguments. They colorfully describe the problem that suggests the need for a change, and they press for a joint problem-solving session. They suggest that a written version of the joint solution be prepared, which will have the force of a contract, or they treat the target persons in ways that develop mutual trust and confidence, using an interpersonal style that prevents negative emotional reactions, since such resistance strengthens opposition.

Resistance. Change agents evoke resistance from target persons if they use an influencing style that arouses anger, fear, or defensiveness. Because the responses of target persons occur on a groupwide basis, they become contagious, and they are stronger, I assume, than they would be on a one-to-one basis. Members tend to reinforce (rather than dampen) one another's emotional reactions. For instance, I have seen target persons encourage resistant behavior among their colleagues by telling members who do not show an emotional response that they should not remain calm in the crazy situation facing them. Resistance in itself is not bad or lacking in excitement and interest. It tends, however, to reduce the chances that a serious problem will be solved sensibly.

The style of activists' behavior, rather than the substantive content of their ideas, causes target persons to resist suggestions. There are many examples of resistance-triggering actions by activists. The change seekers make arbitrary demands of their listeners, so that the latters' acceptance of them is tantamount to admitting defeat (Frank, 1944; Brehm and Brehm, 1981). They ridicule the beliefs or behavior of target persons or make ad hominem remarks about them. They show hostility toward target persons when making their presentation; they talk loudly, speak rapidly, pitch their voices high, reveal tension (a tight throat) in the sounds they make, and display facial and postural signs of aggression. According to linguists, bodily aspects of communication provide much of the total meaning in any message, and so such nonverbal behavior may have more effect than words. The innovators may also threaten to harm the listeners. They propose actions that do not suit the values of the target persons, intimate that they (the activists) have the support of powerful persons in high places, and use dishonest information (such as distorted "facts" and illogical derivations) or other forms of duplicity. In sum, they try to restrict the freedom of the target persons, or they use emotional and false means in their attempts to be convincing. Plainly, such behavior is more likely to occur with constraining methods of social action than with nonconstraining methods because constraining methods are more often employed when agents of change have great faith in the correctness of their ideas, believe that the target persons are evil or wrong, and are zealously determined to convert the listeners to these notions in any way they can.

The members of a group seeking social change ordinarily try to prevent resistance among persons they wish to influence, unless they are confident that they have enough power to overcome it, or unless it pleases them to make the target persons angry or fearful. To calm the others' resistance, the agents of change avoid behaving in ways that generate resistance. They take steps to prevent the anger or fear that may cause resistance, and they attempt to get the decision makers engaged in constructive problem solving by posing a problem for discussion, rather than a solution. For example, they list a number of alternative outcomes for an issue, but they state no preference among these unless asked for one, and they propose a procedure that could be followed to choose among alternatives (creating a task force or study committee, consulting with an expert, gathering data, brainstorming, holding an open hearing, interviewing informed citizens, running workshops, or hiring a professional in organizational development). A major consequence of such activities is that target persons are assured that their own autonomy is being respected.

A different way for reformers to prevent resistance among target persons is to diagnose the origin of resistance in the current situation. The proposers initially gather information that helps them understand why the listeners may become hostile, defensive, or evasive. Once they identify the potential sources of such reactions, they try to eliminate these causes. Clearly, resistance is less likely among the persons addressed if their leaders, or a dominant faction among them, are convinced to accept the need for a change, since the leaders can help convince their colleagues who have not been approached directly by the innovators. High-status persons, I suspect, are more confident of their own views and patience, and so they do not develop resistance as readily, even when they oppose the ideas of activists.

Advocates of a given change will generate less resistance among those they wish to influence if they suggest that the new idea be given a tentative trial before a decision is made about whether to implement it. Rothman, Erlich, and Teresa (1976, p. 23) reviewed writings on the circumstances that determine whether citizens adopt new social practices put before them, and they offer the following generalization: "Innovations that are amenable [to] trial on a partial basis have a higher adoption rate than innovations that necessitate adoption without an anticipatory trial." The authors provide evidence that target persons are most accepting of change if they are given an opportunity to try out parts of the total plan informally, to see how well they work. The same authors also state that an innovation is more likely to be adopted if target persons have an opportunity to see it in action for a trial period and to witness what results it generates, or if they initially test only a piece of innovation. Furthermore, a new plan is most likely to be accepted if it is first used by opinion leaders of the decision-making group.

Rothman, Erlich, and Teresa (1976, p. 25) propose the following general guideline: "Practitioners wishing to promote an innovation in a general target system should develop it initially as a partial segment of the system." Either a part of the innovation may be given a trial, or the whole plan may be tested in a section of the community. The authors advise that an incremental process be used, meaning that separate steps should be taken, one at a time, so that any success on a small scale can be seen by observers to be grounds for promoting the idea or for spreading it among colleagues. Apparently, the more visible an innovation is made, the more it will receive favorable reactions among those who have a stake in it. All in all, Rothman and his colleagues propose that agents of change can avoid resistance by moving slowly and using a trial-and-error approach.

These ways of preventing or reducing resistance may be too bland, however, if refusals by target persons cause reformers to keep up their pressure for a change, come what may. In that case, a two-sided resistance may develop and a circular-causal situation ensue, in which resistance on one side arouses similar behavior on the other. Activists and target persons alike now intentionally act in a defensive manner, even though it hurts the causes of both factions to do so. Mutually hostile feelings and actions escalate. The reactions of target persons arouse correspondingly aggressive responses among activists, and these mirrored emotions cause misperceptions, misunderstandings, or deliberate efforts to coerce the others, on both sides. Chaos takes over.

Thereafter, all discussants see malicious intent in the other side's actions. They distort the comments by their opposite numbers, do not listen to others or try to understand what they are saying, see one another as selfish and untrustworthy, and do not make conciliatory moves, for fear that willingness to compromise may be taken as weakness. They threaten, emphasize how far apart their ideas are, make overwhelming demands, and try to deceive one another into giving up. Although there may be only a few issues at the outset, more and more are brought into the discussion, and more and more persons become involved (Deutsch, 1973; Pruitt and Rubin, 1986; Zander, 1982). Each side is now out to win. It can be seen that things get out of hand during such an escalation. The authors just cited suggest procedures that conferees can use to inhibit or dampen such double-edged resistance. These include the following:

1. Both the agents of change and the persons exposed to pressure state at the outset that they intend to be rational and to control their tendencies to become fearful or hostile. They recognize that resistance and escalation can happen when agents of change present their case to a formal body, and that all involved intend to prevent this.

2. Participants come to the meeting prepared. They know their own views well, have a common belief about the issues, and are able to present their ideas clearly. Such preparation prevents resistance that is due to poorly stated ideas.

3. Participants establish ground rules for appropriate behavior during presentation and discussion.

4. Conferees decide ahead of time who is to make a decision, if any is needed, and how this is to be done.

5. Before the meeting, members among the change agents and the target persons agree on how they will conduct themselves. They agree not to ridicule opposing comments and to pay close attention when rivals speak, use others' ideas to understand and test them, accept their opponents' interests as legitimate, and recognize that their opponents are justified (as they see things) in presenting their views.

6. Participants use, if necessary, legitimate means of conflict resolution established by the community (referees, mediators, arbitrators, judges, or the courts).

7. Discussants work to develop bases for being trusted and for trusting members of the opposite unit. For example, they provide evidence for factual information, bring in witnesses to support ideas that may be questioned, and refer to similarities in the views, friendships, and motives among target persons and change agents. They expand on the fact that some persons in the current gathering have had useful and pleasant interactions in other cases and places and can trust one another now.

8. Participants agree on which values are most important, such as fairness, justice, and equality.

9. Everyone promises to abide by these values.

10. Members on both sides identify similarities between the objectives of the reformers and those of the target persons and declare that all participants are therefore in a cooperative

relationship. Each can help the others reach the common goal. Rivalry and competition are inappropriate and irrelevant.

Following steps like these may prevent each side from becoming too coercive and constraining, on the one hand, or too passive and nonconstraining, on the other. If all goes well, a constructive problem-solving relationship is created, in which the parties can coolly consider the proposed plan for change. The result is a sound solution-reaching process rather than a contest in which the strongest or most abrasive side wins.

Maintaining an Active Organization

Because I have been paying the most attention to how change agents influence target persons, I have concentrated on examples in which just one influence attempt is made by those who advocate a change. Obviously, many groups of activists do not try to win their way just once; they try many times, in many fashions, over a long period. Eventually, some hit on procedures that bring them success. They do so, in part, by evaluating what went wrong in previous trials and by planning how they can improve their approaches to target persons (Zander, 1982). Every community has a few groups of dedicated souls who have been working for a long time to change things in schools, parks, welfare, recreation, health care, police protection, or traffic control. How do these change bodies survive?

We get some useful insights into what helps a group to endure by examining the contrasting qualities of live and lazy groups. Wandersman and his associates have studied the characteristics of active and inactive block organizations (social action groups in urban areas) (Prestby and Wandersman, 1985; Wandersman and others, 1985). They report that active units, as compared to inactive ones, are more likely to have members who are able to do what needs to be done; sufficient money, supplies, and sources of information; elected leaders who listen to the members' ideas; democratic decision making, in which all members have a say; a division of labor that gives everyone a chance to participate; awareness of the need to keep the group alive by recruiting new members and regularly regenerating enthusiasm among them; members who give time to the group; a continuing program of activities; and, finally, a success or two, plus the promise of additional ones.

No one factor guarantees the effectiveness and survival of an organization that wants to improve things. A group's ability to influence target persons requires that attempts to gain social power take place in a healthy and sound organization. These matters deserve more study.

Summary

Innovators influence others when they perform acts that change the behavior or beliefs of those persons. If their influence extends to specific matters or particular persons, we say that innovators have power over those matters and individuals.

Reactions among target persons to an influence attempt depend primarily on how they see the motivational consequences of accepting it or rejecting it. They will adopt a proposed move if they believe that it is in their best interests. Thus, innovators try to help target persons see what is in it for them if they help in a planned change. As a general rule, the stronger the motive or desire that change agents arouse among target persons, and the greater the probability that this motive or desire will be satisfied if the target persons do what activists propose, the more likely the innovators are to influence the target persons successfully.

Initiators of a change may use any among three degrees of vigor in attempting to influence target persons: gentle, moderate, or strong. Gentle approaches tend to employ encouraging or nonconstraining methods; strong approaches tend to use pressuring or constraining methods; moderate approaches use methods in between. When nonconstraining methods are used, the proposed change itself is the incentive for target persons. When constraining methods are employed, an external incentive is offered to (or pressed on) target persons.

Successful influencers counteract the reasons that target persons give for opposing change and get them to give up those reasons. The strength of opposition depends on how different the innovation is, how satisfying current practices are, and how much dissatisfaction is foreseen as proceeding from the new idea. Agents of change try to weaken the impact of these three sources of opposition.

Resistance is evoked when the style used by change agents arouses anger, fear, or defensiveness. Wise innovators try to prevent the development of resistance, but this is difficult to do if they themselves respond emotionally to the reactions of target persons, so that a circular-causal escalation ensues. Escalation can be prevented or controlled once it arises, however. Efforts to control it lead eventually to constructive problem solving. Attempts to cool things down will not work if target persons set out to damage the effectiveness of the change agents' group. (How target persons do this is a matter we shall take up in Chapter Ten.) A group's continuing ability to influence target persons requires the unit to mount such efforts within a healthy and lively organization.

10

~,~

Responses of Decision Makers
to Actions
of Change Agents

Decision makers who are presented with an idea for planned change can ignore, accept, or oppose that plan. Under some circumstances, they reject individuals who bring such proposals; under other conditions, they warm to those activists. Before we consider how receivers respond to the overtures of change agents, let us recall their situation at the time they are approached by reformers.

The reactions of target persons, to make an obvious but not trivial point, occur after the agents of change have acted. Moreover, the listeners probably have not planned how they will reply to the advocates' ideas because the initiators' moves are either unexpected or unpredictable. Thus, the initial responses of target persons usually are unrehearsed attempts to study, supplement, or stall the influence attempts of the proposers. The responders thus become agents of change themselves, either in support of the ideas of the innovators or in defense of their own view. They typically modify their first reactions once they see how the advocates reply to the initial answers. The target persons' behavior toward the activists is determined in good part by the moves that change agents later make in the dance of influence attempts and replies.

The dominant drives of target persons are different from those of reformers. The change agents are primarily concerned with achieving their stated objective, as a group, because doing so will reduce their dissatisfactions or will take advantage of a golden opportunity. Their success will provide a feeling of pride in the accomplishment of their group (or in their own accomplishment). What is more, if the activists fail to attain their goal, they lose only a skirmish; they can try again another day, in a different way, and a failure is seldom a serious source of embarrassment because activists' goals are almost always difficult. Then, too, they derive a measure of pride (plus public applause) from having ventured to reach such hard objectives (Zander, 1977). The prime concern among target persons, in contrast, when they are facing a set of activists, is dread of the public consequences that could follow from any blunder. They may feel some success if they implement the ideas offered by the agents of change. More commonly, however, they will derive little pride from such action because they are proud of their own practices and they have not developed the idea for a change. They may be criticized by constituents who believe that the target persons' decision to act is unwise. In addition, they will gain little approval if they reject a proposal offered by the change agents, unless everyone agrees that the plan will not work. Moreover, rejection of the proposal may cause public disapproval of the target persons if it is a popular idea in the community, and a refusal will arouse anger among those who support the change. All in all, activists have much to gain and little to lose in putting forth a proposal; target persons have little to gain and much to lose by accepting a proposal. They have to be especially cautious in evaluating an idea brought to them by reformers.

If target persons actively work against the ideas of change agents, they may use any of the methods described in Chapters Six and Seven. The method they probably employ most often will resemble the one that the innovators brought into play when initially presenting their ideas, since like behavior tends to beget like behavior (Deutsch, 1973). To illustrate, if the initiators offer advice, argument, intervention, or aggression, the target persons tend to respond with advice, argument, intervention, or aggression, as the case requires. Their tendency to imitate the method used by agents of change may be modified, however, according to whether they like or dislike the innovators' proposal. If target persons welcome the plan and are not put off by the presenters' style, they are more likely to use a nonconstraining method toward the advocates and less likely to oppose or resist them. If they think that the proposal is a poor idea or are repelled by the behavior of the agents, they are more likely to use constraining methods and to offer opposition or resistance. These actions will be stronger, we may assume, as the issue is more important to the target persons. In sum, receivers more readily use permissive (nonconstraining) methods in their responses to change agents if the latter initially behave in those ways and if their proposals are acceptable. They more often use constraining methods if the initiators have used constraining forms and if their ideas are not acceptable. These conjectures, I believe, are worthy of further study.

In this chapter, we consider three broad topics: why target persons may be quite comfortable with a proposal proffered by reformers; why receivers oppose a proposed plan, and how they make their opposition known; and why target persons resist a presentation by initiators, and how they make their resistance strong, even damaging to the agents of change.

Welcoming the Ideas of Change Agents

Several conditions foster target persons' readiness to welcome the ideas of change agents. Among members of a community's established administrative agencies, as an illustration (setting aside for the moment a typical group of change agents), there usually exists an understanding that each organization has a definite job to do, and that the actions of one entity should not invade the legitimate domain of another. Those in a given body may assist persons in other units, cooperate in specific programs, and even make suggestions about how the work of another unit could be improved, but individuals in each of the agencies are careful not to do things that are the prerogatives of others. This interagency understanding exists, according to Warren, Rose, and Bergunder (1974), because each entity has an *organizational rationale*. Such a rationale describes what that organization has a right to do in that community. It denotes the purposes and programs of the body, the special competencies of the members, and the unique policies and principles followed by all who work in that body. Each of the separate agencies in a town knows the organizational rationales of the others.

Warren, Rose, and Bergunder (1974) studied the cross-group interactions among staff members of what they called *community decision organizations* operating within a number of towns, and they were impressed by the lack of rivalry or conflict among the professionals in these separate bodies. When those in one organization unintentionally invaded the turf of a neighbor, representatives from both bodies met to decide what to do about it. All members of these organizations clearly accepted as a given that the rationales of the organizations should not overlap or generate rivalry. Each body was to have its own niche in the community.

Warren and his co-workers developed these ideas while observing how established community agencies work side by side. The kind of body we have been calling a group for social action is seldom structured or enduring enough to be conceived as a formal decision-making body. It is possible, however, for target persons and change agents (as I have been describing them) to define rationales for their separate organizations, prescribing how each can function without invading the domains of the others. Those in each body—the agents of change and the target persons—can learn to recognize and respect their separate legitimate rights. It goes without saying that organizational rationales are more fully respected and obeyed if they are known and accepted by members on both sides. As illustrations of such rationales, members of a reformers' group could ask target persons to accept that the activists can properly request permission to present their ideas at a meeting (perhaps over several meetings), receive thoughtful consideration of their notions, and risk no retribution for raising these points. The targeted persons, for their part, may want the right to stick by the basic rules governing the operation of their body, to drop discussion of a proposal once they have decided on the matter, and to reject presentations by innovators if these are based on coercion or threats. Joint agreement on such rationales probably helps opposition and resistance on both sides.

Community governing agencies make many decisions that affect aspects of life in their town. Gotshalk (1966) believes that such administrative bodies give more thoughtful consideration to plans brought before them by would-be reformers if the administrators' primary aim is to foster the well-being of local citizens, rather than merely to manage the town's affairs, giving little heed to the consequences of their supervisory actions. Officers in a local government are more effective, in Gotshalk's view, if they help people carry through on their ideas for community improvement and if they stand ready to encourage and foster citizens' innovations. They help local people attain their aims in the arts, sciences, agriculture, industry, leisure, or commerce. They facilitate the establishment of programs and encourage ways of making them efficient. They work in addition to create groups that will plan and analyze what the community should have, so that citizens take the most important needs of the community into consideration (as well as their own desires) when thinking about changes that would improve the town. Useful officials do not try to manipulate matters to make their administration appear to be more successful than it actually is. They do not compete with citizens' action groups or impose their own wishes on the programs of those bodies. They make their influence felt, Gotshalk says, only when there is a need for particular services. These include control of crime, sanitation, floodwaters, highways, and the postal service. A government that sees itself as aiding townsfolk to be creative problem solvers is able to deal more constructively with proposals for change brought before it.

Target persons can foster in themselves a calmer consideration of the ideas offered by reformers if they are responsive toward those notions, even though the proposers may be assertive or aggressive (Levitt, 1973). A responsive person is one who listens to what is being said and gives those ideas a reasonable amount of thought. Levitt (1973, p. 6) raises a value-loaded question in discussing the need for responsiveness among target persons: "How can we prevent the reformist forces which are seeking so urgently to produce a more responsive society from ruining that society in the process with their powerful tools of advocacy—the tools of marches, sit-ins, and organized accusation and vilification; their endless stream of diabolistic fault-finding in every nook and cranny of our complex

world—tools whose powers are massively multiplied by the calcu-
lated exploitation of the mass media, particularly television?" He
also asks how persons who are treated in the ways just described can
keep themselves from showing similar behavior when they respond.

Levitt thinks that excessive hostility can be prevented among
advocates if target persons meet with these agents of change, show
sympathy and understanding toward their grievances, reveal good
will while discussing their problems, and, demonstrate that they are
prepared to devote money and effort, if necessary, to improving
things. The decision makers also try to comprehend the issues at
hand, keep in mind that few questions are one-sided, and take for
granted that persons in both parties legitimately can have their own
points of view. They are under no obligation to give in, but they are
obliged to act toward innovators in a way that is "a sensitive and
constructive acknowledgment of their [the change agents'] claims,
at least to the extent of talking about them" (Levitt, 1973, p. 63). All
in all, as Levitt sees it, members of effective decision-making organizations do not let their sensitivity to the style of social pressure
interfere with the possibility that they are being offered ideas worthy
of consideration, even when these are presented in a hostile manner.

Levitt's admonition about the value of responsiveness among
members of the audience is probably correct much of the time, but
one wonders if persons enduring abrasive acts will listen with much
sympathy if they have enough power to stop such confrontations
and avoid having to sit through the full treatment. Will they be
responsive, moreover, if the reformers make it clear that they will
not tolerate a compromise, or that mere refusal will not slow them
down? Alinsky (1971) thinks that target persons who are treated
abrasively will eventually have to insist on responsiveness among
persons on both sides. He taught members of urban neighborhood
councils to be unremittingly angry toward city officials, until the
latter stopped stalling, said they had had enough, and were willing
to bargain (Alinsky, 1971; Lancourt, 1979). Will powerful persons
be responsive to aggressive agents of change if they are not forced to
be? That is a researchable issue.

The importance of such a question is enhanced when we
remind ourselves that the kinds of target persons who will be most
readily responsive are those who have less social power than the

agents of change. Examples of target persons with little social power are community groups being pressured by officials from the state government to allow oil drilling in their city park, parents being told by the board of education that their children's school is being closed and that students will now be transported to a building in another part of town, and citizens who are informed by city hall that current controls on rental rates are being removed. Citizens and parents may protest such powerfully backed plans, but they will be lucky (and weary) if they manage to reverse the ideas of change agents who have enough social power to let criticisms roll off their backs.

Targeted persons probably can deal with activists more con-structively if they recognize that the reformers' goals and their own are similar in many respects. Persons in both parties can then see that actions directed toward their common goals provide gains for all; one group does not benefit more than the other. Because of such compatibility between objectives, the listeners usually are willing to hear the innovators' story, and the latter, for the same reasons, are ready to foster cooperative efforts with the target persons. Both the innovators and those under pressure come to realize that they have comparable beliefs about the need for change, and so they help one another accomplish what should be done, communicate facts and feelings freely, display trusting and friendly interpersonal behavior, realistically recognize what interests are common or irrelevant, and try mutually to influence and be influenced.

Such forms of interaction not only result from a cooperative relationship but also help a cooperative relationship develop and prosper (Deutsch, 1973). Cooperative behavior begets cooperative behavior. What is more interesting, according to Deutsch, is that members in a cooperative relationship become helpful to one another once they have recognized the similarity of their goals. First, cooperating participants see that the issue under discussion is a legitimate one; that it is appropriate to bring up the grievance, opportunity, or desired change; and that it is a matter worthy of attention. Second, discussants accept that it is fair for participants to back their own points of view, that people properly may disagree, and that these differences are not based on malice or greed. Third, those present accept that each conferee is motivated to find a sound solution to the problem at hand, and no one selfishly intends to block attainment of the best answer. Deutsch writes that the most effective way to reduce tension between two groups (where cooperation has been displaced by rivalry) is to induce those in the competing parties to engage in constructive problem solving.

A similar procedure, it seems reasonable to suppose, can facilitate wise give-and-take when activists come before target persons to convince them that a particular change is needed. Pruitt and Rubin (1986) believe that one of three effects results from a joint problem-solving session. One possibility is a compromise. This is an agreement in which each set of participants concedes ground on a relevant matter, in order that all may reach a middle position; each wins a bit and gives up a little. A compromise is more likely to occur if the aims on both sides are only moderately important, time is running short and a reasonable solution is needed, the participants believe that a fifty-fifty division is fair, and the chosen compromise will cause no harm to bystanders. A second effect of joint problem solving is an agreement on the rules to be followed in making the decision. Examples of a decision rule are flipping a coin, deciding in favor of the party that will benefit most, doing what the majority says it wants, requiring unanimity among participants, or giving an executive committee the right to settle the matter as it sees fit. As a third possibility, discussants reach a mutually beneficial solution, one that profits both sides to a reasonable degree, although neither gets all it was hoping for. This solution is called the *preferred outcome* because it may be impossible to agree on any answer at all, unless one is found that is satisfactory to most.

Target persons can ensure that they sensibly handle a request for change by appealing to a third party who has no vested interest in the issue at hand. They request the help of an ombudsman, who has the right to look up information in records not available to everyone else. They turn to a mediator, who helps the principals reach an acceptable solution. They depend on an arbitrator, who likewise helps the discussants but follows precise rules and makes the final decision, binding both sides to obey it. Finally, they may take their case to a court of law and abide by the ruling handed down there.

In summary, target persons are less likely to display opposition or resistance toward agents of change if they think the request for change is wise, if the proposers behave in a way that does not threaten anyone, if persons on each side accept that all participants have a legitimate rationale for their beliefs, if the target persons assume that their proper role is to serve as helpers or facilitators for agents of change (instead of merely being managers of a fixed program), if the listeners are responsive to the actions or views of the activists, if they foster joint cooperative relations, if they engage in problem solving, and if they turn to a third party, as necessary. It is plain that target persons can increase the chances that the views of change agents will be given sober consideration or even approval, but target persons need to take careful steps in the matter; a constructive solution will not just happen.

Limiting the Effectiveness of Influence Attempts

Officials who are pressed by advocates to initiate a change can oppose that proposal for any of a number of reasons. They may think that it is a bad idea, is contrary to their own experience, or will not work. They may believe that the new plan defies logic or good sense. They may feel that there is no reason for changing things, since all is going well and complaints about the current state of affairs are not valid. They may decide that the change will be too difficult or too costly to implement. They may be offended by the innovation because it is unethical, immoral, illegal, or plainly dumb or breaks with long-standing tradition. They may reason that the intended effects of the proposed innovation are uncertain, will create a bad precedent, or can do good for a few people but harm to a greater number. They may view the protesters as troublemakers who have no support in the larger community and who are "interfering with orderly, lawful, and efficient processes of government. . . . By what right [target persons may ask] . . . does this self-interested minority burden and delay the conduct of public business for which society, in its wisdom, has made them, and not the protesters, responsible?" (Caldwell, Hayes, and MacWhirter, 1976, p. xiv).

When decision makers have a plan brought before them that they absolutely cannot accept, they must make their reasons for opposing it clear and convincing. They must refuse in a way that persuades the activists to take no for an answer. This is not always easy to do, since they often have to state their arguments against the initiators' plan in face-to-face meetings, without prior preparation, and while an audience is watching. Their first move, I have observed, is often to try to get more time to consider the matter. Accordingly, they set up a task force to look into the plan, refer the idea to a standing committee, call for a fuller hearing at a later date, or in some other way make it possible to attend to the idea under calmer conditions. Their intent is to make it possible to deny the pressure placed on them, if necessary, without allowing an intergroup conflict to develop that itself would have to be resolved. It is not uncommon, in contrast, for malicious members among the target persons to take delight in asking for definitions of all kinds of terms that change agents have used in their proposal and then to demonstrate that these are inadequate or make no sense. An expert in Socratic questioning can make agents of change sorry that they have appeared in public with their ideas.

Target persons may also propose that those on each side of a delicate discussion agree to be objective, thoughtful, and fair, and to avoid ad hominem remarks. They mention the values of the proposition put before them. They state their reasons for opposing the plan but do not say that it offends them, even if that is the case. They encourage the initiators to respond to their comments against the idea, and they attend to those responses. Points on which there is mutual agreement are identified and set aside as no longer in need of discussion.

Target persons describe the limits on their freedom to change things—laws, the charter of their organization, their basic purpose, or the bounds that another body has placed on them. They also indicate what kinds of matters they can or cannot modify without the approval of others. These latter things must be said early because reformers often appeal to the wrong body when seeking support for a change they want made. (Students usually blame the regents of their university for actions by a teaching department, actions that the regents know nothing about.) Target persons also make sure that the activists fully understand the reasons for their final decision. They invite change agents to listen to and observe all discussion of the matter. They make all minutes of their meetings available, and they open relevant files of correspondence, reports, and data to the innovators. If necessary, they appeal to a larger constituency, to get those persons' opinions on the matter into the record.

If they finally decide to reject the plan, they try to explain the reasons for their refusal in a way that generates minimal resistance among the change agents. They do this because they sense that resistant acts too often displace rational ones. Lancourt (1979) describes a number of other things that officials can do to keep things calm, none of which is a full-fledged response to the proposal. One is to offer a reward that has symbolic value to the activists but does not imply agreement with the proposal, such as asking them to become an advisory committee for the target persons. Another is to agree to do a few of the things requested by reformers, but only those that are easy and inexpensive (token acquiescence). An additional move is to respond favorably to matters that clearly are crises and properly should have attention, allowing the rest to go by the board. Still another method is to make the demands of the advocates appear unreasonable, in light of facts to the contrary. Finally, target persons may postpone any decision, on the grounds of pressure from regular duties or a need to find more data on the issue at hand.

Effectively Resisting Proposals

Resistance, as we saw earlier, is an unfavorable emotional response among target persons to the style used by reformers in presenting their ideas. This response is based on fear, anxiety, anger, envy, or greed aroused by the activists' actions. When target persons resist, they defend themselves from the innovators and at the same time use methods that constrain the freedom of the change agents. Toward this end, they may appeal for help from bystanders (lawyers, police, thugs) and may even try to weaken or destroy the change group.

Target persons may resist proposals for one or more reasons. They decide that the persons pushing a particular plan want primarily to benefit themselves or to deprive others (including, perhaps, the ones to whom the plan is submitted). The decision makers do not trust the validity of the information used by the innovators to

support their case and believe these data are deliberately or acciden-
tally based on misinformation. They perceive that the proposal
offers a solution but does not indicate which problem is supposed to
be solved. They see the reformers as abrasive, discourteous, uncivil,
hostile, and loud.

When target persons are faced with unpleasant behavior,
their impulse is to counter these actions with similar ones of their
own. Emotions will usually increase on both sides as the obnoxious
coercers, upon receiving a dose of their own medicine, feel impelled
to return more and better of the same. Such mutual attacks seldom
develop into full-fledged conflict, however, if sensible heads recognize that calmer forms of interaction are needed and that otherwise
hostility will continue to grow and waste everyone's time. Leaders
among the target persons point out that it is unwise and unbecom-
ing for discussants to be caught in a cycle of coercive reactions, as
they now are, and that it would be better to develop rational efforts
among all participants. Before they can facilitate a more thoughtful
demeanor, however, the target persons must curb their own feelings.
They can do so by facing the mindless nature of their behavior and
figuring out why it occurs. They try to understand why a need to
win is dominating their actions. They identify what the reformers
do that arouses resistance, and they describe these acts to the agents
of change. The explainers also urge the agents of change to make a
similar diagnosis of their own feelings, to ask themselves what the
target persons do that arouses resistance and to point these things
out. Ideally, after such two-sided evidence is assembled, all participants will discuss what they must do to create a mode of constructive problem solving and to minimize defensiveness among
themselves. The kinds of moves they may try in such a situation
have been described in the writings of Cordes (1986), Deutsch (1973),
Pruitt and Rubin (1986), and Zander (1982). Some such suggestions
were noted in Chapter Nine, in the discussion of how change agents
plan to minimize resistance among those they hope to influence. It
will be useful to review these actions—this time, however, from the
standpoint of the target persons.

One way that decision makers can forestall two-way resistance is to foster standards of intergroup behavior that forbid the use
of contentious tactics. They can prepare a code of courtesy, which

prescribes proper actions for participants if discussion becomes too heated. These norms are put in writing, and everyone pledges to follow them. The rules cover such matters as listening attentively to comments by individuals on the other side, using the others' ideas in one's own responses, avoiding personal remarks, and giving logical reasons for opposing others' assertions, instead of rejecting their ideas out of hand. To prevent two-sided resistance, all must understand its damaging consequences and how difficult it is to stop its spiraling excitement once it begins. A further way to prevent bad interpersonal relations is to recall any strong social bonds developed among discussants in other settings and to assert that the same connections can be developed here. Long-standing friendships, common memberships, or similarities in background can be reviewed, to remind the discussants about how much everyone can depend on the others for support.

Target persons can do several things to urge that participants on both sides become constructive problem solvers. First, they declare that they intend to keep the tone of discussion turned away from rivalry, pressuring, or efforts to outdo others and toward a cooperative approach that will improve the chances of a mutually beneficial outcome. They explain that they support such intentions, not because they feel weak, but because they believe it is the wisest procedure to follow and will facilitate constructive conferring. They make it clear that they are more willing to change their goals than their basic values or principles. In addition, they state that cooperative efforts to solve the joint problem will lead to solutions that all can appreciate. They point out that a useful solution will be more likely if the discussants consider many alternatives than if they consider only a few. They describe what values they see in the ideas that agents of change are proposing, and they emphasize that they themselves have had questions about the problems now under discussion. Statements like these indicate that the target persons are prepared to talk openly and are willing to make concessions, if and when they are convinced that a better way is available.

It helps, moreover, to acknowlege that sweetness and light will not always prevail during a discussion because some persons will wish to emphasize certain points, and their heavy-handed comments can generate more heat than understanding. These flare-ups will not be frequent or enduring and will be noted and regretted when they appear. Meanwhile, successes (useful points of progress in the discussion) are to be identified and applauded when they are reached.

Sometimes no one suggests that participants try to calm things down. Instead, target persons take unilateral steps simply to suppress the moves of the activists. At the outset, they may avoid contact with the agents of change, allow the reformers only a brief time for a presentation, make no coherent response to their ideas, assign their proposition to a subcommittee (which takes its time deciding what to recommend), or postpone consideration of the proposal. Some assertive forms of action against troublesome reformers require more coercion and less concern about adherence to due process than leaders in most American communities wish to display, except under much duress. Nevertheless, the use of aggressive social control by administrators is not uncommon, either in history or today. Nisbet (1953) gives numerous examples of deliberate efforts by government leaders to restrict social activists in certain times and to encourage their efforts in other periods.

The ultimate effort of target persons against a threatening organization is to reduce that group's power to influence anyone. The things they do toward that end are already familiar to us. Early on, they may try to prevent the group from even getting under way or from continuing in operation if it manages to get started. They solicit help from lawmakers and police in implementing curfews against the activists, antisubversion laws, regulations to restrict the nature of bargaining, tighter rules on demonstrating, prohibitions against parades, taxes on unwelcome activities, evictions from public places, restrictions against disturbing the peace, and narrow rules for gatherings in parks. They justify requests for such measures by contending that the change agents are a threat to law and order and that the community must defend itself against potential disorganization, or they argue that the change agents are putting forth ideas and plans that are seductive to the young and weak in the community and that such views must be suppressed (Toch, 1965). Wise politicians can often short-circuit the demands of change agents—for example, by coming forth with a building program (an emphasis on "change" of their own) or a festival that fosters pride in the city. Once these moves are under way, the leaders assert that the activists are enemies of the people, as well as complainers and cynics who try to tear down citizens' love of their community. These are old tricks to disparage unwanted rivals.

Decision makers may not need to act at all if a program proposed by change agents is effectively blocked by others. Hornblower (1988) reports protests by citizens' groups that objected to new and unusual developments in their neighborhoods—a foster home for infants, a drop-in center for the emotionally disturbed, lodging for the homeless, a hospice for persons ill with AIDS, and a hazardous-waste incinerator. The objectors held that such activities were good things and that they approved of them, but they said, "Not in my backyard!" These forms of antisocial activism occur more often today because more persons need social services, Hornblower says; thus, there is a greater need to provide these in residential parts of towns.

Crowfoot, Chesler, and Boulet (1983) believe that decision makers can aim direct attacks at an unpopular group (of change agents, for example) by undermining the cohesiveness of such a body or the support that the community provides it. As an illustration, target persons under pressure from change agents may work to divert the loyalty of the participants in the agents' group. The target persons then try to convince the participants that they are being duped or misled by their self-seeking leaders, or that the group's programs are not appreciated by local citizens and will not succeed. The attackers then tell the participants that they will be better off in a different entity and push them toward this other organization. Another way to weaken a group of activists is to provide no response at all to their proposals. As a result, the activists perceive that their ideas are having no effect, and they give up. Still another approach is to weaken or remove the leaders of the social action by having them arrested, kidnaped, or overthrown by persons whose ideas are acceptable to the attackers. Officials who are being badgered by change agents may also seek support from citizens, asking them to express their opposition in public or to form a body that will present a contrasting point of view. Such an approach gives the agents of change several sets of opponents with which to contend.

Target persons also may attempt to persuade community

members that the upstarts have no sensible message. Toward this end, they give the activists labels that make them unacceptable— illegal aliens, hoodlums, naive dreamers, sexual deviants, Communists, self-serving socialists, or deceivers—or they may spread unfavorable information about the leaders of the activist group, whether these are facts or half-truths. A different line of attack is for target persons to withhold or block resources that the unit needs to operate. The target persons evict the innovators from space they are occupying, have their funds cut off, deny means to recruit new members, allow no publicity for their new ideas, or prevent them from demonstrating or parading. The target persons sabotage the products of the change agents by deriding, damaging, or destroying these.

Even more direct forms of action may be needed against activists who employ coercive methods. One is to disparage the abrasive ways of the change agents by publicly declaring that their procedures are unfair. The weight of this accusation can be enhanced with suggestions that the change agents use more acceptable manners. Another tactic is to foster conflict within the group of reformers by giving support to a dissident set among them. Still another is to try to reduce the members' motivation and perceived probability of success by telling them that no one wants to hear their message.

If change agents deliberately generate fear among target persons, it is difficult for the frightened individuals to control the activists without help from experts trained in methods of dealing with extreme aggression, or terrorism. A number of writers have described ways of meeting harmful hostility. Hyams (1975), for instance, says that terrorists can be overcome only by counterterrorism. Reactive violence is seldom effective, however, if the aggressive groups are small units that quickly hit, hurt, and hide, because such squads are hard to find, infiltrate, arrest, or convict. Eliminate one such team, moreover, and another takes its place. Netanyahu (1987) holds that the only remedies for attacks that are intended to provoke fear are refusal to yield to demands and deployment of overpowering force toward those who start the violence. Because of the secrecy surrounding the planning and performance of such acts, countermoves are more likely to succeed if they are based on inside information. Informers are hard to recruit, however, from within a fanatical hostile organization, and it is difficult to infiltrate such a small, aggressive body. Modern methods used by police in detecting crime and countering gang-related illegal activities (including drug sales) suggest procedures that could be useful in responding to hostile and impatient demands for social change. Pfaff (1986), for instance, says that aggressive hostility can be overcome only by infinitely patient police work. Such efforts should include careful and slow negotiation with cornered violent persons (such as kidnapers or hostage takers), who are promised everything they request but not given any of these things, and who are alternately cheered and depressed during continual conversations, until they become too tired and disoriented to think straight or persist (Flinn, 1988).

The kinds of actions we have been noting have been called forms of deterrence by students of intergroup and internation hostility. Lebow and Stein (1987, p. 6) define *deterrence* as "an attempt to influence another actor's assessment of its own interests. It seeks to prevent undesired behavior by convincing the party who may be contemplating such action that its cost will exceed its possible gain." The three assumptions behind deterrence, according to these authors, are that people make decisions in response to a cost-benefit calculus; that initiators of social action can influence this calculus; and that the best way to have this kind of influence is to increase the cost side of the ledger, to prevent people from taking action because of the consequences (pain, expense, fatigue, jail, ridicule) of being caught. The authors caution, however, that many people may not be deterred by high costs; if they want something badly enough, they may move aggressively to get it, even though the costs of doing so are high (they reason that they may not have to pay these). Deterrence may even provoke people into acting immediately, before it is too late. Deterrence can work, these writers believe, if the deterrers precisely define what behavior they wish to forestall, tell the aggressors they will be punished if they engage in such acts, deny them the goals they want to reach, and make it clear to the aggressors that punishment will be forthcoming. Deterrence works best if the persons who are to be turned away from aggression are motivated by the prospect of gaining something, rather than by the fear of losing something, and if they are able to restrain themselves, are not misled by distorted ideas about what the deterrers can or cannot do to them, and are ready to stop their hostile acts when they see that counter-aggressive threats from the deterring persons will be backed up with action. It is best if attempts at deterrence are made early, before the agents of change have had a chance to act, become committed to their efforts, and end up too busy to pay attention to demands that they stop.

When both opposition and resistance develop among target persons, which has the greater impact on their behavior? Target persons who oppose the content of the ideas offered by innovators tend to do so on rational grounds. In arguing against a proposal for change, they employ facts and logic to explain their stance and discuss these matters openly with the activists. Their opposition becomes less objective, however, if they also react emotionally to the latters' style of behavior. The emotion in resistance reduces the rationality in opposition; thus, resistance serves as the more powerful determinant of target persons' behavior. It seems likely, moreover, that target persons will resist more than oppose if change agents use constraining methods. They will also resist more if the change agents intend to serve their own desires, regardless of the effect their behavior will have on others. Thus, when officials are pressed by a selfish group that uses coercive methods, they are more likely to resist than to oppose and more likely to be emotional than rational as they respond. These views should be given more study in community life.

In some cases, opposition by target persons causes activists to perform poorly and to spoil their own efforts. For instance, Douglas and Wildavsky (1982) observed small squads of activists who were pressing industrial organizations to protect the environment. These authors were struck by the pessimism of the participants in these bodies. The members tended to give up after having their proposals rejected one or more times, and then they spent more effort deploring and complaining about the evil state of affairs they had wished to transform than they spent developing a program for influencing decision makers. Utopias that are ignored by nonmembers, despite the desire of the utopians to change the economic basis of society, seldom last long; the participants quarrel among themselves about strategy and tactics, according to Hine (1953). Lipset and Raab

(1970) aver that reactionary, rightist reform bodies that are engaging in what these authors call "the politics of unreason" eventually decline, since a group created to support bigotry or narrow and selfish aims usually has incompetent leaders who do not supervise the organization well and sooner or later are caught in dishonest acts. When target persons consistently refuse to accept the proposals made by agents of change, the latter probably see those refusals as increasing the difficulty of their goal. A tougher objective is more attractive, as we have noted, but it is also less likely to be reached; thus, it leads to discouragement or to willingness to drop the issue (Zander, 1971, 1985).

Suppose that target persons accept the proposal made by reformers and do their best to implement the change. There is reason to expect that the transformations they put in place often will not work out as intended; things go wrong. Sieber (1981) has collected examples in which the implementation of a social innovation turned out to be a "fatal remedy," meaning that it was of no help at all or that it caused more harm than good. Hirschman (1989) has demonstrated that such perverse consequences have appeared throughout history. They are often cited by opponents of progressive moves as arguments against the reforms ("They will only make things worse!"). There are many examples of social interventions that have had these outcomes. An increase in the benefits paid to subscribers of old-age security insurance made the elderly beneficiaries ineligible for Medicaid, and so they ended up with less money than they had been getting. More generous payments to local welfare clients attracted hundreds of unemployed outsiders to a certain community, and so there was not enough money to cover the costs of welfare for everyone. New "magnet" schools, built to provide special instruction for less competent students, reduced the funds available to other schools, and because the teaching was better in the magnet schools, they lured the bright youths, and there was not enough room for the less able. A group of community colleges, originally created to reduce the number of students enrolled in the first two years at state universities, have sent only a few of their graduates on to universities; 95 percent have stayed at home and gone to work. A city council that passed a law to improve recreational facilities failed to provide funds for the improvement because council members felt that this "service" was really a boondoggle. Police charged with finding instances of environmental damage caused by local industry were so busy citing small companies that the big ones got no policing and did more polluting than ever.

Synonyms for what Sieber (1981) calls a "fatal remedy" are *counterproductivity, negative result, backlash, boomerang effect, perverse incentive, two-edged sword,* and *going to sea in a sieve.* Actions to introduce social change, labeled *social interventions* by Sieber, are defined as "any sort of deliberate effort to alter a human situation in some desired direction, such as a modification of a program for social welfare, a military expedition, an organizational structure, or a law" (Sieber, 1981, p. 9). These may be efforts to do good, to dissent, or even to disrupt. Sieber uses the term *regressive* to mean that the intervention "rendered the original end in view less attainable, or . . . caused a deterioration in the conditions it was supposed to alleviate" (p. 9). He is concerned with interventions that turn target persons away from the original goal, but he is not merely interested in unfavorable side effects (meaning unpleasant consequences that occur along with good ones). He believes that reversals of social innovation occur when new laws or social interventions interfere with natural processes, such as the law of supply and demand.

Sieber discusses seven kinds of reverse effects caused by awkward interventions:

1. *Functional disruption:* some useful function of the community is damaged because an "improvement" to it causes it to be overloaded, unbalanced, or modified too severely.
2. *Exploitation of the intervention:* a change is used in a way that subverts or reverses its intended outcome.
3. *Goal displacement:* means or instrumental values are taken to be ends.
4. *Provocation:* an attitude, desire, or passion is aroused that leads to a reversal of results from those initially intended.
5. *Classification:* persons are derogated, required to defer to rules, or unfairly exempted from certain services as a result of a classification scheme based on age, citizenship, ethnic origin, educa-

tion, income, health, or religion, or persons are granted degrees of deference that they do not deserve.

6. *Overcommitment:* resources are inadequate, or expectations are higher than is reasonable, and thus sufficient changes do not occur.

7. *Placation:* persons are appeased by those who want support for new activities; the placation leads to exasperation and to rejection of the changes that are offered.

The main point is that mechanisms like these may generate regressive effects that weaken or destroy the value of new practices introduced by agents of change. Wise target persons examine the potential side effects of a given change and make sure that these will not damage or destroy the consequences they hope for.

In sum, if target persons feel forced to make changes that they know they will regret, their best defense may be to wait for the reformers to run out of steam or for the proposal to develop undesirable side effects. They then can expect to get support from citizens in their efforts to get rid of the plan that is causing consequences other than those they want.

Summary

Persons put under pressure to initiate specific changes may accept these proposals, oppose the substance of the plans, or resist (react unfavorably to) the style that agents of change employ in presenting the new ideas. Target persons' behavior in response to actions by initiators is flavored by a fear of making an unwise decision and suffering embarrassing consequences.

Certain conditions apparently make target persons more willing to accept a new idea, or to be less likely to oppose or resist it. These conditions are agreements among members on both sides that each has its own unique organizational rationale, eagerness of target persons to facilitate proposals made by innovators, willingness of target persons to be responsive toward the acts of reformers, readiness of persons on both sides to recognize similarity in goals, and skill in using constructive problem solving.

Target persons may have many reasons for opposing an idea

put before them. These include their perception that it is unworkable, not sensible, not needed, too difficult, too costly, unethical, conducive to a bad precedent, unfair to others, and not in the public's interest. To make their refusal acceptable to reformers, target persons may state clearly the reasons for their opposition, encourage activists to comment on this explanation, decline to discuss items on which both sides agree, suggest that all participants keep calm, describe matters that the targeted group is not free to change, win the concurrence of bystanders, and try to prevent the flowering of situations that generate resistant reactions among those on both sides.

Target persons react negatively to the style used by innovators when they believe that the activists intend primarily to benefit themselves, use misinformation to bolster their cause, and behave in abrasive and uncivil ways. If the group being put under pressure is an established administrative agency, its members tend to be less flexible and more resistant to change. Their resistant reactions, moreover, generate more of the behavior among reformers that initially stimulated the resistance. A cycle of escalating hostility begins.

The target persons may recognize that a heated interchange is accomplishing little and attempt to convince initiators that they ought to cease their provocative behavior. If that effort fails, they try to diminish the effectiveness of the change agents' unit by limiting the reformers' freedom to associate or demonstrate, preventing their influence attempts, destroying members' loyalty to their group, disparaging the group's goals and methods, demonstrating to members that their efforts are a failure, or fostering rival organizations that develop their own plans for change. In general, I suspect, resistance determines the behavior of target persons more than opposition does.

In the long run, target persons who are not in favor of the ideas proposed by reformers can be assured that the latter will be pessimistic about their chances of reaching their objective, fail more often than they succeed, give up, or generate consequences that are exactly the opposite of what they intend. Target persons under unwanted pressure may be wise to stall, bide their time, and wait for the agents of change to lose heart.

11

Organizing, Managing, and Studying Action Groups

We have examined a number of concepts concerning community social action by groups of ordinary citizens. In this chapter, I summarize the central ideas from previous chapters in a way that emphasizes their utility. These comments are addressed to two separate audiences: first, to organizers, leaders, or consultants of groups for community improvement, all of whom I will call *managers;* second, to students of group behavior or social action, whom I designate as *scholars.* For the managers, I consider how social action groups are developed, nurtured, and directed. For the scholars, I offer a review of topics worthy of investigation.

Managing Groups for Social Action

Starting an Action Group. A person who sets out to improve a situation in a community through group action takes preliminary steps toward that end by finding a few neighbors who feel as he or she does about that matter. Participants in this small set define the circumstances under question and consider whether to take some kind of action. Although they may be dissatisfied with the issue at hand, they probably will not move on it unless they believe that they or others are more deprived than they deserve to be.

If planners decide that they ought to do what they can to modify the situation, they still will not try to form a larger unit unless they can identify things that a group could do to improve matters. Moreover, these ideas for action must suit the abilities, resources, and values of persons who would join such a body. Before they will join, potential recruits want to know what the chances are that the entity will be successful. Ordinarily, they will be more attracted to the group if they perceive that there is a good probability of its success.

If the initial subset decides to develop a group, it looks for persons who can be helpful to the body being planned. For instance, the organizers choose persons who are disposed to take an active part in such a unit, feel strongly that things should be improved, have talents that will be useful, accept the group's purpose, and can withstand the embarrassment that may arise if they meet opposition or resistance among officials or neighbors.

Choosing Group Objectives. Compared to groups in business, education, health, or government, groups engaged in community action are likely to have clearer objectives. This is because the goal that brings a social action group together is often a good group goal in itself. The unit's objective comes up for discussion early, since the newness of the group causes its members to think about such matters. They choose a goal that offers the best likelihood of satisfaction for members or significant others, one that target persons may also wish to see achieved.

It can happen that members do not choose an objective at the outset because they prefer to do whatever appeals to them most, regardless of the consequences of that action. They want to vent their anger, get revenge, win attention for their cause, or see what will happen if they simply try to address target persons. Sometimes they may have difficulty selecting an objective because members do not know enough about themselves, the situation, the methods they could use to bring about change, or the views of target persons. Therefore, they choose to make some move, any move, because esprit de corps will come alive in the group during this action, and the experience will help members find an objective for the unit. In such a case, they ordinarily take up a task that they believe they can perform, such as getting the traffic commission to place a stop sign on a busy corner. A wise developer helps members set goals that provide a challenge that is neither too easy nor too hard.

Arousing Enthusiasm. Individuals who take part in a change group are notorious for the zeal they invest in their activities, and managers foster such enthusiasm. The leaders learn what motives recruits bring with them (such as yearnings for higher status, approval, power, security, or pride), and they choose purposes and procedures that may satisfy these hopes. Often, group managers induce colleagues to develop wishes that they previously have not had. The members may be led, for example, to worry about fluorine in the water, the arrival of new immigrants in their town, or the lack of funds for the local golf course. They may be shown the value of having new sewers in the neighborhood, the best high school hockey team around, or a local playground. They may be stimulated to fight against the creation of community gardens next door or to seek relief from too much automobile traffic moving through the neighborhood. All of these are self-oriented wishes in the sense that members of the change group will want to accomplish these ends for their own personal benefit, paying little attention to the potential effects of their efforts on fellow group members or on others in the community. In contrast, managers and members may be most interested in creating satisfaction for persons outside their organization (homeless, sick, or deprived persons). In fulfilling desires like these, participants can also gratify personal motives, but their main urge is to bring about benefits that are not directed inward. An organizer of a group concerned with initiating change tries to have participants pleased with being part of this body. To do this, he or she creates an attractive incentive for members. An *incentive* is a state or outcome that provides satisfaction when it is attained. A group's purpose is an incentive (or should be) for all members.

A supervisor of a group increases the value of its goal by assuring members that they will be able to attain that incentive and will be satisfied when they do this. The manager increases members' total motivation by enhancing each of three factors: the strength of the motive or desire, the value of the group's incentive for the participants, and the perceived probability of success in attaining that objective. The three factors are multiplicative; each one strengthens (or weakens) the effect of the others.

Choosing a Method. In this kind of group, the biggest decision that managers and members make concerns the method they will employ in attempting to exercise influence. They assume that they cannot introduce an innovation entirely on their own because some group of decision makers (a council, committee, commission, company, corporation, or board) is responsible for the practices currently being followed. The advocates have to convince those officials or their constituents to introduce a change. These decision makers (or their supporters) are the *targets* of efforts by change agents to bring about an innovation. Activists have different approaches available to them in trying to influence the target persons. The method that reformers choose to use should be the one they believe will best convince target persons. It should suit members' talents, should not violate their values about right or wrong behavior, and should be satisfying in itself to carry out.

Nonconstraining Methods. Responsible agents of change may use permissive methods, ones in which they tell target persons that a given situation deserves to be changed and then let the listeners decide what, if anything, should be done toward that end. In this instance, the initiators exert no direct pressure over the decisions or motives of the target persons. Examples of nonconstraining methods include acting as a model, providing information about what other communities have done, informing townsfolk about the condition that warrants transformation, giving advice to officials when asked for it, and negotiating toward a common point of view about the issue. Managers of reform groups will prefer permissive methods like these if they believe that the target persons would resent being put under pressure, that the target persons know best what changes ought to be made, and that target persons would rather work for pride in their own achievement than to win applause, approval, and rewards or avoid a penalty from change agents and townsfolk.

Constraining Methods. Managers of a social change group may urge members to employ pressuring methods against target persons if they believe that the latter are deeply attached to the current state of affairs and will not adopt a change plan unless they can benefit (or not lose) from doing so, or if the persons seeking improvements believe that there is only one right way to fix things. Activists who hold such views put pressure on receivers by offering them a reward to behave as requested (the reward is the incentive for making a change), persuading them that their current activities are unwise, spreading distorted or unfair propaganda about the target persons, bargaining strongly with them, presenting ideas in a way that deliberately creates conflict, threatening to harm target persons or others, actually harming target persons or their surrogates, making it difficult or impossible for target persons to operate their organization, or describing penalties that target persons will receive unless they do what they are pressed to do or stop doing what they are doing.

Agents of change are more likely to threaten target persons with harm if they decide to polarize the issue ("us against them"), in order to be sure that officials will seriously consider it. They also may wish to demonstrate their courage, fearlessness, and strong feelings. They are willing to employ the strategies and tactics that these methods require and to develop the discipline and strict rules that are needed when reformers set out to force a change. They have the necessary resources for seizing hostages, such as money, skill, and equipment, and are trained in hiding, bribing, behaving ruthlessly, bargaining, and withstanding attacks made on them. They are prepared to deal with hostile or fearful reactions among target persons or bystanders, and they plan primarily to charge through any resistance, until they get their way or until target persons are willing to bargain in good faith. Furthermore, they are prepared to monitor any postagreement behavior of decision-making officials, to be sure that the innovation is actually established and maintained. The activists are willing to conduct such surveillance by spying on target persons' activities, bribing insiders for information and requiring them to make periodic reports, getting appropriate laws passed so that police can enforce the rules, or hiring private detectives. Clearly, a change pressed on target persons tends to generate prickly relations among agents of change and the pressured ones. The fact is, however, that activists often do not care whether poor interpersonal conditions arise; they want to have their way, even if they lose friends among those they wish to influence.

Collaborative Methods. Instead of employing permissive or pressuring methods, the managers of an action group may refer to use procedures that emphasize thoughtful interaction and allow participants on both sides to collaborate in the creation of a joint plan. An example is the process of problem solving, wherein the point at issue is treated as a dilemma, alternative solutions are listed, and the best among these is chosen. Ideally, agents of change and target persons participate equally, and the final decision is one that satisfies all conferees. Discussants may also decide to bargain over a course of action while adhering to rules that prevent persons on either side from gaining more than they deserve. They may wish to negotiate, which means that they compare ideas, feelings, and facts until they have a common point of view about the issue, without trying to find a solution for it. Finally, they may sense that none of these approaches will work and that it would be best to get a third party involved (a mediator, arbitrator, umpire, or judge). In all collaborative methods, the emphasis is on the objectivity and rationality that each participant is to employ toward goals that everyone values.

Even though innovators may prefer to use collaborative methods, it is not always easy to do so. For one thing, reformers may have little influence over target persons at the outset. Thus, if agents of change ask decision makers to enter into a problem-solving process, their request may be refused because the target persons are not allowed, on legal grounds, to let others have a part in decision making, do not feel that the issue warrants time-consuming treatment, or do not need the views of the change agents. The same kinds of barriers may arise if the reformers seek to negotiate. Activists may then pressure target persons either to bargain or to negotiate, using coercive and abrasive behavior (threats or acts of harm), until those put under this pressure agree to talk. Activists may take their complaint to court instead, provided that the issue is legitimate and that the plaintiffs have standing in the eyes of the judge. A court hearing is expensive and slow, however. Lawyers and witnesses must be paid, and the process is useful only if the matter is not urgent.

Reformers try to persuade target persons that it would be best if the issue were treated as a problem worthy of attention. They assert that they have a right as citizens to bring the issue before the decision makers, as well as to have a say in its solution, because they have to live with whatever decision is made. Any conclusion may be sounder if it is based on views from all sides. Agents of change may demonstrate that they prefer to work in rational ways and to avoid actions that cause anger, fear, or defensiveness among target persons, thereby reassuring the latter.

Group Structure. Whether members of a change-seeking body decide to use a permissive method, a pressuring method, or a conferring one, they have to organize their group for action. If they plan to employ practices that place few constraints on target persons, developers of the group usually will keep the group's structure loose, informal, and flexible, so that informing, advising, nurturing, or stimulating can take place in whatever ways seem to arouse the greatest interest among the decision makers. If group members intend to press for a specific solution, developers will prefer a group that is tightly controlled, follows strict rules, and has carefully defined roles for members and relations among these, along with a strict hierarchy of duties and offices. If they wish the group to engage in problem solving, the developers create an organizational plan that helps members find and develop information about the issue, list a number of alternative solutions, and create the trusting interpersonal relations needed for an effective conference with target persons.

Attempting to Be Influential. Having chosen a group objective, a method for appealing to decision makers, and a structure that is suited to those ends, the activists are ready to see if they can influence the persons whose help they need to introduce and maintain a change. The group leaders recognize that target persons, when they are approached with a proposal, will want to know what is in it for them if they do what the initiators suggest. Thus, any attempt to influence is framed in a way that promises to provide satisfaction for the target persons. If, for example, the activists believe that target persons want to please their constituents by removing a local problem, functioning as effective administrators, or attaining a difficult goal, the reformers are more likely to use methods that allow these officials to set their own incentives and gain their own satisfaction. The assistance of the innovators is lighthanded here, yet it serves to arouse motives like those just noted. This approach also suggests objectives that will satisfy these motives, proposes methods that may be used to accomplish the goals, and encourages target persons to believe that they can reach those goals.

If the activists realize they can convince target persons to take action only by appealing to their desire for status, power, money, security, or freedom from harm, they employ a procedure in which gratification of one of these desires is offered. The activists may promise praise and publicity, more prerogatives, pride in serving the community, or authority over a wider range of community activities. The reformers may also threaten that they will interfere with the work of target persons, call a strike, distribute propaganda about the listeners, work to unseat them, hold them hostage, threaten them with harm, or do damage to valued persons or objects unless the decision makers do as they are asked. Here, the activists provide an external incentive. The actions of the reformers are intended to urge the target persons to move in one direction and no other. This pressuring approach arouses a motive, offers a specific incentive, and assures the targets that they will gain the incentive if they make the change being backed by the activists.

If the managers of a change group believe that the most important outcome of interaction with the target persons will be the one that satisfies themselves and decision makers alike, they will emphasize the value of working toward a solution that benefits as many persons as possible, and they will try to encourage this desire among target persons. Accordingly, they will suggest that the issue being raised by the reformers be treated as a problem to be solved, as a matter to be bargained over lightly, or as a question to be cleared up through negotiation. They will arouse a motive (to benefit all concerned), an objective (a sound solution), and a means for reaching that end.

Whatever motives, desires, incentives, objectives, or procedures activists bring before target persons, they are more likely to get the listeners to take action if they can strengthen the latter group's total motivation. The motivation of target persons will be stronger if the activists can convince them of three things: that the aroused motive or desire is valuable, that achievement of the group's objective will satisfy it, and that the odds are good that the objective can be reached.

Overcoming Opposition. It is not enough for leaders among agents of change to present their case to target persons in an attractive way. They also must prevent receivers from opposing the ideas contained in the proposed plan, since opposition can keep target persons from taking action. Innovators therefore try to learn as much as they can about the opposing views and to prepare arguments showing that those ideas are not sound. They take further steps to prevent decision makers from opposing the plan. These include demonstrating that there is not much difference between the proposals being offered and the procedures usually supported by the listeners, showing target persons that the current situation has not been satisfying, and demonstrating that the suggested reforms have many attractive features and few unfavorable ones. In most situations, opposition from target persons is based on reasonable grounds. Therefore, proposers must make their case on its merits and expect that a rational presentation, given the goodness of their cause, will receive a fair hearing from receivers.

Sources of Resistance. Activists recognize that target persons are resisting when the latter show anger, fear, or defensiveness. Activists may arouse resistance by making arbitrary demands of target persons, shouting, or showing hostile feelings. They threaten to harm listeners who do not give in. They use dishonest means, such as incorrect "facts," distorted arguments, illogical derivations, or lies. They ridicule the target persons. They chant slogans and emotional phrases over and over, creating a din. They interrupt members of the audience and do not allow speakers with disliked ideas to hold the floor. They attach unfair and unfavorable labels to the target persons, or they use tones and inflections intended to upset the targets. Interpersonal behaviors like these may intentionally be used to provoke resistance or unwittingly employed by agents of change who do not expect target persons to be sensitive.

Origins and Resolution of Two-sided Resistance. When target persons resist the behavior of activists, their actions tend to duplicate those of the change agents; they, too, become hostile and demanding. The agents of change then respond in turn, increasing their aggressive behavior, which causes further resistance among the listeners. Such a cycle, in which like begets like, creates escalating two-sided coercion. A proposal for change has turned into a contest in which members on each side try to win. Such a circular-causal relationship seldom solves the initial problem.

Leaders of the reformers may seek to prevent resistance among target persons by behaving in ways that they think will not arouse it and by attempting to get the decision makers interested in listening to and thinking about the proposition put before them. They show why the issue is worthy of efforts to solve it. They deal most directly with the dominant faction among the target persons because it is easier to work with fewer persons, these individuals are less likely to become uneasy about considering a change, and such people, if they are converted, will influence others. The agents may also suggest that any plan for a solution be given a tentative trial in a limited setting, so that a commitment to action is not too large or too difficult to revoke.

If these measures to prevent resistance do not work, activists may move along a different line. They say that they will stop their resistance-arousing behavior if the target persons will agree to bargain in good faith, engage in a problem-solving process, or establish a procedure for solving the problem (such as a task force, a public hearing, or an appeal to a consultant on community social action). They may try to dampen any resistance by pledging to behave in a courteous manner, calling for an appeal to a referee or a mediator, repressing tendencies to be fearful or hostile, agreeing on ground rules for appropriate intergroup behavior, deciding on decision rules, or defining commonalities in the goals of presenters and listeners, so that actions by those on each side are directed toward common and jointly valued ends, not separate and rivalrous ones.

Target persons can help prevent escalation of resistance on both sides if they are willing to generate conditions that lead to constructive problem solving. They are more likely to do this if they assume that it is their duty to set the tone by granting initiators the right to bring up an issue and by taking responsibility to be helpful. They will assert that this kind of matter should be treated as a dilemma for which an answer can be sought and that problem solving requires proper procedures and rationality on both sides.

Suppressing a Coercive Action Group. If the proposers will not take no for an answer, persist in presenting their case in ways that arouse resistance among receivers, or do not calm down when asked to do so, the target persons may work toward diminishing the effectiveness of the activist organization or even abolishing it. In so doing, they restrict the freedom of the activists, set up rival organizations, emphasize the group's failures, damage leaders of the group, or restrict the availability of resources that the reformers need. Whether these measures restrain the innovators depends on the innovators' motivation and skill in winning support from residents of the community.

Topics for Research on Social Action Groups

Ideas in this volume may stimulate scholars to study aspects of influential action by community groups. To encourage such interest, I offer here a list of topics that warrant investigation. Some of these have been mentioned in earlier chapters.

1. Do altruists prefer to use permissive methods in their attempts to influence target persons? Do self-serving persons favor constraining methods? How large a part do activists' values play in helping them decide which method they will use and what style they will employ in presenting their case?

2. Under what conditions is the method chosen by agents of

change most likely to influence the properties of their group? When is it likely to do so? Do constraining methods foster formation of formal groups? Do nonconstraining methods encourage the creation of informal groups?

3. In what circumstances will persons prefer to join a group for social action, in contrast to acting alone to create change?

4. Do persons who join a group of change agents have particular personal characteristics? Are the personal qualities of agents who use constraining methods different from those of persons who employ gentler means?

5. What causes an action group's purpose to be more influential with members than their own personal desires are? Can agents of change be more motivated to benefit others than to benefit themselves? How? Do formal groups have clearer (or muddier) goals than informal groups?

6. What is the precise relationship between an individual's self-oriented motives and that person's desire to benefit neighbors, citizens in need, or the community as a whole? Do these desires operate the way motives do? Do changes that benefit others function as incentives for individuals?

7. Under what circumstances do members of a social action group lose interest in their group's objective or give up their group's cause?

8. Does greater strength of members' motivation make them more likely to use constraining methods? Does weaker motivation result in permissive methods?

9. After change agents fail to influence target persons, are they likely to make their group's structure more formal when planning how to enhance their chances for success?

10. Which arouses a member's actions more strongly—cognitive commitment (promise) to behave in a particular way, or awareness that achieving a given incentive will satisfy a particular motive or desire? Is a commitment to work toward a given objective largely an indication that the goal is highly valued?

11. In what kinds of situations are members more likely to take action as a group, without caring where these efforts lead them?

12. Does resistance among target persons outweigh opposition? Generate opposition?

13. Will agents of change be more successful in their attempts to influence target persons if they are trained in ways to prevent the arousal of opposition and resistance? Can they be trained effectively in these matters? Can a community teach its citizens both to seek social change and to avoid becoming coercive protesters?

14. Are opposition and resistance less likely to arise if change agents and target persons participate in constructive problem solving? In what ways can a two-sided escalating resistance best be calmed down? Can administrative officials be taught to use these cooling procedures sensibly?

15. Will reformers be more effective in influencing target persons if they are taught the nature of social power and how it works?

16. Will target persons follow through more fully in their efforts to introduce change if they are influenced by activists who use permissive methods or by those who use coercive methods?

17. In what ways does the psychology of a small face-to-face social movement differ from that of a large social movement? Why?

References

Alinsky, S. *Rules for Radicals.* New York: Random House, 1971.

Bailey, F. *The Tactical Uses of Passion.* Ithaca, N.Y.: Cornell University Press, 1983.

Barbrook, A., and Bolt, C. *Power and Protest in American Life.* Oxford, England: Martin Robertson, 1980.

Bar-Tal, D. *Prosocial Behavior: Theory and Research.* New York: Wiley, 1976.

Bellah, R., and others. *Habits of the Heart.* New York: Harper & Row, 1985.

Berry, J. "Beyond Citizen Participation: Effective Advocacy Before Administrative Agencies." *Journal of Applied Behavioral Science,* 1981, *17,* 463–477.

Berscheid, E., and Walster, E. *Interpersonal Attraction.* Reading, Mass.: Addison-Wesley, 1978.

Bollinger, L. *The Tolerant Society: Freedom of Speech and Extremist Speech in America.* New York: Oxford University Press, 1987.

227

Boulding, E. "Image and Action in Peace Building." *Journal of Social Issues,* 1988, *44,*17–38.

Brehm, S., and Brehm, J. *Psychological Reactance: A Theory of Freedom and Controls.* Orlando, Fla.: Academic Press, 1981.

Brill, H. *Why Organizations Fail.* Berkeley: University of California Press, 1971.

Caldwell, L., Hayes, L., and MacWhirter, I. *Citizens and the Environment.* Bloomington: Indiana University Press, 1976.

Capraro, J. "The Revitalization of Chicago Lawn: A Private Sector Response to Local Decline." *Commentary,* 1979, *3,* 11–14.

Carter, A. *Direct Action and Liberal Democracy.* New York: Harper & Row, 1973.

Cartwright, D. (ed.). *Studies in Social Power.* Ann Arbor: Institute for Social Research, University of Michigan, 1959.

Cartwright, D. "Influence, Leadership, and Control." In J. March (ed.), *Handbook of Organization.* Skokie, Ill.: Rand McNally, 1965.

Cartwright, D., and Zander, A. *Group Dynamics: Research and Theory.* New York: Harper & Row, 1968.

Chamberlain, D. "Town Without Pity." *Image,* Aug. 2, 1987, pp. 23–28.

Commager, H. *The Era of Reform, 1830–1860.* New York: Van Nostrand Reinhold, 1960.

Cordes, C. "Responding to Terrorism." *The Monitor,* 1986, *17,* 12–13.

Crowfoot, J., Chesler, M., and Boulet, J. "Organizing for Social Justice." In E. Seidman (ed.), *Handbook of Social Intervention.* Newbury Park, Calif.: Sage, 1983.

Deci, E. *Intrinsic Motivation.* New York: Plenum, 1975.

Delbecq, A., and Van de Ven, A. *Group Techniques for Program Planning.* Glenview, Ill.: Scott, Foresman, 1975.

Delgado, G. *Organizing the Movement: The Roots and Growth of ACORN.* Philadelphia: Temple University Press, 1986.

Deutsch, M. *The Resolution of Conflict.* New Haven: Yale University Press, 1973.

Diringer, E. "Earth Lovers Tell Why They Turned Tough." *San Francisco Chronicle,* Dec. 7, 1987, p. A-8.

Douglas, M., and Wildavsky, A. *Risk and Culture.* Berkeley: University of California Press, 1982.

Fanon, F. *The Wretched of the Earth.* New York: Grove Press, 1966.

Flinn, J. "Playing Mental Games." *San Francisco Examiner,* Jan. 21, 1988, p. B-8.

Frank, D. "Experimental Studies of Personal Pressure and Resistance." *Journal of General Psychology,* 1944, *30,* 23–41.

Fraser, J. *The Chinese: Portrait of a People.* New York: Summit Books, 1980.

French, J., and Raven, B. "The Bases of Social Power." In D. Cartwright (ed.), *Studies in Social Power.* Ann Arbor: Institute for Social Research, University of Michigan, 1959.

Fuchs, L. "The Role and Communication Task of the Change-Agent Experience of the Peace Corps Volunteers in the Philippines." In D. Lerner and W. Schramm (eds.), *Communication and Change in the Developing Countries.* Honolulu: East-West Center, 1967.

Funk, D. *Group Dynamics Law: Integrating Constitutive Contract Institutions.* New York: Philosophical Library, 1982.

Gamson, W. *Power and Discontent.* Homewood, Ill.: Dorsey Press, 1968.

Gamson, W. *The Strategy of Social Protest.* Homewood, Ill.: Dorsey Press, 1975.

Gerlach, L., and Hine, V. *People, Power, and Change: Movements of Social Transformation.* Indianapolis, Ind.: Bobbs-Merrill, 1970.

Goodenough, W. *Cooperation in Change.* New York: Russell Sage Foundation, 1963.

Gotshalk, D. *Human Aims in Modern Perspective.* Yellow Springs, Ohio: Antioch Press, 1966.

Gusfield, J. "The Study of Social Movements." In D. Silk (ed.), *International Encyclopedia of Social Sciences.* Vol. 14. New York: Macmillan, 1968.

Hammond, K., and Adelman, L. "Science, Values, and Human Judgment." *Science,* 1976, *194,* 389–396.

Hanley, R. "The Hot Dirt Rebellion." *San Francisco Chronicle and Examiner,* Sept. 14, 1986, p. A-5.

Hine, R. *California's Utopian Colonies.* New Haven: Yale University Press, 1953.

Hirschman, A. "Reactionary Rhetoric." *Atlantic Monthly,* May 1989, pp. 63–70.

Hitchens, C. "Wanton Acts of Usage." *Harper's,* Sept. 1986, pp. 66–76.

Holsti, E. "Crisis, Stress, and Decision Making." *International Social Science Journal,* 1971, *23,* 53–67.

Hornblower, M. "Not in My Backyard, You Don't." *Time,* June 27, 1988, pp. 44–46.

Hyams, E. *Terrorism and Terrorists.* New York: St. Martin's Press, 1975.

Janis, I. *Victims of Groupthink.* Boston: Houghton Mifflin, 1972.

Janis, I., and Mann, L. *Decision Making.* New York: Free Press, 1977.

Kahneman, D., and Tversky, A. "Prospect Theory: An Analysis of Decision Under Risk." *Econometrica,* 1979, *47,* 239–291.

Kanter, R. *Commitment and Community.* Cambridge, Mass.: Harvard University Press, 1972.

Kiesler, C. *The Psychology of Commitment.* Orlando, Fla.: Academic Press, 1971.

Knoke, D., and Wood, J. *Organized for Action: Commitment in Voluntary Associations.* New Brunswick, N.J.: Rutgers University Press, 1981.

Kweit, M., and Kweit, R. *Implementing Citizen Participation in a Bureaucratic Society.* New York: Praeger, 1971.

Lancourt, J. *Confront or Concede.* Lexington, Mass.: Heath, 1979.

Langton, S. "Current Reflections on the State of the Art." In S. Langton (ed.), *Citizen Participation in America.* Lexington, Mass.: Heath, 1978.

Lanternari, V. *The Religions of the Oppressed.* New York: Knopf, 1963.

Laqueur, W. *Terrorism.* Boston: Little, Brown, 1979.

Lebow, R., and Stein, J. "Beyond Deterrence." *Journal of Social Issues,* 1987, *43,* 5–71.

Levitt, T. *The Third Sector: New Tactics for a Responsive Society.* New York: American Management Association, 1973.

Lindgren, H. "The Informal-Intermittent Organization: A Vehicle for Successful Citizen Protest." *Journal of Applied Behavioral Science,* 1987, *23,* 397–412.

Lippitt, R., Watson, J., and Westley, B. *The Dynamics of Planned Change.* San Diego, Calif.: Harcourt Brace Jovanovich, 1958.

Lipset, S., and Raab, E. *The Politics of Unreason.* New York: Harper & Row, 1970.

Liversidge, D. *The Luddites: Machine Breakers of the Early Nineteenth Century.* New York: Watts, 1972.

Luttwak, E. *Coup d'état: A Practical Handbook.* New York: Knopf, 1968.

Macaulay, J., and Berkowitz, L. *Altruism and Helping Behavior.* Orlando, Fla.: Academic Press, 1970.

Madison, A. *Vigilantism in America.* New York: Seaburg Press, 1973.

Marris, P., and Rein, M. *Dilemmas of Social Reform.* New York: Lieber-Atherton, 1967.

Mayer, A. "The Significance of Quasi-Groups in the Study of Complex Societies." In M. Banton (ed.), *The Social Anthropology of Complex Societies.* London: Tavistock, 1966.

Meier, B. "Citizen Suits Become a Popular Weapon in the Fight Against Industrial Polluters." *Wall Street Journal,* Apr. 17, 1987, p. 17.

Moreland, R., and Levine, J. "Socialization in Small Groups: Temporal Changes in Individual-Group Relations." In L. Berkowitz (ed.), *Advances in Experimental Social Pscyhology.* Vol. 15. Orlando, Fla.: Academic Press, 1980.

Morgan, G. *Images of Organization.* Newbury Park, Calif.: Sage, 1986.

Moscovici, S. *Social Influence and Social Change.* Orlando, Fla.: Academic Press, 1976.

Moynihan, D. *Maximum Feasible Misunderstanding.* New York: Free Press, 1970.

Netanyahu, B. *Terrorism: How the West Can Win.* New York: Farrar, Straus & Giroux, 1987.

Newcomb, T. *The Acquaintance Process.* New York: Holt, Rinehart & Winston, 1961.

Newhouse, J. "The Diplomatic Round: A Freemasonry of Terrorism." *The New Yorker,* July 8, 1985, pp. 46–63.

Nisbet, R. *The Quest for Community.* New York: Oxford University Press, 1953.

Nisbett, R., and Ross, L. *Human Inference: Strategies and Shortcomings of Social Judgment.* Englewood-Cliffs, N.J.: Prentice-Hall, 1980.

Olsen, M. *Participatory Pluralism.* Chicago: Nelson-Hall, 1982.

Osborn, A. *Applied Imagination.* New York: Scribner's, 1957.

Perlman, J. "Grassroots Participation from Neighborhoods to Nations." In S. Langton (ed.), *Citizen Participation in America.* Lexington, Mass.: Heath, 1978.

Pfaff, E. "Reflections: The Dimensions of Terror." *The New Yorker,* Nov. 10, 1986, pp. 122–131.

Piven, F., and Cloward, R. *Poor People's Movements: Why They Succeed and How They Fail.* New York: Pantheon, 1977.

Prestby, J., and Wandersman, A. "An Empirical Exploration of a Framework of Organizational Viability: Maintaining Block Organizations." *Journal of Applied Behavioral Science,* 1985, *21,* 287–305.

Priscoli, J. "Implementing Public Involvement Programs in Federal Agencies." In S. Langton (ed.), *Citizen Participation in America.* Lexington, Mass.: Heath, 1978.

Pruitt, D. "Methods for Resolving Differences of Interest: A Theoretical Analysis." *Journal of Social Issues,* 1972, *28,* 133–154.

Pruitt, D., and Rubin, J. *Social Conflict: Escalation, Stalemate, and Settlement.* New York: Random House, 1986.

Robertson, M. "A Penchant for Protest: Why the Bay Area Likes to Demonstrate." *San Francisco Chronicle,* Mar. 25, 1988, pp. B-3–B-4.

Rogers, E. "Social Structure and Social Change." In G. Zaltman (ed.), *Process and Phenomena of Social Change.* New York: Wiley, 1973.

Rogers, E. *Diffusion of Innovations.* New York: Free Press, 1983.

Rosenblatt, R. "The Demogogue in the Crowd." *Time,* Oct. 21, 1985, p. 102.

Rosener, J. "Matching Method to Purpose: The Challenge of Planning Citizen Activities." In S. Langton (ed.), *Citizen Participation in America.* Lexington, Mass.: Heath, 1978.

Rothman, J., Erlich, J., and Teresa, J. *Promoting Innovation and*

Change in Organizations and Communities. New York: Wiley, 1976.

Rude, G. *The Crowd in History: A Study of Popular Disturbances in France and England, 1730–1848.* New York: Wiley, 1964.

Ruffner, F. (ed.). *Encyclopedia of Associations.* (5th ed.) Detroit, Mich.: Gale Research Co., 1968.

Schachter, S. *The Psychology of Affiliation.* Palo Alto, Calif.: Stanford University Press, 1959.

Seligman, M. *Helplessness: On Depression, Development, and Death.* New York: W. H. Freeman, 1975.

Sieber, S. *Fatal Remedies: The Ironies of Social Intervention.* New York: Plenum, 1981.

Stone, C. *Should Trees Have Standing? Toward Legal Rights for Natural Objects.* Los Altos, Calif.: Kaufmann, 1974.

Thum, G., and Thum, M. *The Persuaders: Propaganda in War and Peace.* New York: Atheneum, 1972.

Toch, H. *The Social Psychology of Social Movements.* Indianapolis, Ind.: Bobbs-Merrill, 1965.

Trotter, R. "Stop Blaming Yourself." *Psychology Today,* 1987, *21,* 31–39.

Tversky, A., and Kahneman, D. "Causal Schemata in Judgments Under Uncertainty." In M. Fishbein (ed.), *Progress in Social Psychology.* Hillsdale, N.J.: Erlbaum, 1978.

Unger, D., and Wandersman, A. "The Importance of Neighbors." *American Journal of Community Psychology,* 1985, *13,* 139–169.

Vander Werf, M. "Sign Man Calls 'Em, Wears 'Em." *Arizona Republican,* Oct. 4, 1987, p. B-1.

Vogel, E. *Modern Japanese Organization and Decision Making.* Berkeley: University of California Press, 1975.

Walton, E. "Establishing and Maintaining High Commitment in Work Systems." In J. R. Kimberly, R. H. Miles, and Associates (eds.), *The Organizational Life Cycle: Issues in the Creation, Transformation, and Decline of Organizations.* San Francisco: Jossey-Bass, 1980.

Wandersman, A. "A Framework of Participation in Community Organizations." *Journal of Applied Behavioral Science,* 1981, *17,* 27–58.

Wandersman, A. "Citizen Participation." In K. Heller, R. Price,

S. Rienharz, and A. Wandersman (eds.), *Psychology and Community Change: Challenges of the Future.* Homewood, Ill.: Dorsey Press, 1984.

Wandersman, A., and others. "Getting Together and Getting Things Done." *Psychology Today,* Nov. 1985, 64–71.

Wandersman, A., and others. "Who Participates, Who Does Not, and Why? An Analysis of Voluntary Neighborhood Organizations in the United States and Israel." *Sociological Forum,* 1987, *2,* 534–555.

Warren, R. *Social Change and Human Purpose: Toward Understanding and Action.* Skokie, Ill.: Rand-McNally, 1971.

Warren, R., Rose, S., and Bergunder, A. *The Structure of Urban Reform.* Lexington, Mass.: Heath, 1974.

Weick, K. *The Social Psychology of Organizing.* Reading, Mass.: Addison-Wesley, 1979.

Wicker, A. "Behavior Settings Reconsidered: Temporal Stages, Resources, Internal Dynamics, Context." In D. Stokols and E. Altman (eds.), *Handbook of Environmental Psychology.* New York: Wiley, 1987.

Wilson, J. *Introduction to Social Movements.* New York: Basic Books, 1973.

Woito, M. *To End War: A New Approach to International Conflict.* New York: Pilgrim Press, 1982.

Wood, J., and Jackson, M. *Social Movements: Development, Participation, and Dynamics.* Belmont, Calif.: Wadsworth, 1982.

Zander, A. *Motives and Goals in Groups.* Orlando, Fla.: Academic Press, 1971.

Zander, A. *Groups at Work: Unresolved Issues in the Study of Organizations.* San Francisco: Jossey-Bass, 1977.

Zander, A. *Making Groups Effective.* San Francisco: Jossey-Bass, 1982.

Zander, A. "The Value of Belonging to a Group in Japan." *Small-Group Behavior,* 1983, *14,* 3–14.

Zander, A. *The Purposes of Groups and Organizations.* San Francisco: Jossey-Bass, 1985.

Zander, A., Forward, J., and Albert, R. "Adaptation of Board Members to Repeated Success or Failure by Their Organizations." *Organizational Behavior and Human Performance*, 1969, *4*, 56–76.

Zander, A., and Newcomb, T., Jr. "Group Levels of Aspiration in United Fund Campaigns." *Journal of Personality and Social Psychology*, 1967, *6*, 157–162.

Index

A

Action-taking, group, 89–90

Activists, 10, 93

Adelman, L., 119

Advisers of organizations, 51–53, 89

Advising target persons. *See* Counselor groups

Agents of change: as activists, 93–94, 167; cooperation between, 65; as experts, 103; as innovators, 93–94, 167; as models, 8, 100–102, 130–132; as nurturers, 130–132; qualities of, 46, 49–50; questions facing, 2–3, 163–170, 213–215; as reformers, 10, 93, 130–132, 140, 164; social power of, 121–122, 140–143, 148–149, 174–190; talents of, 167–168; as teachers or coaches, 104–109. *See also* Methods and techniques (change agent)

B

Albert, R., 40

Alinsky, S., 20–21, 50, 65, 148, 196

Alliances, 65–66

Altruism, 26–29, 42, 72, 77–78, 130–132, 169

Animal rights activism, 33–34

Antisocial activism, 205

Arbitration, 126, 128

Assertive tactics, 142–143

Association of Community Organizations for Reform Now (ACORN), 20–21

Attention-getting activities, 93, 102–103, 144; publicity, 144, 152–154. *See also* Demonstrations

B

Bailey, F., 135, 137–138, 142

Bar-Tal, D., 26, 131

Barbrook, A., 17

237

Bargaining, 129, 140–143, 154–155, 175
Behavior, beliefs *vs.* overt, 8–9, 94, 145, 147, 161
Behaviors of bystanders, 89, 93, 145, 150–151, 169–170
Behaviors of change agents: motivation and, 69–70, 74; resistance provoking, 10–11, 136–137, 143, 186–188
Behaviors of target persons, overt, 8–9, 94, 145, 147, 161
Beliefs, 62; behavior *vs.*, 8–9, 94, 145, 147, 161; in group action, 44–49; transcendentalism, 50–51; in violence, 158–160. *See also* Goals and objectives (group); Values, group
Bellah, R., 71
Beneficiaries of social action: animals, 33–34; change agents and, 61, 72, 77–78; cultural objects, 33; determining the, 3, 7; disadvantaged persons, 38–41, 45, 130–132; group members, 22–25, 42, 164, 215; members and others, 29–34, 38–39, 164; methods adjustment to, 163–169; natural objects, 33–34, 78; outsiders, 26–29, 38, 164, 215
Bergunder, A., 63, 193–194
Berkowitz, L., 26, 131
Berry, J., 19
Berscheid, E., 49
Black power movements, 31–32, 85, 98, 148
Block organizations, 188–189
Bollinger, L., 139
Bolstering, 120
Bolt, C., 17
Boulding, E., 81
Boulet, J., 53, 205
Boycotts. *See* Demonstrations
Brainstorming, 115–116
Brehm, J., 184
Brehm, S., 184
Bribes, 142, 144
Brill, H., 19, 21, 89, 149, 156

Bystanders, roles of, 89, 93, 145, 150–151, 169–170

C

Caldwell, L., 199
Capraro, J., 26
Carter, A., 149
Cartwright, D., 60, 63–64, 69, 84, 94, 106, 174, 181–182
Celebrities, use of, 100–102
Challenge goals, 87
Chamberlain, D., 32
Change agents. *See* Agents of change
Change organizations, 14–15, 34–35; citizen action groups as, 20–21; citizen participation groups as, 17–20; community groups for social action as, 21–34; conditions working against, 181–188; improvement associations as, 16; maintaining, 188–189; pressure groups as, 16–17; social movements as, 15–16; structure of, 63–68. *See also* Groups for influential action
Chapters, groups with, 15
Chesler, M., 53, 205
Chicago, 20, 26–27, 65
China, 95–96, 156
Citizen action groups, 20–21
Citizen participation groups, 17–20
Civil disobedience, 96–97, 151–152
Civil rights movement, 21, 28–29; anti-discrimination, 77–78; black power movement, 31–32, 85, 98, 148
Classification, 210–211
Clean Water Act, 127
Cloward, R., 21
Coercion. *See* Constraining (pressuring) methods
Commager, H. S., 51
Commitment: consequences of, 87; effects of, 86–87, 135; methods of group, 84–86; nature of, 83–85, 90
Commune groups, 23, 83–84, 96
Community attitudes: approval, 147; of governing agencies, 194–195;